P9-CFA-486

Radwan Ziadeh is a Visiting Scholar at the Carr Center for Human Rights of Harvard University and Visiting Fellow at Chatham House (The Royal Institute of International Affairs) in London. He is the founding director of the Syrian Center for Political and Strategic Studies in Washington DC, and has been a Senior Fellow at the United States Institute of Peace. He was awarded the MESA Academic Freedom Award in 2009.

LIBRARY OF MODERN MIDDLE EAST STUDIES

Series ISBN: 978 1 84885 243 3

See www.ibtauris.com/LMMES for a full list of titles

92. *Orientalism and Conspiracy: Politics and Conspiracy Theory in the Islamic World*
Arndt Graf, Schirin Fathi and Ludwig Paul (Eds)
978 1 84885 414 7

93. *Honour Killings: International Human Rights and Crimes Against Women in Turkey*
Leylâ Pervizat
978 1 84885 421 5

94. *Gender and Identity in North Africa: Postcolonialism and Feminism in Maghrebi Women's Literature*
Abdelkader Cheref
978 1 84885 449 9

95. *Kurds of Modern Turkey: Migration, Neoliberalism and Exclusion in Turkish Society*
Cenk Saraçoğlu
978 1 84885 468 0

96. *Occidentalisms in the Arab World: Ideology and Images of the West in the Egyptian Media*
Robbert Woltering
978 1 84885 476 5

97. *The Army and the Radical Left in Turkey: Military Coups, Socialist Revolution and Kemalism*
Özgür Mutlu Ulus
978 1 84885 484 0

98. *Power and Policy in Syria: Intelligence Services, Foreign Relations and Democracy in the Modern Middle East*
Radwan Ziadeh
978 1 84885 434 5

99. *The Copts of Egypt: The Challenges of Modernisation and Identity*
Vivian Ibrahim
978 1 84885 499 4

100. *The Kurds of Iraq: Ethnonationalism and National Identity in Iraqi Kurdistan*
Mahir Aziz
978 1 84885 546 5

101. *The Politics and Practices of Cultural Heritage in the Middle East: Positioning the Material Past in Contemporary Societies*
Irene Maffi and Rami Daher (Eds)
978 1 84885 535 9

102. *The Politics and Poetics of Ameen Rihani: The Humanist Ideology of an Arab-American Intellectual and Activist*
Nijmeh Hajjar
978 1 84885 266 2

103. *The Transformation of Turkey: Redefining State and Society from the Ottoman Empire to the Modern Era*
Fatma Müge Göçek
978 1 84885 611 0

POWER AND POLICY IN SYRIA

The Intelligence Services, Foreign Relations and Democracy in the Modern Middle East

RADWAN ZIADEH

I.B. TAURIS
LONDON · NEW YORK

Published in 2011 by I.B.Tauris & Co Ltd
6 Salem Road, London W2 4BU
175 Fifth Avenue, New York NY 10010
www.ibtauris.com

Distributed in the United States and Canada Exclusively by Palgrave Macmillan
175 Fifth Avenue, New York NY 10010

Copyright © 2011 Radwan Ziadeh

The right of Radwan Ziadeh to be identified as the editor of this work has been asserted by the editor in accordance with the Copyright, Designs and Patents Act 1988.

All rights reserved. Except for brief quotations in a review, this book, or any part thereof, may not be reproduced, stored in or introduced into a retrieval system, or transmitted, in any form or by any means, electronic, mechanical, photocopying, recording or otherwise, without the prior written permission of the publisher.

Library of Modern Middle East Studies 98

ISBN: 978 1 84885 434 5

A full CIP record for this book is available from the British Library
A full CIP record for this book is available from the Library of Congress
Library of Congress catalog card: available

Printed and bound in Great Britain by CPI Antony Rowe, Chippenham
from camera-ready copy edited and supplied by
Oxford Publishing Services, Oxford

FSC www.fsc.org MIX Paper from responsible sources FSC® C013604

Contents

Acronyms and Abbreviations

CIA	Central Intelligence Agency
EU	European Union
HRAS	Human Rights Association in Syria
MERIA	*Middle East Review of International Affairs*
MERIP	Middle East Research and Information Project
MP	Member of Parliament
NPF	National Progressive Front
PKK	*Parti Karkerani Kurdistan* (Kurdistan Workers' Party)
UAE	United Arab Emirates
UN	United Nations
UNIFIL	United Nations Interim Force in Lebanon
UNDP	United Nations Development Programme

To my wife Susan
For her love and support

Preface and Acknowledgements

The year 2010 marked the tenth anniversary of Bashar al-Asad's presidency of Syria. In 2000, on the death of President Hafez al-Asad, Bashar's father, Syria underwent a brief period during which, for the first time since the Baʾth military coup of 1963 (which initiated the ongoing state of emergency), a period of intense debate about political and social issues culminated in calls for reform. This brief flowering came to be known as the 'Damascus Spring' and the national debate (*Montada Al-hiwar Al-watani*) that took place at that time had important consequences for the society. This book is an attempt to recount the inside story of Bashar al-Asad's first decade in power.

Although the manner in which the presidency was transferred from al-Asad senior to al-Asad junior outraged most Syrian people, the period following the transition nonetheless gave them an opportunity to participate in politics and to express their fears about their country's future. Intellectuals and activists took advantage of the situation to launch a 'friends of civil society' movement to foster critical dialogue between the people and the state and the Syrians suddenly rediscovered politics.

Riyāḍ Saif, a former Syrian member of parliament turned political dissident, set up the Forum for National Dialogue (*Montada Al-hiwar Al-watani*) and became its main leader. The forum was launched on 13 September 2000 with a lecture on the importance of civil society. Having written *The Path of Human Rights in the Arab World* (Beirut, 1999), now banned in Syria, I attended the lecture and was overcome by a desire to become a political activist in the movement. Further lectures were held and were eventually collected in a publication entitled *For a Civil Society in Syria: Debates of the Forum for National Dialogue*. The lectures attracted considerable interest and were reported in the Syrian, Arab and international media.

The story of the Forum for National Dialogue is the story of the

Damascus Spring. Its closure in February 2001 and the clamp-down and arrest of Riyāḍ Saif marked the beginning of the end of the Damascus Spring. An attempt to reopen the organization on 7 September 2001 resulted in the Syrian government closing it by force and arresting five of its active members – Riyāḍ Saif, Walīd al-Bunnī, Fawwāz Tal-lū, 'Ārif Dalīlah and Kamāl al-Lubwānī. I, along with 40 other activists, then set up the Human Rights Association in Syria (HRAS) and I became the first editor of a periodical it published in Syria called *Tyarat* (*Trends*). When the regime banned the publication in 2002, three members of its editorial board were brought before a military court.

During this turbulent period, Syrian military intelligence, the Ministry of Defence and the Ministry of the Interior subjected me to dozens of interrogations, which would begin with a phone call or unsigned letter on official stationery. The sessions sometimes lasted six or seven hours and occasionally would not begin until I had been kept waiting for an entire day. I was repeatedly questioned about my human rights activities, articles I had written, my affiliations to various bodies, conferences in which I had participated and my contacts inside and outside the country.

In 2004 I joined a group of Syrian intellectuals and human rights activists who were planning to draft a Damascus declaration for democratic and national change. In May 2005, my travel ban was lifted for the first time since 2001. The release of the Damascus declaration on 16 October 2005 coincided with a group of Syrian and Lebanese intellectuals starting to hold monthly meetings to discuss Syrian–Lebanese relations. Meanwhile, in November 2005, a Damascus Centre for Human Rights Studies was launched. When the Damascus–Beirut declaration was made public in May 2006, it was publicly branded a 'threat to Syria' and 12 of its signatories were arrested and I was again issued with a travel ban. Even when I was allowed to travel, I had to obtain permission for each trip and, more often than not, this was withheld.

In June 2007 a new order banning all travel was issued against me. I had written an article analysing the structure of decision-making in Syria and the head of security summoned me for interrogation.

During the course of the interview he implied that the next time I would be arrested. I left Syria in 2007 to take up a senior fellowship at the United States Institute of Peace in Washington, DC. I have not been back to Syria since then because, in January 2009, my lawyer informed me that the Syrian security branch had issued an order for my arrest.

Although I have written eight books in Arabic, in which I covered different aspects of Syrian politics and history, this is my first book to be published in English.

Finally, I would like to thank the many people who have lent me their support, first and foremost my father, who unfortunately died before seeing the book in print, but who discussed many of its ideas with me, and of course my mother about whom I always think. I would especially like to thank my wife, to whom I dedicate this book, for she gave me all the support I needed and much more. I thank Judy Barsalou, Steven Heydemann, Mona Yacoubian and Scott Lasensky from the United States Institute of Peace, and my research assistant, Cory Julie. To my friends in Syria, who helped create the Damascus Spring, I should like to say that I feel sure we shall see a lasting one in the future.

Radwan Ziadeh
Washington, DC

1

Birth of the Third Republic and Establishing Syrian Authoritarianism

In the 1950s, in the aftermath of Syria's acquisition of independence, the old values from the independence period collapsed and more radical political parties began to attract Syria's intellectual elites. This political confusion, manifested in the incapacity to sign a national agreement that would bring together all political parties and parliamentary blocs, had led to a series of government resignations. In 1954 alone, for example, more than four consecutive governments were formed and dismantled. The defeat of the Arab forces in the first Arab–Israeli war in 1948 made the situation worse. It had a direct bearing on political life in Syria because it encouraged a form of ideological thinking that not only rejected the current situation, but also weakened the country's already fragile democratic institutions. Consequently, it was easy for these institutions to fall prey to the kind of dogmatism that came to dominate the Syrian elite at that time.

The Third Republic[1] and Syrian Authoritarianism

After independence in 1946, Syria witnessed two important events that had a strong influence on what was happening in the political, economic and social spheres. In the period after independence, the political elite, as well as the Syrian people in general, thought that it would be possible to build a modern nation based on the separation of the legislative, judicial and executive authorities within the cabinet and to spell out the relationship of the army and intelligence agencies to these authorities. Later on, the growth of the latter two institutions deeply affected the structure of the other constitutional institutions.

The first challenge to civilian control of the army occurred in 1958, or more precisely February 1958, with the creation of the Syrian–Egyptian unity movement. The second was when the Baʿth Party seized power in Syria, which later ushered in the third republic on 8 March 1963. It is necessary to state here that if these two important events appeared to have stemmed from arbitrary personal or military decisions, the two republics did not see them that way from the outset, for at that time they were clear expressions of the mentality of the political, economic and military elite. The only dilemma the elites of each of these sides faced was over the decision when to seize power to achieve what were, in effect, the same ends. With the power of the liberal political elite gradually eroding, its representatives had become far more likely to support social leftist than liberal constitutional ideologies, so there were no competing alternatives. Unlike Egypt, Syria had no constitutional movement whose mission was to protect a founding document that everybody had to abide by and respect. Rather, because the Syrian constitution had undergone periodic and regular amendments, it no longer retained its 'sanctity' in the national public perception.[2]

The first republic reached its nadir, or 'political looseness',[3] right after it crashed into the lap of Syrian–Egyptian unity. The constitutional institutions formed after independence, which imitated a French style of government and constitution, seemed to be very fragile after successive military coups had deprived the Syrian people of their sense of security and patriotism. Consequently, there was a marked shift in Syrian perceptions towards nationalist ideologies, encapsulated in the Syrian nationalist, socialist and communist political parties; even political parties known for their pro-feudal or bourgeois positions, such as the People's Party,[4] started to lean towards a way of thinking that encouraged social justice. The only way to interpret the victory of Khālid Bakdāsh in 1954, the founder and leader of the Syrian Communist Party, appearing on the same ticket as Khaled al-ʿAzem, the descendant of an ancient Damascene aristocratic family, is with reference to the Syrians' pro-leftist anti-Western mentality. That many

Syrians backed both Khaled al-ʿAzem and Khālid Bakdāsh – referred to as 'al-Khalidain' (the two Khaleds) on the Syrian street – was an indication of the extent of social transformation in Syrian society. Meanwhile, there was an Islamic current reinforcing the trend and some leftist 'foolishness' began to appear in the lectures and books of, for example, Muṣṭafá al-Sibāʿī, the general supervisor of the Muslim Brotherhood in Syria.[5] All this created an anti-American ethos not least because of America's support of Israel on the Security Council and in international resolutions.[6] At the same time, national, Nasserite and leftist-blowing winds began to undermine liberalism in Syrian policy, culminating in the fall of Fāris al-Khouri's government on 7 February 1955. This was a 'turning point' in Arab policy: the leftists seized the initiative and the curtain went down on traditional liberal policy having any further influence on social, economic or political life in Syria. A group of individuals tried to take charge, but their scattered voices had no real effect. From that point onwards, the political instability of the first republic in Syria meant that many governments came and went, eventually to clear the way for the second republic (the United Arab Republic).

After his victory, Egyptian president Gamal Abdul Nasser not only received unparalleled mass support from the Arab people but also came to dominate the entire Arab scene. Consequently, politicians in Syria lost any sense of direction they might once have had. They seemed dazzled by Nasser's ability, based on a total institutional and constitutional abandonment of the first republic, to stand up to Western pressures. Abdul Nasser advocated a full merging of the two governments, which meant dismantling Syria's parliament and political parties, and replacing the judicial, constitutional and security institutions in Syria with new ones based on both territories – northern (Egypt) and southern (Syria).

To Syria's elite, Abdul Nasser seemed careless of the minor details that had for so long preoccupied and corrupted political minds in Syria. Nasser faced Western pressures when Syrians could not: furthermore, the Syrians could not agree on how to withstand these pressures. It is safe to say that the political system in Syria was on the verge of a complete breakdown. The reservations of Khaled al-ʿAzem (the then Syrian prime minister) about Syrian–Egyptian unity, which he described as irrational impetuosity, were ignored.[7] His was perceived to be an odd and singular voice against the myriad of political, military, intellectual and economic minds in Syria who thought of unity as salvation from international conspiracies such as the Eisenhower Doctrine or the Baghdad Pact, not to mention more local territorial alliances (starting from east Jordan to Iraq and ending in Egypt and Saudi Arabia). There were also the permanent military threats from Israel and pressures on the Turkish border that threatened to become actual invasions.

When Syria entered the second republic, it became alienated from the institutional and constitutional principles on which it had been based since independence, and so succumbed to the temptation of handing the affairs of state over to the Free Officers movement. Patriotic military men were thus placed in charge of the country's social, economic and political affairs and allowed to achieve their goals without having to engage in all the political confusion of the democratic game of vying for alliances and supporters. Although Syrians had suffered under al-Shīshaklī's dictatorship, Syrian officers seemed eager to relive the experience. One justification for military rule, apart from the failure of the constitutional and judicial institutions, was the revolutionary content of such power. Neither Shīshaklī nor Husni al-Zaʾim had enough charisma to attract the crowds, but the 'revolutionary philosophy' of Abdul Nasser consisted of more than words – it embodied the social, economic and political views of the average Egyptian man on the street. Furthermore, Abdul Nasser's support for the Arab liberation movement in Algeria and other places was evident in the international stands he took. For all these reasons, the second republic seemed to be an extension of a dream in Syria. However, the unity was not to last long politically, for the clash it brought between two such different political systems was inevitable, deeply affecting the Syrian elite intellectually, politically and emotionally. When Syria entered the third republic, its political and ideological conflicts were still raging and these could not to be settled until the era of long-term political stability under the rule of Hafez al-Asad and later his son Bashar al-Asad.

When Syria left the United Arab Republic in 1961, its political elites became divided between those who supported unity with Egypt and wanted it restored, and those who called the separation 'the blessed uprising' and wanted to revert to the Syrian constitutional institutions based on the French model that had characterized Syria after independence.[8] The rise of the military elite, however, with its ideological tendencies, had the final word in deciding that 'revolutionary legitimacy' was the obligatory choice for Syrians. The Nasserite and Baʿthist elements made an alliance and took power on 8 March 1963, ushering in the beginning of the third 'revolutionary' republic, which was, from the state's point of view, an implicit continuation of previous policies, but under cover of a discourse that claimed a change in policy.

After the failure of unity with Egypt, Syria suffered badly from a general lack of direction. The people had grown used to the idea of a choice between separation and partnership, but had failed to find a place for any discourse of national agreement or partnership based on differences. This led the country into what has been described as a 'fragile state',[9] a state that lasted until a new type of government, a 'revolutionary state', took over in Syria. This phenomenon was not new to Third World countries, for revolutionary states tended to proliferate wherever a metaphoric state could be found – in Latin America, Africa or Asia. This 'revolutionary state' has certain features:

- The legislative, executive and judicial branches are integrated and brought under government control.
- There is a centralized hierarchy with the commander in chief of the revolution at the top of the pyramid. As the French thinker Edgar Moran put it, the government controls society, the party leads the government, the central committee directs the party and the revolutionary leader dominates the central committee.
- Governmental institutions and budgets are merged into the political party organization, with the result that promotions are more likely to be secured through loyalty than efficiency. Eventually, this leads to the concentration of power in the hands of the party leaders, with the same budget serving all purposes. So long

as the party and state operate as a unit, there is no need for separate budgets.

The 'revolutionary state' was created in Syria after the events of 8 March 1963 culminated in the Ba'th Party seizing the reins of power. Here, the view of 'Abd Allāh al-'Arawī, in his evaluation of the modern Arab state, seems to be significant. He calls for the separation of the state from its apparatuses on the grounds that the latter might well be strong and developed even although the state *per se* might be weak and backward. The modern Arab state often has strong well-developed apparatuses, yet in many Arab countries, even the larger ones, the state itself, is always questionable.[10]

Separation left its scars, especially on the Syrian political and factional elite. The insignificant liberal groups in Syria supported the separation as soon as it took place – witness the doubtful attitude of Khaled al-'Azem towards the success of Syrian–Egyptian unity. Some 62 significant figures signed the 'separation document', which they described as the 'revolution' or 'blessed uprising'. These were the leaders of the National Party, People's Party, Arab Liberation Movement, Ba'th Party and a few elite tribal and sectarian leaders. Five Ba'thist politicians signed the document, the most significant of whom were Akram al-Ḥawrānī and Muḥammad Bahjah al-Bīṭār,[11] but their pro-separation stand backfired in that it was decisive in the breakup of al-Ba'th itself. Al-Ba'th was not the only party to suffer from the break-up; the split hit all Syrian political elites, for the pro-separation and pro-unity subdivisions dominated all other ideological and social issues.[12] Al-Ba'th had witnessed many breakaways, the most crucial of which was that of 'Abd Allāh al-Rīmāwī in Jordan, after an argument with Abdul Nasser in 1960, followed by that of Fu'ād al-Rikābī in Iraq and, most seriously, that of Akram al-Ḥawrānī in Syria. This last rift was basically much like putting an end to the companionship between *al-Ba'th al-Arabi* (the Arab Ba'th Party) and *al-Arabi al-Ishtiraki* (the Arab Socialist Party). All this resulted in a new group, known as the Socialist Unionist Movement, breaking away and taking quite a few Ba'thist intellectuals with it. This group had criticized its party for failing to protect the unity and for accepting Muḥammad Bahjah al-

Bīṭār – who signed the separation document – as its leader. The separatist coalition led by Riad al-Mālikī was called 'the *alquṭrīyīn*' because of the regional (*qutri*) tendencies it manifested and its hostile attitude to Abdul Nasser and the Ba'th leadership.[13]

After separation, as former nationalist intellectuals broke into numerous factions to promote their various ideological and historical differences, the Syrian elite became highly ideological and solidly middle class. The Cairo-oriented Unionists, who were later known as 'Nasserites' and whose members came mostly from the urban middle classes and were students, teachers and workers, established three strong urban organizations. The first of these was the Socialist Unionist Movement, which 50 former Ba'th members established only one week after separation. It called for immediate unity with Egypt and represented a wing of al-Ba'th. The second was the Arab Nationalist Movement, which in Syria grew from being a prominent closed nationalist fraternity to a public movement with thousands of industrial workers among its members.[14] Researchers often attribute the confusion about the notion of a Syrian national state to the Syrian elite's obsession with separation. Despite the reservations about unity of Communist Party general secretary Khālid Bakdāsh and liberal prime minister Khaled al-'Azem, the separation could not be justified on nationalist grounds because the principles of true unity had never been disputed. Separation could only be justified in terms of the failure of the Egyptian central bureaucracy and evidence of a police state.[15]

Ideological awareness reached its peak through the experience of forming and running political parties, and their proliferation in Syria was a true reflection of how active these various rather doctrinaire parties were after separation. Independent intellectuals and old-style national liberal parties were, on the other hand, deathly quiet. Al-Ba'th held its fifth national (*Qawmiyah*) conference in Homs in May 1962 at which the main thrust was to get rid of the outmoded separatist system and resume unity with Egypt. It produced a number of dissenting political voices, including Akram al-Ḥawrānī and his colleagues, Regional Leadership Trend (*Tayyār al-Qiyādah al-Quṭrī*), the Socialist Unionist Movement and the National Leadership Trend (*Tayyār al-Qiyādah al-Qawmīyah*) (Michael 'Aflak and his colleagues).

The Communist Party, on the other hand, was active in the post-separation government led by Bashir al-ʿAsma from 16 April to 14 September 1962, as were the Muslim Brotherhood, so it is possible to say that ideological parties took over the national government of Syria (the post-separation government) and the unity government at the same time. Syria's intellectual elite was highly politicized and its public activities were restricted to seizing or sharing power to achieve its ideological goals.

Alongside the activities of the intellectual elite, officers in the Syrian army also took an active role in trying to reshape political life, which they did by mounting a series of military *coups d'état*. The revolutionary movement that ʿAbd al-Karīm al-Naḥlāwī led in an attempt to detach Syrian territory from the united republic provided a gateway through which Baʿthist military organizations could benefit from a failing military movement to succeed eventually in establishing a new government after the coup of 8 March 1963.

When a coup in Iraq successfully toppled ʿAbd al-Karīm Qasim on 8 February 1963, many Baʿthist military organizations were encouraged to attempt to attack the already crumbling government of Bashir al-ʿAsma. Consequently, just one month later, on 8 March 1963, a clique of Nasserite-leftist Syrian army officers mounted a successful *coup d'état* that brought the Baʿth Party to power.

The 8 March 1963 coup ushered in a dualistic form of Syrian government. Although it is true that this was not the first military takeover in Syria's history, the legality of the military intrusion was different in each case. The army's rationale for the pre-unity coups was to sort matters out on the political, economic, social and even military fronts. (Liberating Palestine was a rationale for all subsequent revolutions.) These coups often caused legal and constitutional embarrassment, which was usually resolved by the elected president abdicating, as in the case of al-Zaʾim, or through assigning a nominal president, so that actual power lay in the army, or through fake referendums and elections. However, the military recognized that people resented its intrusion in policy, which is why it withdrew completely from that role after the 1954 Shīshaklī *coup d'état*.

The Syrian–Egyptian style of unity, especially the kind Abdul

Nasser devised, with its single political party, militarized society and abandonment of any factional diversity, let alone a parliament or democratic elections, led Syria's national and leftist elite to adopt revolutionary economic and social measures to pursue its course of independent development and its external political goals. This ideology – whether in a Nasserite, Baʿthist, Islamic or communist guise – saw little virtue in a state based on legislative and constitutional institutions and a social contract between power and society. For them, the state was nothing more than a tool through which to realize the revolution towards achieving a 'united socialist Arab society'.

This fragile image of the state among the Syrian elite and intellectuals encouraged the military to implement what the intellectuals themselves were unable to achieve quickly or efficiently. For this reason, during the unity era the Syrian army was split into contradictory ideological and paramilitary blocs. These were the Damascene officers' bloc (*al-Shwam*), which signed the separation; the socialist officers' bloc (*al-Ḥawrānīyīn*); the Baʿthist independent bloc, secretly subsumed in the 'military committee'; and the Nasserite bloc. Although the latter was the largest front, the Baʿthist bloc was the most organized and cohesive. It put all the leaders of units at the mercy of its lower officers. While all four blocs – Damascene, socialist, Nasserite and independent – generally represented the urban middle class, the leaders of the 'military committee', which consisted mainly of a cadre descended from 'Alawi, Durzi and Ismaeli Islamic minorities, had the stranglehold on the rural population.[16]

The rise of the 'military committee' in the Baʿth Party, which assumed power, really meant one thing: it meant the exclusion of the intellectual Baʿthist elites from decision making and replacing them with members of the newly emergent military elite. The intellectuals then assumed the role of thinkers rather than policy makers. In his book *Theoretical Starting Points* (*Baʾd al-Muntalaqat al-Nazariyah*), which the party approved in 1963, Yāsīn al-Ḥāfiẓ vividly describes the exchange of roles between the intellectuals and the army.

The military committee, which was established and operated in Cairo during the unity period,[17] looked upon Abdul Nasser's method of building a socialist state as an ideal prototype that it wanted to replicate in its own image. Despite previous military interventions, as I mentioned earlier, this one took on a totally different aspect, especially after the al-Bīṭār and Michael ʿAflak defeat of 23 February 1966 when the army's own ideological position supplanted that of the Baʿthist intellectuals. As Salāmah rather creatively described it, the position developed as follows: when notables and their nationalist followers fought over power, the army would interfere to put an end to the squabble. In 1963, although al-Baʿth had by then Baʿthized the political field, the same dynamics continued. While the politicians and ideologues carried on debating and throwing accusations at one another, the military would stand by as the debate progressed from outside to inside the party and then seize the appropriate moment to pounce and seize power.[18]

Salāmah concluded that, in terms of its political and social changes, Syria was no different from any other Arab Levant country. The inhabitants were 'urbanized', but power was first 'ruralized' and then taken by the army. In Damascus, Aleppo, Lattakia and other Syrian cities that expanded at the expense of the countryside, the formerly rural newcomers had great difficulty merging into the native population. This was because of the high population growth in Syria, which went up from 3.5 per cent in the 1950s to 4.4 per cent in the 1960s. It was highest in Damascus and Aleppo, moving from 1.3 per cent in the 1950s to 6.4 per cent in the 1960s, while in Lattakia the population doubled between 1960 and 1970,[19] when it reached 4.6 per cent.

This new concentration of populations resulted in the destruction of urban traditions and a failure to modernize rural culture, which remained at loggerheads with the urbanized elites. It is necessary to bear in mind, however, that the arrival of new rural generations to the city does have positive benefits in that educational opportunities are expanded, and certain economic and social needs are fulfilled. In fact, these are necessary prerequisites for building a modern country. The loss of legal traditions, especially in the political field, ushers in another different form of power monopoly. Power in the hands of notables did not actually represent the society's classes. The deputies were mostly urban, rich landlords, yet, despite their defects, their function as a channel for the civil society was somehow ensured. They felt a constant tension between achieving power and representing the people who could, somehow, exclude them from their offices, or at least, decrease their presence through the pressure of popular activist groups.

The society's political bodies are becoming more representative of the people, though not necessarily in a predictable or even intentional way. The last elections of 1954, for example, were the best and most honest, for there the influence of public pressure on the deputies was noticeable. The first council (the general Syrian conference), was driven by popular patriotic pressure to make more progressive moves than its members probably wanted. In other words, although representation on the council was not a true reflection of all the elements of society, the council was, nevertheless, prepared to act as a channel through which mounting pressures or opinions could be directed. Civil society was being politicized, even if in an unintended way.

Nowadays, indirect representation for people has improved in the council, government, leading party and popular organizations. Direct representation, on the other hand, was very weak, mainly because the different elements of civil society did not choose its leaders from among the group they represented. The relative economic independence of notables from the state was useful in that, unlike their successors, they were not reliant on the state for their positions – for income, privileges and sometimes just the wherewithal to live an ordinary (apart from a political) life.[20] This marks the main difference between post-independence and post-revolutionary political systems. Post-revolutionary systems have no room for freedom of expression other than from revolutionary intellectuals, especially since announcement 'No. 1' cancelled first newspapers, then political parties. At that point the state identified with the revolution, so ideological debates, mostly leftist ones, flared up. The state's left-wing debates consisted mostly of propaganda that could sometimes descend to an immature and primitive level, especially if we look closely at the three doctors' (President Nour el-din al-Atāsī, Prime Minister Yosif Zaʿien and Minister of Foreign Affairs Ibrāhīm Makhus were all physicians, which was why many scholars called the Syrian regime at that time the 'three doctors' regime) formal arguments after the defeat of June 1967.

Despite the loss of the Golan Heights, this regime considered Israel its main target, even though no such war could be won, especially given that Israel's real goal was to overthrow the regime in Syria. That these debates should reach their greatest intensity during national *qawmī* and regional *quṭrī* conferences was an indication of the presence of ideology and absence of reality. When the political elite began to focus its thoughts and theories on battling over social, economic and political offices, the debates had become nothing but mental abstractions and brain storming. Meanwhile, a different tune was being heard in the society at large when, to the joy of the public, on 16 November 1970, a military coup intervened to steer the Baʿth Party onto a correct path. This coup, later referred to as the 'corrective movement', was proof that only army intervention and military coups could solve political arguments. The military thus took full control over policy, leaving only a marginal role to the politicians and intellectuals.

Quarrels between revolutionary leaders would continue to plague the 'revolutionary state' and the coup of 23 February 1966[21] was itself the product of competitive conflicts between revolutionary groups. Consequently, whenever difficulties arose over local public issues in the country or among members of the civilian population, there was a tendency always to revert to the internal contradictions.

In brief, the military started a new chapter after 1966. This was a chapter in which the countryside predominated over the city, the minority over a fragile mix between the majority and minorities, military men over citizens, realism over utopia, and the army over the party. Since then, the Baʿth Party has been no more than the tool of the military, or more precisely, of a few officers. Its only use is to disseminate propaganda, recruit members and reinforce legitimacy. The new 'extremely leftist' path adopted in Syria by Salah Jdaʿed (1966–70) was to some extent an attempt to escape from all these 'victories' with a view to establishing a legality based on new elements.[22] The party came to resemble a leftist military cadre. It restricted the rights of active members who led public organizations set up as substitutes for the previous civil society institutions to vote, nominate and elect members to senior Baʿth positions, even though these organizations and trade unions functioned only as adjuncts to help the party gain access to the wider society. At a trade union level, it started from the idea of political unionism rather than from the notion of a form of trade unionism that made claims to promote the interests of its members, which was considered a liberal bourgeois form of trade union activity. As a party in which a trained member and an active member had to undergo *fidāʾī* (militia) courses, it was like a camping party in which a 'People's Army (*al-jaysh al-shaʾbi*)' was created alongside the 'doctrinaire army' in an attempt to recruit the whole society.

Because ideological, class and loyalty criteria determined the acceptance of officers and non-commissioned officers as professionals into the army, and because military service was mandatory when the military structure was national, there was a 'ruralization' of the professional military elite, which in turn politicized what became known as the 'doctrinaire army'.[23]

The coup of 8 March 1963 saw the natural demise of 'revolutionary legality' and a notable reduction in 'constitutional legality'. In fact, after seizing power in 1963 and appointing Hafez al-Asad as president in 1971, the Baʿth Party made no attempt whatsoever at even a pretence of organizing local, legislative or presidential elections. Granted, some elections were held afterwards, especially during Hafez al-Asad's tenure, but with no accurate data and wholly predictable results, they were mere charades and nothing more than a game. Their purpose had less to do with legality or confidence than with giving the outward appearance of a democratic political process going on within the autocratic pyramid of power.

So long as there were no constitutional or legal issues to worry about, the Baʿthist elite that ruled after 1963 did not really care about the charade. It aimed mainly through the use of revolutionary methods to achieve independent social and economic development, and to maintain its foreign political objectives.

The party that emerged first from the revolutionary council's axe and later from that of its leader has existed since 8 March 1963 and, apart from some marginal changes, which were sometimes essential, its pyramidal structure of autocratic power based on one party with the president at its head has remained unchanged. This structure characterized the third republic from its establishment until President Hafez al-Asad set it in stone first by rewriting the constitution and then by reorganizing the constitutional, legislative and judicial institutions in a way that would prevent them from thinking outside the previously designed framework. Later on, non-governmental organizations, trade unions and various other associations, which the Baʿth Party had kept in reserve, were brought out of obscurity to express the party's more public face[24] by playing a role in running the various trade unions and campaigning movements that 'shaped' civil society.

The Third Republic and the Pyramid-building Theory

Getting to know what mechanisms underlie decision-making in Syria is a highly intricate and difficult task. This is due less, for example, to the complexity of the process than it is to the secrecy that surrounds a given legal formula, which inevitably results in different research projects proceeding from different viewpoints.

Even although there are not all that many academic studies on Syria compared with other neighbouring countries such as Jordan or Lebanon, those that do exist tend to place too much emphasis on a particular Syrian leader without attempting to study what mechanisms lie behind the political system.

Patrick Seale, for example, who wrote a biography of President Hafez al-Asad,[25] claimed that Asad is Syria, and Syria is Asad, while Lucian Peterlan echoed the same sentiment in describing Asad's foreign policy[26] and Moshe Maʿoz referred to him as 'the Sphinx of Damascus'.[27] There are others, however, like Hinnebusch,[28] Heydemann[29] and Batatu,[30] who have tried to compare the Syrian system with those of other similar authoritative regimes. Volker Perthes, who studied economic policy under Asad,[31] was perhaps one of the earliest to analyse economic and political decision-making in

Syria, and Eyal Zisser wrote a book that looked into 'decision-making in al-Asad's Syria'.[32]

Despite the seriousness of these specialized studies and the thorough way in which they pursued their investigations even into decision-making under the regime of President Bashar al-Asad, they seemed to adopt a behaviourist position to explain decision-making in Syria: they assumed that al-Asad's behaviour and personal characteristics were enough to explain, or at least provide answers to, the political and economic troubles he faced.

The 1973 Syrian constitution, issued during President Hafez al-Asad's period in office and still in force, confirms that the republic's president assumes responsibility for foreign policy, while the prime minister, despite his overall responsibility for it, does not play any distinct role in the field of foreign policy. This is because, in Article 94, the constitution stipulates that the president of the republic lays the foundation for the foreign policy of the state and supervises its implementation through deliberation with the Council of Ministers, while according to Article 71 of the constitution the duties of the legislative power do not extend beyond discussing the ministers' policy and ratifying international treaties and agreements related to the security of the state.[33]

Article 8 of the Syrian constitution gives the president of the republic wide powers, apart from being the secretary-general of the Ba'th Party, to lead both the state and society. According to Article 103 of the constitution he also holds the position of supreme commander of the army and armed forces and high commander of the central leadership of the National Progressive Front (NPF). His authorities exceed those of any other executive or legislative authority because he has the right to break up the People's Assembly (Article 107), legislate at times when the council is not in session (Article 111), dismiss office holders (Article 108 of the People's Assembly rules of procedures), appoint one or more vice-president and determine their powers or acquit them from their positions, appoint the prime minister, his deputies and the ministers and acquit them from their positions (Article 95), declare a state of war (Article 100) and declare or cancel a state of emergency (Article 101).[34]

The state president's authority in the Syrian constitution reflects the extent of his 'constitutional' power over the state's other institutions. The shape of the state and the development of its institutional structures in a pyramid-like presidential system have resulted in a constitutional, legal and actual concentration of power in the hands of the state president.

One of the main characteristics of the Syrian system that emerged with the 'third republic' was the concentration of political power in the hands of an elite with rural and military origins. Consequently, throughout his long years in office, Hafez al-Asad was able to concentrate this power in a steeply pyramidal way in which bureaucracy played a decisive role in invalidating the numerous competitive roles represented by the state's different legislative, judicial and executive institutions. This gave the president free rein to express his personal wishes and orientations, which in turn led to military, economic and social networks and interests based on personal relations or affiliations being established on the fringes of state institutions, or in some cases even completely outside them.

This happens when the methods used to secure previous security agreements, and to which the different ministries of the state as well as the citizens are bound, are used by the state to exercise its authoritative control over society in all civil, informational, social, economic, political and even charitable matters. What results is a bureaucratic atmosphere imbued with the kind of fear that characterizes all authoritative regimes in the world.

With increased educational provision in the countryside, alongside the accompanying need for these newly-educated people to migrate to the main cities to improve their social standing, many sought employment in the various state institutions, particularly the army, for which they needed fewer educational or other formal qualifications. At the same time, the majority of these rural elites, particularly the sons of the Alawite and Druze minorities,[35] felt drawn to the more doctrinaire ideologies, especially socialism, which promised a more egalitarian distribution of power and wealth, and access to the new Syrian social and political system encapsulated in the third republic. The ruralization of the city led gradually to the ruralization of the authority itself, and this eventually undermined the legal traditions founded by the civic elite that took power after independence. This does not, however, exempt these elites from the serious mistakes they made in their administration of the state and its institutions. Still, although they sometimes violated or neglected them, they nonetheless maintained and valued the terms of the constitution. With deep demographic changes and rapid social development taking place in Syria, it was hardly surprising that the country should produce a new political elite coming from different social origins and in which a military background played a decisive role.

The Ba'th Party's seizure of power in 1963 coincided with a notable strengthening of the military committee within it. This committee would later take on the decisive role of deciding who assumed and controlled power, which meant that the military developed in such a way that it presented an obstacle to the smooth running of civilian institutions and sometimes paralysed their work, as witnessed in the consecutive military coups that took place between 1949 and 1970.

During his rule, Hafez al-Asad relied heavily on his comrades in the military struggle. As a result, the two most decisive qualities he sought in the people he chose for office were first of all loyalty, which he placed above all else, and then a person's military background, which was the secret component of the civil state he tried to create.

On taking up power al-Asad tried to restructure the political system on a new and different basis from the one that had prevailed since 1963 when the Ba'th Party assumed power. In 1971 he set up the parliament (or People's Assembly of Syria) and appointed members to it. A year later, in 1972, he established the NPF, which, given that it brought together all the political parties in Syria that supported the Ba'th Party and ratified the charter that acknowledged the permanent leadership of al-Ba'th, was looked upon as a kind of political federation. In 1973 he announced a new constitution amending the temporary one of 1969. This new constitution attached the legislative powers to the Council of Ministers and was later further amended so that the system became a presidential one.

The main disagreement that the corrective movement led by President Hafez al-Asad attempted to resolve in 1970 centred on the government's general orientations, political strategies and economic programme.[36] The result, eventually, was a more open form of government triumphing over the more doctrinaire one that wanted to run political and economic affairs according to the ideological strictures of the Ba'thist programme. In fact, these ideological restrictions exacerbated the Ba'th Party's internal crisis because whenever any new regional or central developments floated to the surface the internal discords would merely intensify.

Asad with the Ba'th Party behind him seemed to be willing to enter a new relationship with society and its various political forces. The beginning of this had been the formation of a coalition government under the auspices of the National Progressive Front. This coalition contained representatives of five parties with two ministers for each party in the NPF except for al-Ba'th, which secured the majority for itself.

At the beginning, Asad tried to get out of the shackles of the leftist Ba'thist doctrines. Discord within the Ba'th Party centred on the division between the 'factional wing' headed by Salah Jda'ed and the military wing that he, Asad, led. Asad's programme can be summed up in the statement that the priority is 'national liberation' defined as retrieving the Arab territories occupied by the Israelis. The conflict between the 'Arab nation' and 'Israel' was paramount; hence, all other political, ideological and social contradictions were secondary. This required the realization of an 'active Arab solidarity' – externally, transcending the ideological political discords with Iraq and Jordan and, internally, liberation from the 'leftist' closed characteristic of the party. His domestic programme involved establishing a constitution that would ensure popular participation in government, made possible by the election of a People's Assembly and the formation of a National Progressive Front that would consolidate national unity. Jda'ed, on the other hand, reiterated his leftist 'theory' that 'the outer aggression has an internal objective which is the overthrowing of the progressive revolutionary system in both Syria and Egypt, and that the program suggested by al-Asad is no more than the practical execution of the internal part of the aggression.'[37]

The front that al-Asad wished for would essentially be a 'National Bloc' that would include parties of different ideological trends united in a common purpose of nation building. The charter of the NPF committee was ratified on 22 May 1971. It stated that the NPF constituted the political leadership that decided matters of peace and war, approved five-year plans, determined general political orientation and consolidated the basis of the popular democratic system. The charter also gave the Ba'th Party leadership of the NPF by ensuring that it always had majority representation in it. The Ba'th Party had a monopoly of the political work in two crucial sectors – the students and the army. The party programme and its conference decisions would be the main guide to the NPF in formulating its general policy and executing its plans.[38]

Thus, al-Asad tried to widen the base of political and popular support for the existing regime, and, at the same time, give it a legal status by clothing it with the attire of the civic institutions.[39]

He founded institutional structures to provide the democratic façade behind which he could exercise the real power of his party. At the same time, it was necessary to rebuild the popular organizations of the workers, peasants, unions, Ba'th Party itself and others on a basis that would ensure complete loyalty in a way that could not be done merely by widening the governmental administration, the army or the security organs. This process was made possible by an increase in state finances, thanks to the many Arab contributions given to Syria after the war of 1973 and, then, to the revenue from Syrian oil discovered a little later.

This allowed Asad to build a bureaucratic cadre to fill the various Syrian institutions that had been established in a pyramidal form with the head of the state standing on top of the pyramid and its three sides all leading up to him – these were the government administration, the army and security organs (the intelligence), and the party.[40]

These three organs descend from the leadership down to the city, the village and the quarter.

The Governmental Administration

Governors represent the president at the regional level of government. There are 14 governors in Syria who directly execute the president's commands – administering and supervising the departments attached to the central government ministries and overseeing the public sector in and around the governorate. The governor is the executive head of the administration and in this capacity he also heads the municipal council in the governorate and, in cases of an emergency, becomes the leader of the police and army. Correspondingly, the secretary of the Baʿth Party branch in the governorate is also a representative of the central authority. The secretaries of the party branches in the governorates are subject to precise vetting by the president in his capacity as secretary-general of the party to whom they directly send their reports. The party branches in the 14 governorates supervise the education, health, cultural affairs, technical development and sport institutions. Moreover, the secretary of a branch may take the place of the governor in case of the latter's absence from his governorate. On the third and last level the different activities of both party and administration on all levels are under the daily control of the Syrian security organs.

The Baʿth Party

The Baʿth Party is considered the ruling party or 'the party that leads both society and the state' according to the eighth article of the Syrian constitution, while the regional leadership (*al-Qiyādah al-Quṭrī*) of the party suggests the name of the presidential candidate. The number of those joining the party has been dramatically increasing since 1963, the year when the party held sway, despite the fact that the number of party members at the time had not exceeded a few hundreds.[41] Later, in 1971, when president Hafez al-Asad assumed power the number rose to almost 65,000,[42] but when he died in 2000 the number had reached 71,573 active members (*ʿudw ʿamil*).[43]

The so-called 'policy of Baʿthization' was adopted. It entailed doubling the number of members affiliated to the party and giving them priority for jobs in government administrations and educational missions. It also meant that all important senior military, security, ministerial and administrative positions were limited to them.

The newly affiliated member is called '*nasir*' (meaning advocate or supporter). He needs to be trained for two years before attaining full membership, called 'active membership', which after a certain period of time entitles him to vote and to stand as a candidate for office. Students account for 53.71 per cent of the intake because the majority of affiliated members are recruited from among students in preparatory and secondary schools. Workers constitute 20.62 per cent of party membership and peasants 16.53 per cent.[44]

According to social structure analysis, the overwhelming majority of Ba'th members came from Syria's various rural areas, since the sons and families of established cities such as Damascus, Aleppo, Homs, Hama and Lattakia continued to be cautious about joining the Ba'th Party, which historically had raised its flag in defence of workers and peasants.[45] When President Hafez al-Asad assumed power, the party was reorganized into a pyramidal semi-military structure. Since 1971, local conferences have ceased to elect the leaders of branches and subdivisions; rather, they have been elected by the regional leadership (*al-Qiyādah al-Quṭrī*) that superintends the work of local branches according to the principle of 'centralized democracy' approved by the party. This principle requires that members elect their representatives to the regional conference (*almout 'amar al-quṭrī*), which, in turn, selects the members of the regional leadership (*al-Qiyādah al-Quṭrī*) from among them. In fact, the regional leadership has always influenced the election of representatives to the conference through supporting its nominees, recommending them and putting pressure on competing nominees to withdraw. The regional conference (*almout 'amar al-quṭrī*), which directly elects the members of the regional leadership (*al-Qiyādah al-Quṭrī*), remained unchanged until 1975, but in 1980 this conference made appointments only to the central committee, which, in turn, elected the members of the regional leadership (*al-Qiyādah al-Quṭrī*) from among its members.[46]

In 1985 the conference authorized President Hafez al-Asad personally to appoint the central committee.[47] This committee, however, has not convened a meeting for itself since the eighth regional conference (*almout ʿamar al-quṭrī*) in 1985; even the party had not convened its general conference for 15 years, that is until 2000, the year of President Hafez al-Asad's death, despite it being the ruling party.

Although the regional leadership (*al-Qiyādah al-Quṭrī*) was supposed to constitute the political leadership of the ruling Baʿth Party, it more or less lost its power to make political decisions with the arrival of President Hafez al-Asad to the regime in 1970, at which point the regional *Quṭrī* conferences became no more than theatrical festivals for celebrating the symbolic significance of 'our leader forever'. As long as al-Asad chose the members of the regional leadership (*al-Qiyādah al-Quṭrī*) it owed him loyalty and, therefore, during the last decade of his rule, he never attended its meetings, contenting himself with sending 'his commands' on a paper to be read and ratified at once, or resorting to the telephone in the case of an urgent event that could not be postponed.[48] A member of the regional leadership (*al-Qiyādah al-Quṭrī*) described Asad thus: 'For us he was tantamount to an imaginary voice coming through the phone.' With al-Asad's withdrawal from domestic affairs (except through daily security reports coming by phone), there emerged the concept of '*ḥiẓwah*' (meaning 'favour' or 'preference'). The number of people he met became very limited, restricted to close favourites who came to have special influence.

As for the national leadership (*al-Qiyādah al-Qawmīyah*), which is theoretically an institution organizationally higher than the regional leadership (*al-Qiyādah al-Quṭrī*)[49] because it includes both the Syrian and the other regional leaderships, it was changed into an honorary body. According to Volker Perthes a position in the national leadership became a synonym for unemployment.[50]

The party was changed into a governmental bureaucratic institution, which paradoxically deprived it of its ideological and political leadership, despite it having been in power since 1963. Its role as a political party was mixed up with its role as part of the regime and the two functions were incorporated into the state institutions. This is contrary to the concept of a party competing for power and submitting to an electoral process that gives a vote of confidence to a particular party to assume power for a limited length of time. The mixing up of these concepts started with the Syrian constitution, which defined the role of a political party as a leader of both society and the state and joined its budget to that of the government to an extent that the party funding comes mostly from governmental financial resources. In 1983, 80 per cent of its budget, which reached $129 million (the equal of the Ministry of Finance budget at the time) came as allocations from the state.[51]

The party is theoretically subject to the authority of the security organizations that supervise its activities; however, its branches often submit reports to the security services and help them survey people in their areas. Syrians often joke about the Ba'th Party being no more than an additional arm of state security.

The Security Organs

There are four bodies concerned with security. These are General Intelligence Administration (state security) officially subordinated to the Ministry of the Interior; political security, which is another Ministry of the Interior department; military intelligence; and branches of the air force that are nominally subordinated to the Ministry of Defence.

The National Security Bureau supervises these different organs, which are subordinated to the regional leadership (*al-Qiyādah al-Quṭrī*) of the Ba'th Party. These bodies (except for the air force, which is charged with special missions) are responsible for local surveillance and have branches in all governorates as well as central branches in the capital, Damascus.[52] Because of intense competition among these different bodies, the role of some security branches expanded hugely even at the expense of the administration to which they were subordinated. This contributed to the influence and power of the branch head, which were often inflated because of the direct relationship of this post to the president. These branches (enjoying legal immunity) always went beyond their competence, thus becoming an influential factor in political or administrative decisions. They came to consider themselves as directly responsible, ahead of President Asad, and thus were encouraged to grow in an alarming way.[53]

Some 65,000 people were employed full time in different Syrian security organizations, with several hundred thousand employed part time. According to this reckoning, there is a member of the intelligence service for every 257 Syrian citizens. Since only 59.5 per cent of the Syrians are above the age of 15, there is a member of the intelligence service for every 153 adult citizens – one of the highest ratios in the world.[54]

Using the language of numbers to illustrate the extent of bureaucratic extension in the different state departments under the third republic, we find that the number of public sector personnel in the different government administrations rose from 70,000 in 1965, to beyond 685,000 in 1991 and exceeded 900,000 in 2004, while the number of those working in the army and different security organs rose from 65,000 in 1965, to 530,000 in 1991 and exceeded 700,000 in 2004.[55]

This tremendous bureaucratic build-up of the pyramid's three sides creates an Orwellian system of surveillance. Political opposition or civic organizations could have very little if any impact because it is very difficult in such a situation to escape the surveillance of so many different state organizations, unless the state itself tries to penetrate them and change them into 'subjugated' or at least cooperative institutions.

It is ironic that, despite the three different surveillance levels the governmental institutions represent, the first two levels, namely the party branches and security organizations, have gradually faded out of the picture, despite the importance of their role in building the political and institutional structure. They have lost ground to the third level (the security organizations), which has lost no time in taking over all the important security and political decisions.

Thus, since the emergence of 'the third republic' in 1963, the Syrian political system has been based on a pyramid-like structure with each of its three sides leading up to Hafez al-Asad at the apex. These three facets constitute the structure of Syrian totalitarianism. They provide a safety system that prevents some part of the regime from breaking away with its leadership, while at the same time giving the regime a veneer of legitimacy by virtue of its various judicial, political and legislative institutions.

Within this complicated framework of bureaucracy and legal institutions, there developed a system of allegiances and patron-client relationships that played a crucial role in both protecting the regime and, at the same time, providing it with the cement necessary to bind the pyramid's three facets to each other.

The pyramidal structure of the regime provided the office of president with constitutional and legal safeguards. Any threat to the presidency had been completely removed by the end of the 1980s when al-Asad could rearrange the security organizations and military units that threatened his position as president.

The appointed date for the presidential referendum that would give President Hafez al-Asad an additional fifth constitutional seven-year period in office was set for 8 February 1999. Because of the death of King Hussein of Jordan, however, al-Asad suddenly decided to postpone the referendum to a later date. There was no constitutional difficulty in doing this so long as the People's Assembly was the party authorized to do it. In practice, all that was needed was a telephone call from al-Asad declaring the date to which he wished the referendum to be postponed. In fact, this made no difference because he would get his 99.98 per cent of the vote irrespective of when the referendum took place. On the appointed day, however, when all the various political leaders were awaiting his arrival at the polling station, he suddenly changed his mind and turned up at a girls' school instead, quite contrary to what had been planned for him.[56]

Asad's behaviour during the so-called referendum was a reflection of his general leadership style, particularly during the last years of his life. As I have already mentioned, he rarely attended the meetings of the Ba'th Party's regional leaders even though, constitutionally and politically, this was the highest governing body in the country; rather, he would content himself with conveying his instructions to the meeting by telephone, instructions he would immediately expect to see ratified and executed.

He was completely and single-handedly the one decision-maker who could set in motion any all-inclusive system at his disposal.[57] He did not allow independent, let alone critical, media to emerge. The three official newspapers – the only newspapers in the country – were instructed to report and follow up any expressions of praise or thanks from observers in the Arab region or world at large and to repeat them with a lot of veneration and pomposity. The media, therefore, were characterized by a deadly type of repetition and monotony, which the Syrians took as a tool of Asad's hegemony rather than as a means of providing the citizens with accurate information.

The same can be said about what are called decision-making centres (think-tanks) or independent research centres: each was attached to one or other of the intelligence branches and would provide them with whatever studies and information about Syria were deemed necessary, but they had no advisory function. Al-Asad had no permanent consultants, but sought advice on certain occasions, usually to get a technical opinion, though the final decision rested with him. The absence of ambassadors from all Syrian embassies abroad during the last years of his regime[58] seems to confirm this and reveals his indifference to his image abroad.

The regime's pyramidal structure reinforced the hereditary tendencies. Thus, the transition from al-Asad senior to al-Asad junior, which the various security, military, political and legislative institutions administered, reflected the extent to which familial links penetrate these institutions. The transition was highly organized and efficiently carried out: on a single day, 11 June 2008, power was quietly transferred under a constitutional cover from al-Asad the father to al-Asad the son.

The People's Assembly quickly assembled to amend Article 83 of the Syrian constitution, which states that 'the age of the State President shall not be less than forty years'; the required age became 34, Bashar's age at the time. Article 88, which appoints the president's first deputy as a ruler in the case of a president's death – in this case ʿAbd al-Ḥalīm Khaddām – was removed. It was essential that there should be no opening for a challenge while the authority was being transferred from father to son. Asad's symbolic heritage built up over the course of three decades would be shaken if there were any break in continuity, even if for only a few days. Thus, the catchwords 'change under the wing of continuity' and 'renewal under the wing of stability' immediately became current. For many years, stability in Syria has been linked with the name of Asad, as the Syrian media continually remind us.

Asad's Heritage

Asad's heritage can be read from the effects of his internal policy on the different educational, social, economic and political sectors. Political life was firmly based on the parties of the NPF being recognized as legal agencies, even although no body existed in Syria to regulate the work of political parties. The NPF was created to consolidate the foundations of the regime President Hafez al-Asad established by neutralizing any possible opposition – particularly the opposition of groups that had traditionally been considered Baʿth rivals – and by widening the base of President Asad's political support beyond the Baʿth Party. Moreover, the NPF enabled the Syrian regime to portray its political structure, even if only rhetorically, as based on political and factional plurality.[59]

The NPF included the two wings of the Communist Party (one led by Wiṣāl Bakdāsh and the other by Yūsuf Fayṣal), the Arab Socialist Union (which underwent many breakups and considered itself part of the movement), the Socialist Federalist Movement (which dissociated itself from the Baʿth Party after Syria's break with the United Arab Republic in 1961), the Democratic Socialist Federalist Movement (which had parted from the last movement in 1974) and the Arab Socialist Movement (which also separated from al-Baʿth in 1964.)

Representatives of these parties attended the periodical meetings held by the central leadership of the National Progressive Front, regarded as the highest political leadership in Syria. Even before joining, however, these parties had ratified the NPF's charter, which stated that it (the NPF) was a 'political supreme command which decides peace and war issues, the five-year plans, consolidates the foundations of the popular democratic system and leads the general political orientation'. Also, through formulating the majority (half+1) principle, the NPF supplies the Baʿth Party with its leaders. The constitution of the NPF allowed the Baʿth Party to monopolize political work in the army and among students, and stated that 'the party program and its conference resolutions are the main guide to the Front in formulating its general policy and executing its plans.'[60] This charter was considered tantamount to a directory guide for the NPF's policy, so its parties could not raise any questions in an NPF meeting, just as they could not open headquarters or get licences to issue their publications before Bashar al-Asad's arrival to power.[61]

The NPF parties lost their credibility, which some of them, particularly the Communist Party, had acquired historically, just as they lost their popularity because of their dependence on the Baʿth Party. This meant that they were forced to support the regime's policy, even if it flew in the face of their ideological principles. The personal perks the leaders acquired, as well as party splits and conflicts, had the effect of decreasing the number of members to just the few thousand who had benefited personally. Wiṣāl Bakdāsh's wing of the Communist Party officially claimed 8000 members, Yūsuf Fayṣal's wing between 9000 and 10,000, the Socialist Federalist Movement 5000, the Democratic Socialist Federalist 1000 and the Arab Socialist Movement 1000. However, these figures are all greatly exaggerated.[62]

The opposition, whose existence al-Asad never acknowledged, had ever since his assumption of rule in 1970 been subjected to an organized campaign of political arrests. Those arrested included his political opponents, particularly supporters of his mortal enemy in the Baʿth Party Salah Jdaʿed, as well as Baʿth members suspected of being followers of the party's Iraqi wing. The arrests increased considerably after 1979 following a bloody armed conflict with the Muslim Brotherhood and this time they included members of the independent syndicates (of lawyers, doctors and engineers) who declared a general strike in 1981 and called for democracy, freedom, the principle of the rule of law and respect for human rights.[63] These syndicates were broken up and many of their members were imprisoned. When the National Democratic Coalition was established and advocated pursuing a midway path between supporting the regime and armed opposition, the majority of its activists were arrested. At the same time, there was a widespread campaign of arrests against members of the Muslim Brotherhood and a law was passed (Act 49) that prescribed the death penalty for anyone who joined the Muslim Brotherhood and refused to provide documentary evidence of withdrawal within one month.[64] With respect to the regime's opponents abroad, a long-arm policy of assassination came into force[65] and a number of hostile Lebanese journalists such as Salīm al-Lawzī[66] were liquidated in Beirut. At that point al-Asad decided that it was necessary to 'intensify the campaign politically and in the field of security to clear the Muslim Brotherhood band and get rid of its support in both society and the state'.[67]

Deciding to resort to the military option in the wake of the escalation of violent action, al-Asad bombed the city of Hama in February 1982, which resulted in the deaths of many civilians whose precise number is still unknown (between 5000 and 15,000). Most of them died beneath the debris of the city, which had been levelled to the ground.[68] Then followed a haphazard campaign of arrests during which thousands of activists, opponents and even advocates of the regime were arrested; the number exceeded 100,000.[69]

A large number of those prisoners were victims of forced disappearances and, to this day, their families know nothing about their fate. Human rights organizations estimate that about 17,000 people are unaccounted for. This horrific record of human rights violations is comparable to the losses following a natural disaster. But al-Asad remained indifferent to the consequences, thus creating a negative impression of Syria, which acquired a reputation for being an authoritarian police state. Campaigns of random and collective arrests continued up to the last year of al-Asad's rule,[70] and did not stop under his successor Bashar al-Asad.[71]

Furthermore, Asad had never taken an interest in the economy or dedicated any time to it except when an economic crisis[72] threatened the security and stability of the country. In 1986 a period of economic stagnation paralysed all productive sectors and a foreign currency crisis[73] hit consumer prices. At one point there was no bread flour obtainable in the markets and this threatened to trigger a serious social crisis, which the Syrian authorities decided to deal with gradually. By the end of 1987 the exchange rate for the Syrian pound had officially fallen from 3.95 to 11.2 for one US dollar, but the real rate was closer to 40 Syrian pounds for one dollar.[74]

Cultivating wheat as a strategic crop was encouraged. For fear of repeating the flour crisis that had exposed Syria to so much economic pressure, the state would buy the entire crop, which would be stored in large silos and warehouses. These measures were accompanied by savage cuts in basic provisions, a widening gap between rich and poor and the rise of a new, extremely greedy and wealthy class.[75] Corruption was widespread in the government and elsewhere.[76] For two full decades, networks of corrupt officials inside the regime monopolized commercial relations, thereby undermining any trust that there may have been in the monetary system, foreign investments or any of the other economic or legal measures taken to serve the interests of the regime. The competition and transparency necessary for the development of an economic sector were therefore lost.[77]

The pillar of the economy was thus the public sector, which employed about one-quarter of the work force and supported companies with annual losses continually running into billions of pounds – losses that the state automatically covered. Despite the state support, this sector was unable to absorb the increasing numbers of unemployed young people. According to approximate statistics, at least 25 per cent of young people aged between 15 and 30 were unemployed.[78]

The increase in economic stagnation since the second half of the 1990s has reduced citizens' purchasing power and led to a severe deterioration in their standard of living. A study by the United Nations Development Programme showed that in 2005 there were 5,300,000 Syrians living below the poverty line.[79]

All these clear indications made no impression on al-Asad. Consequently, Syria now faces extremely difficult economic challenges. Today the country depends mainly on its oil, since oil constitutes 60–70 per cent of Syrian exports as well as 40–50 per cent of state revenues. Even that, however, is uncertain because, according to international estimates, Syrian oil reserves are likely to run out in 2012.[80]

Also, there has been little development in the field of education; only 60 per cent of men and 50 per cent of women have benefited from schooling, which is a much lower percentage than in neighbouring countries such as Jordan for example.

In the area of social development, al-Asad worked towards establishing new civil associations to regulate the more active and politically significant trade unions. In practice, these were a resource for the regime because their main objective was to tame public protest by absorbing the people into semi-official institutions in which the regime directed and determined their main aims and activities.[81] Already existing organizations were also transformed to serve the same purpose. These included the Ba'th Pioneers (*Talā'al-Ba'th*), the Revolutionary Youth Union, the National Union of Syrian Students, the Peasants' Union, and the General Union of Women. Their function was threefold – representation, recruitment and control. First, these organizations would ensure that their legitimate interests, particularly their social and cultural concerns, were represented in the political system; the political leadership would prioritize these interests and decide which of them should be considered legitimate. Second, these organizations would recruit personnel from among their particular sectors of society who would support the regime for the purpose of realizing 'the revolutionary objectives'; they would also work towards developing their productive capabilities and implementing the general political programme of the state. Third, these organizations would serve as tools for establishing censorship over these sectors and containing them politically.[82]

These organizations differ with respect to the level of compulsion in their membership. Joining the Ba'th Pioneers and the Revolutionary Youth Union is semi-compulsory for elementary and secondary school pupils and both these organizations play a key role in inculcating the strict slogans and rules of a 'Ba'thist upbringing'.[83] Although it is not compulsory to join such organizations, people from outside them are not allowed to come together to form a parallel body with objectives that differ from or are contrary to those of the officially recognized 'popular organizations'. These organizations play a role in completing the bureaucratic circle. Because the Ba'th Party always selects the leaders of these popular organizations, it maintains a permanent hold over them. Again, because each of these organizations is exclusively responsible for the social group it represents, they never compete with one another. Their members carry out semi-governmental tasks, which are usually restricted to offering monetary payments to members by way of pensions, health security and social services. They have exclusive authorization to represent their members in official bodies, on committees and in the People's Assembly and, for that matter, they all hold leading positions in the Ba'th Party.[84]

Thus, the popular organizations never exceed their brief, which is to provide services to their members, a role the regime set to ensure that the organizations did not get out of hand. In other words, a labour union is committed to defending the workers, but only within a prescribed context. It has no role, for example, in negotiating wage increases, because its task is to defend the regime's policies, not to carry out procedures for the benefit of its members (such as promoting strikes). In this respect, the role of the labour union was not only to refrain from supporting its members but also to cooperate with the security organizations in suppressing them.[85]

This pervasive censorship that permeates all aspects of life is also visible in the paucity of non-governmental organizations. A detailed map of civil institutions in Syria reveals that there are remarkably few popular and charitable associations, as well as non-governmental organizations. And this is mainly because legal (or rather security cum political) obstacles make it virtually impossible to set up civil associations and organizations with different objectives. Although Syria was one of the first Arab states to establish civil organizations and associations, under al-Asad it became the poorest in this respect. There were no more than 750 such organizations in Syria in 1990, whereas there were more than 17,000 in Egypt and 25,000 in Morocco. In 2000 there were only 504 charitable, religious, educational, scientific, cultural, social and legal associations in the whole country. In other words, there were 246 fewer associations than there had been ten years earlier.[86]

Civil society in Syria, particularly trade unions, non-governmental organizations and syndicates, were deeply penetrated by the regime. These were changed, especially after the syndicate crisis in 1980, into organizations appended to the state and used for maintaining political control over the societal sectors they represented. They became, in effect, semi-governmental organizations for the purpose of implementing the regime's policy rather than expressing the legitimate interests of the groups and sectors they represented and defending them legally, politically and economically.[87]

In short, this was the heritage al-Asad left behind with respect to his domestic policy. He put all his effort, especially in the last decade of his rule, into foreign policy, particularly peace negotiations with Israel. But he died without achieving peace, leaving Syrians to pay the price with their living standards.

The Syrian Elite and Democracy

As I have already mentioned in this chapter, Syria inherited a legacy of pluralism, democracy and the peaceful transition of power. The period following political independence in 1946 was full of active discussions among political elites and different ideologically-oriented political parties. In 1950 Syria gained the privilege of a constitution – apparently one of the first in the Arab region – that in a number of articles assured equality between the sexes, public freedoms and respect for citizens' basic freedoms and human rights.[88]

Women were granted the right to vote in 1949 and the right to run as a candidate in 1953, that is to say a long time before such rights were granted in some European countries. At the same time Syria benefited from a pluralistic parliamentary system and a free press that gave expression to the different sections and groups of Syrian society despite their racial, sectarian and regional diversity.

It is true that this situation did not last long before the country suffered a series of military coups beginning in 1949, yet it constituted a democratic heritage of which many Syrians are still proud, and which democratic and other politicians remember as evidence that Syrians can handle the freedoms and privileges of democracy. Despite the Baʿth seizure of power in 1963 and the events that followed – the state of emergency, martial law, the dissolution of political parties and the banning of newspapers – some critical thinking emerged among the country's intellectuals.

Anyone who looks closely at Syrian cultural life at the end of the 1960s and early 1970s will be aware of the highly distinguished contribution that Syrian scholars made to political thought: the efforts of Yāsīn al-Ḥāfiẓ, Ilias Murqus and their comrades in what is called the democratic dimension of nationalism led the way, very early on, for all nationalist parties in the Arab world.[89] Their thinking represented a reconciliation between the concepts of socialism and democracy.

The same can be said of the Muslim Brotherhood; some of its more prominent personalities were familiar with a collection of up-to-date legal studies that reconciled traditional and modern jurisprudence. Jurists like Muṣṭafá al-Zarqā, ʿAlī al-Ṭanṭāwī, Muhammad al-Mubārak, Fatḥī al-Darīnī and others played a role in what would later be called the *al-Shām* (Greater Syria) school of jurisprudence, which gained a reputation for its sound reasoning and cool intellectual authority. Thus, one could say that the cultural life of Syria was like an arc stretching from the utmost left to the utmost right. It was vigorous and productive despite its marginalization and enforced exclusion from the general political domain. Islamist and nationalist renewal, which coincided with the emergence of nationalist voices in the Communist Party, called for disengagement from the Soviet Union and a new approach to national issues.[90] The indications are that Syrian intellectuals, regardless of their different ideological tendencies, were at the forefront of Arab intellectual life and made a considerable impact on Arab Islamist, leftist and nationalist thought.

These critical voices, however, had not yet made their democratic choice. In other words, they were yet to acknowledge democracy as the only means of transferring power and of administering and organizing political and social life.

In much the same way as the Syrian elite's position on the first military coup had been to resist constitutional legitimacy, for democratic reasons the leftist and nationalist parties failed to oppose the National Progressive Front when President Hafez al-Asad used it to impose his nationalizing and monopolizing policy. Rather, they opposed it for 'leftist ideological' reasons, for they were wary of the Baʿth Party's powerful position in it. Democracy, therefore, had been completely absent from the political awareness that was around at that time. Leftist and nationalist parties, which were actually the elite parties, believed in a democracy void of any opposition, since what they wanted from democracy was to keep themselves where they were.

Thus, it can be said that the Syrian political elites had not yet 'internalized' the idea of democracy. They wished to assume power without having a clear idea about how they would administer it later on. Democracy was not the greatest preoccupation among the Syrian elites until the period of the 'Damascus spring', which we shall talk about in a later chapter.

2

Inheriting Syria from Father to Son: Hafez al-Asad's Last Days

With President Hafez al-Asad having ignored the warning signs, the economic, social and political crises were sooner or later bound to blow up in his successor's face. The economic recession that had been undermining Syrian markets since 1996 had reached a point of total stagnation. There was widespread disaffection over the failure to implement laws to promote economic liberalization, modernize banking and finance, upgrade the education system and regulate the property market (a rent law had been on the statute books for 50 years). There was also widespread popular dissatisfaction over the poor provision of such amenities as water, electricity, roads and transport, and the deteriorating living standards of citizens, especially public employees. Indeed, the state was at a standstill during the last days of Hafez al-Asad's rule, by which time Syrians had noted the signs of feebleness in him and his rare appearances in the media.

In his last year, al-Asad tried to arrange the succession in such a way that his policies would be maintained and his son Bashar would succeed to the presidency without opposition.

In a speech on 11 March 1999, when taking the presidential oath before the new presidential term, President Hafez al-Asad said that any institution failing to fulfil its role and to take responsibility for decision making would weaken the country and the popular democratic regime. This was the first time he had indicated that widening the scope of decision-making and encouraging debate and popular participation would strengthen democracy, enrich the country and sustain its progress. He said that the people's involvement in making decisions and implementing them would strengthen the patriotic spirit, thus guaranteeing both stability and progress.

The most interesting part of the speech, however, was how much time he gave to economic and legal issues compared with the amount of time he gave to foreign policy (especially the peace process) and the recital of his own achievements. He explicitly called for a reconsideration of investment law, with a view to eliminating the weaknesses that were slowing down new investments, and suggested developing and modernizing the banking system in order to attract savings and investment funds to promote development. Identifying a future agenda for the government in the next phase, he announced that it should continue to 'modernize the agricultural investment instruments, reduce production costs and create markets for agricultural products so that the mass production in which we are engaged will become a resource rather than a burden on the national economy'. The government should also 'address the defects in the land reclamation and dam construction schemes that are delaying the completion of projects, increasing costs and causing loss of future resources'.

Al-Asad emphasized that the public sector not only constitutes the main basis of the national economy but that it also has the role of creating social and economic balance. He urged the government, in cooperation with the Trade Union Federation, to study the workings of this sector with a view to liberating its companies:

> freeing them from the financial and administrative constraints that impede development, to developing financial and administrative systems that will allow the company to act as an independent legal entity working within the state overall plan, and increasing the administrative efficiency of the sector and its employees' professional and technical capacity.

Though al-Asad did not explicitly mention corruption, he pointed out that 'some [people] have lost their sense of responsibility and are guilty of negligence and more serious offences' and warned that 'modernization of the state requires an increased sense of public service.'[1]

This speech of Asad's introduced a new atmosphere of public debate on reform, corruption and the need for change. The presence of al-Asad's son Bashar at the 'Syrian Economic Sciences Society' lectures enhanced the pace of debate and made it more urgent. The lectures in fact turned into an open discussion about the government's failure to implement certain economic, administrative and developmental reforms.[2]

This gave the green light to the continuation of the unprecedented public criticism of the Syrian government. But, although the political debate had been opened up, it was cautious. It coincided with the parliamentary elections that preceded the referendum and saw intense competition for the seats of Independents, numbering 83 of the 250 seats in the Syrian parliament.

During this election, new slogans appeared that focused on combating corruption and modernizing the administration. They urged the prompt launching of a process of reform to put a stop to the waste of public resources. MP Riyāḍ Sayf from Damascus, who kept his seat for a new term, was the most prominent in propagating these slogans, while the former dean of the faculty of economics, ʿĀrif Dalīlah, failed to win a parliamentary seat.[3]

In Middle East politics it is often said that the 'jungle hides what it hides'. It was not just the faltering peace process that motivated al-Asad to stimulate the Syrians' appetite for open debate, a right of which he had deprived them for so long, but he also wanted to reorganize his domestic affairs in preparation for his approaching death and need to secure the succession.

It could be argued that the transfer of power was almost secured in 1999 though it did not actually happen formally until June 2000. In 1999 al-Asad consolidated the internal situation with considerable caution and confidence. In July 1998 he issued a decree to retire Major General Ḥikmat al-Shihābī and to install Major General ʿAlī Aslan in the position of chief of general staff.[4] General Bashir al-Najjār, the head of the 'General Intelligence Administration', was also forced to resign and to auction his properties. He was later put on trial and sentenced to 15 years imprisonment for having exceeded his brief by attempting to blackmail some ministers whom he wanted to involve in some disputes with him by videotaping them with a female dancer, but he died in August 2002.

Meanwhile, four officers were promoted from general to major general, which was an unusual proceeding. As a result of these promotions, Major General ʿAbd al-Raḥmān al-Sayyid, along with Major General Ḥasan Turkmānī, became deputy chiefs of staff. Major General ʿAlī Ḥabīb, who had been appointed as a leader of 'Special Units' in the Syrian army had replaced General ʿAlī Ḥaydar since 1994. Also promoted were Major General Tawfīq Jalūl and Major General Fārūq ʿĪsá Ibrāhīm.[5]

He also made changes in the field of security, the most influential body in the country along with the military forces. In April 1999, President al-Asad dismissed General Muḥammad Nāṣīf from his position as head of the internal security branch of the General Intelligence Administration and, in September, appointed General ʿAlī Houriah to the post of deputy head of the same department as a member of the civil staff.[6] General Muḥammad al-Khūlī, the head of air security, was also made to resign in June 1999,[7] as was Major General ʿAlī Dūbā, the head of the Military Security Department, whom General Ḥasan Khalīl replaced. General Āṣif Shawkat assumed control of the forces' security branch, which was considered the most influential post in this department.

These changes could be regarded as normal periodic replacements, especially since most of the 'security figures' had reached the eligible age of retirement. However, retaining some and excluding others seems undoubtedly to carry a clear political message, especially considering that al-Asad relied on 'his men' to maintain his authority. During this process, al-Asad showed a great deal of loyalty to all those who had worked with him and been committed to his approach. So, no political, military, security or even administrative member of staff was changed unless he had committed a serious crime or made a flagrant mistake, in which case he would be removed from his post but could retain his social status, provided he kept out of the limelight. On the other hand, the exceptionally severe treatment meted out to al-Najjār was to act as a deterrent for him and the others (for example Muḥammad Ḥaydar, the former deputy prime minister) who had started to extend his activities beyond their defined limits. These cases were an exception to the second golden rule that al-Asad adopted to guarantee his regime's stability. No member of his regime should become self-sustaining, but must derive his power from al-Asad alone. If al-Asad cut off the sustenance he would be extinguished and forgotten. There is a long list of men with whom al-Asad dealt in this way, especially if he felt they had started to assume a more important role than the one he had entrusted to them (such as ʿAlī Dūbā, Ḥikmat al-Shihābī and ʿAlī Dayūb, the governor of rural Damascus).

The most surprising step was the rise of al-Asad's son, Bashar, who started to conduct open and official tours[8] that attracted a remarkable amount of coverage in the official press,[9] even although he had not assumed any official position at that time. He conducted lengthy political interviews,[10] which reflected his adequate knowledge of and familiarity with internal matters. He was also well informed on the complex details of the Lebanese problem, an issue that had been the responsibility of ʿAbd al-Ḥalīm Khaddām, the vice president who later became responsible for the Iraqi file. The Lebanese file did not involve heavy responsibilities, but there were conflicting personalities and policies that required careful scrutiny and judgement.[11]

Meanwhile, arrangements were made for his periodic promotion. Early in 1999, he was promoted to staff colonel.[12] A clear message was sent to his most prominent rival to the succession, his uncle Rifaʾat al-Asad, by challenging his illegal ownership of a port in Ṭarṭūs and warning him that he would stand trial if he returned to Syria.[13]

To protect the succession from any unpredictable shocks al-Asad fostered good relations with other countries in the region. In this context, al-Asad's unexpected visit to Jordan to attend King Hussein's funeral, though his participation had been unplanned, initiated a fresh phase in relations with the new king of Jordan. He tried, through his personal presence, to show the new king his support after a long period of cold and suspicious relations between the two countries during King Hussein's reign. Bashar al-Asad also visited Jordan to present his condolences,[14] which King Abdullah II reciprocated by paying a visit to Damascus, where the two parties declared that they had decided to open a 'new page' in their relations[15] on the basis of looking forward to the future.

Al-Asad succeeded in building friendly relations not only with Jordan – the ever doubtful neighbour – but also with Iraq, where he reinforced Syrian openness towards Baghdad by establishing an 'office for interests'.[16] He also turned over a 'new page' with Turkey towards reaching mutual understanding by signing commercial and economic agreements after coping with the 1998 crisis.[17] Khātamī's first visit to Damascus in May 1999 to lay the foundations of a future 'political partnership' based on an understanding that any improvement in Syria's relations with the USA or Israel would never be at the expense of its 'fraternal relationship' with Iran, clearly improved Syria's strategic relations with Iran.[18]

Syrian–American relations had experienced a real honeymoon; Clinton had been the second American president, Nixon being the first, to visit Damascus, but he was the only one who met al-Asad three times (twice in Geneva) and there were also frequent and lengthy telephone calls between the two of them. Generally, al-Asad made use of his peace negotiations with Israel to reinforce his relations with the United States.

The peace issue that had absorbed his attention for the last decade of his life, in fact so fully that he set aside all domestic considerations, had reached its final stage and there was nothing standing in the way of signing the peace agreement save the last step. Al-Asad had been willing to sign the agreement in Geneva in March 2000 after his meeting with President Clinton, but Israeli Prime Minister Barak's fear, hesitation and weak political influence inside his government made him back down from what his predecessors had committed themselves to and what he, personally, had committed himself to.[19] As a result, al-Asad died without achieving what he had set out to accomplish.

The year 1999, therefore, can be said to have placed Syria at a crossroads domestically, regionally[20] and internationally. At the beginning of the year 2000, events at home took an unfamiliar turn. With the end of peace negotiations in Shepherdstown in January 2000, and the failure to set a definite date for resuming negotiations, al-Asad turned his attention again to the domestic affairs that had for years suffered serious neglect. Attending the periodical meeting of the regional leadership (*al-Qiyādah al-Quṭrī*) had been a rare event in the full sense of the word and a significant indication that matters would be settled at the level of government and party. Asad had for years absented himself from the meetings of the regional leadership (*al-Qiyādah al-Quṭrī*), resorting instead either to sending written 'commands' to be directly read out and ratified, or speaking on the telephone should a pressing or hastily arranged decision need to be made. Al-Asad's personal attendance at the 17 February 2000[21] meeting of the regional leadership (*al-Qiyādah al-Quṭrī*), the highest political ruling institution in the country, therefore released a rush of expectations and rumours, and was the subject of conversation among Syrians for weeks. The rumours were not denied and many of the expectations were met. For example, Prime Minister Mahmoud al-Zu'bi, who had been in office since 1987, was summarily dismissed from office under a barrage of criticism about his government's poor performance, which was unprecedented behaviour and previously forbidden. Newspapers circulated a personal statement from al-Asad in which he described al-Zu'bi's government as 'the worst ever witnessed by the country' and claimed to be 'ready to step into the street to demonstrate against it'.[22] This was a case of responsibility for the economic deterioration being deflected onto the government and not onto al-Asad, even although it was he who had supervised its every function.

On 13 March 2000 al-Asad announced the formation of a new government headed by Muḥammad Muṣṭafá Mayrū, the former lord mayor of Aleppo. While most ministries with a sovereign portfolio, such as defence, foreign affairs, the economy and finance, kept their ministers,[23] it was rumoured that Bashar al-Asad played a significant role in choosing the names of other government ministers. Accompanying the formation of a new government were promises of reform, particularly with regard to renewing and developing the laws that went back to the time of the French mandate for Syria and that had remained unchanged for more than half a century. Mayrū outlined the reforms in his first speech to his new government.[24] An apparent reappearance of political freedom was expressed in the symbolic step of releasing a number of political detainees of leftist orientations.[25] (In 1999 al-Asad had issued a general amnesty that included hundreds of political detainees from the Muslim Brotherhood.) An appointment to the Baʿth Party ninth regional conference (*almout ʿamar al-quṭrī*) was fixed after it had been postponed many times.[26] (The eighth conference had been held 15 years previously.)[27] The campaign against corruption was stepped up.

It was announced through the mass media that Bashar al-Asad would lead the campaign to modernize the state and reform the economy and administration. This was surprising because at the time he had no official political position and his father had repeatedly denied that he wanted him as his successor.[28] The campaign peaked with Mahmoud al-Zuʾbi, the deposed prime minister, being stripped of his membership of the Baʿth Party and relegated to a judicial role dealing with accusations of corruption and abuses of power.[29] Al-Zuʾbi's dismissal from the party took a dramatic turn when he committed suicide at his home by shooting a number of bullets into his head.[30] Salīm Yāsīn, al-Zuʾbi's deputy for economic affairs, and Mufīd ʿAbd al-Karīm, his minister of transport, were brought before the court of economic security on charges of corruption, particularly over the 'air bus' bargain.[31] Many officials were suspected of corruption and interrogated accordingly.[32] Through the official newspapers it was announced that the property of Major General Bashir al-Najjār, former head of general intelligence, had been confiscated following his sentence to 12 years' imprisonment.[33]

This accelerated programme of reforms preceded the ninth regional conference (*almout ʿamar al-quṭrī*) of 17 June 2000, when some people expected to see Bashar al-Asad appointed to a position in the regional leadership of the Baʿth Party.[34] However, a few days before the conference (on 17 June 2000) al-Asad died, leaving the Syrians to confront a new reality. For 30 years they had been accustomed to al-Asad as president, but now they suddenly found themselves facing a choice for which they were ill prepared, despite its inevitability. At the time of the 8 March 1963 movement, when the Baʿth Party took power, the Syrian population had been 5.3 million but by the time al-Asad died it had increased to 17.5 million. In other words, 12 million

Syrians were of the 'revolution generation' and had never known a president other than al-Asad.[35]

Transfer of Power

Within a single day (11–12 June 2000) the transfer of power from father to son took place in a way that reflected the extent of the regime's total control. The People's Assembly was asked to convene to amend Article 83 of the Syrian constitution, which, as mentioned earlier, stipulated that the president of the republic has to be at least 40 years old. This was amended to 34 so that Bashar could assume power. The details of how the transfer of authority took place are still obscure, but before it happened there was clearly enough agreement among military, security and political elites to allow President Hafez al-Asad to carry out radical changes in these sectors, which had had exceedingly stable leaderships since the 1980s. In May 1999 Asad the father met a number of political personalities, particularly from the constitutional branch of the administration. The most prominent of these was the head of the People's Assembly, ʿAbd al-Qādir Qaddūrah, and al-Asad consulted him on what constitutional steps needed to be taken to secure the safe transfer of authority to his son Bashar. He was advised to appoint his son Bashar as his deputy as soon as possible, and to appoint other deputies, through presidential ordinances, so that he could guarantee the transfer of authority to his son Bashar. The idea of carrying out constitutional changes before his death did not, however, appeal to al-Asad, whose personal preference had been not to hand authority over to his son while he was still alive.[36]

Thus, it was clear that the succession in Syria had been finally decided in favour of Bashar al-Asad. By the end of 1998 and during 1999, President Hafez al-Asad carried out the necessary procedures to incapacitate any local centres of power that were likely to oppose the new regime. The most powerful figure among these was ʿAbd al-Ḥalīm Khaddām from whom the most sensitive and influential Lebanese portfolio was drawn and handed over to Bashar al-Asad. General Ḥasan Khalīl and his deputy, General Asef Shawkat, replaced ʿAlī Dūbā as head of the Military Intelligence Department; ʿAlī Aslan, who had a close connection with Bashar because of his son Aws's intimate friendship with Bashar, replaced Major General Ḥikmat al-Shihābī as head of the general chief of staff.

Moreover, there had been extensive changes among the commanders of the army divisions and heads of sensitive security branches in an attempt to exclude anyone likely to oppose the hereditary principle and to appoint known supporters, such as General Bahjat Sulaymān (who later became a major general and took over the interior security branch from Muḥammad Nāṣīf).

During the sessions of the party's ninth conference in June 2000, it was agreed to appoint Bashar al-Asad as a member of the regional leadership (*al-Qiyādah al-Quṭrī*) and, at the same time, a political caucus in support of Bashar al-Asad was formed and led by the minister of defence Major General Muṣṭafá Ṭalās, who openly declared in an interview with the French journal *Express* on 16 July 1998 that: 'Bashar will take his father's position, but this will be only after eight years, because President Asad will run as a candidate to succeed himself at the beginning of next year (1999). This means that his son will succeed him in 2006.'[37]

The second person was Minister of Foreign Affairs Farouk al-Shar'a, who either contacted or met Bashar al-Asad almost every day. In a rare interview with the Lebanese newspaper *al-Mustaqbal* just two months before President Hafez al-Asad's death, he gave the most decisive indication that Bashar al-Asad would succeed his father when he said: 'Staff Colonel Bashar al-Asad told me more than once that President Asad does not intend to bequeath me a dishonourable peace and that he himself does not accept it either.'[38]

This interview was in the wake of the failure of the Geneva summit between Asad and Clinton in March 2000 when rumours were rife about the serious deterioration of al-Asad's health. Al-Shar'a also attended the summit, for it is well-known that he was the distinguished trustee of Syrian foreign policy during the last ten years of al-Asad's rule. Al-Shar'a, therefore, did not need to tell the newspaper that Bashar al-Asad had told him that his father would not bequeath him a dishonourable peace, for the relationship between al-Shar'a and President Asad was close enough for al-Shar'a to report this speech directly from al-Asad's father. In reality, the dialogue was a clear internal and external message that the issue of succession had been fully decided in favour of Bashar al-Asad.

Immediately after al-Asad's death on the morning of 10 June 2000, Minister of Defence Major General Muṣṭafá Ṭalās carried out all the necessary arrangements and assigned everyone his previously decided mission.[39] General Asef Shawkat played a sensitive role in securing adequate military support, as did Bashar al-Asad's youngest brother Maher al-Asad, an influential officer in the fourth squad in the Syrian army charged with special missions.[40] Alongside these two was General Bahjat Sulaymān, then in control of espionage.[41] Vice-President ʿAbd al-Ḥalīm Khaddām issued legislative decrees numbers 9 and 10 proclaiming the promotion of Staff-Colonel Bashar al-Asad to the rank of lieutenant-general and then appointing Lieutenant-General Bashar al-Asad commander in chief of the army and armed forces.[42] The ninth regional conference was held on 17 June, which had been shortened to dedicate time to rehearsing 'the noble deeds of the eternal leader, Hafez al-Asad'. At the end of this conference Bashar al-Asad was appointed general regional (*Quṭrī*) secretary of the party.[43] The People's Assembly then hastily discussed the regional leadership's (*al-Qiyādah al-Quṭrī*'s) suggestion that Bashar al-Asad be put forward as a candidate for presidency according to the constitution and he was elected unanimously. The day selected for the referendum was 10 July and Bashar al-Asad got 97.92 per cent of the vote.[44] Bashar al-Asad was officially proclaimed president of Syria, thus combining the positions of commander in chief of the army and armed forces, general secretary of the party and head of the National Progressive Front with the political position of president of the country.[45]

Bashar al-Asad was now in a very favourable regional and international position. The United States backed by Europe was concerned only with securing stability and did not deal with the Syrian regime except with regard to its role in administering the peace process. Thus, all external pressures pertaining to internal political or even economic policies disappeared, for the mechanism of the transference of authority had been extremely controlled. There were no internal splits or disturbances, except for some 'hostile' press releases in the mass media, which came only from Rifaʾat al-Asad and the Syrian opposition abroad. The situation, therefore, seemed to be extremely stable and this encouraged both the Arab neighbours and the international community quickly to approve the way authority had been handed down.

American President Bill Clinton, for example, expressed his 'willingness to make every possible effort to honour al-Asad's memory'. Although domestic political pressures prevented him from attending al-Asad's funeral, he was represented by Madeline Albright who expressed her respect for 'the historical personality represented by al-Asad'.[46] During her meeting with Bashar al-Asad she confirmed her good impression of the existence of 'a system which works in an organized faultless way and which smoothly arranged the question of succession in Syria'.[47]

Bashar al-Asad and the Game of the 'Old Guard'

With the advent of President Bashar al-Asad to power, questions arose over how much control he actually had over political decision-making in his country given the powerful influence of the 'old guard'.[48] Most studies of President Bashar al-Asad's term of office have concentrated on his view of things and his ability to grasp the reins of power. Consequently, they are based on the logical assumption that the structure and rules of the Syrian regime have basically remained the same, even though the faces have changed.

With the arrival of President Bashar al-Asad to power, two factions appeared within the Baʿth Party. This arose because in the new regime that emerged after the Baʿth Party's ninth regional conference (*al-moutʿamar al-quṭrī*) in 2000, a few days after al-Asad's death, most of the country's former leaders maintained their old positions; in other words, they formed what the Arab and Western media named the 'old guard'.

The military corps, however, dominated the party's central committee.[49] This 'new/old' leadership of the country seemed willing to play a role it had not played in the era of President Hafez al-Asad, which was often characterized as stagnant, unresponsive to new political and economic ideas, narrow minded and sometimes obstructionist. It also accused activists and its opponents, particularly during the 'Damascus Spring', of treason[50] and similar crimes.

The average age of the country's politicians was in excess of 60 years and almost all of them had risen through the ranks of the Ba'th Party. Most of them had no academic qualifications or educational expertise and, furthermore, few had been given the opportunity to travel or to observe administrative, technical, scientific, political and social developments in the West. For this reason, the country's leaders often had negative views of the projects introduced during the first two years of President Bashar al-Asad's rule, particularly regarding private universities, private banks and other economic innovations.

Bashar al-Asad tried, from the beginning of his term, to avoid confronting the power structure he had inherited from his father. He sought to deal with the potential opposition to his attempts to change policies through circumvention, with the result that in the end his measures failed to bring about genuine reform. Instead, they created an alternative regime that preserved the power structures he had inherited from his father while at the same time adopting a long-term strategy to change the character of the regime gradually.[51]

The huge size of the bureaucracy that served the three faces of the Syrian state's pyramid-like administration clearly exacerbated Bashar's difficulties. This structure made it well nigh impossible to reframe political and economic policy, for resistance to change was much more powerful than the good intentions or capabilities of the individuals wanting to implement the reforms. Any steps towards even partial economic openness invariably confronted the traditional Ba'thist mentality that found it difficult to think beyond the socialist ideology with which the regional leadership (*al-Qiyādah al-Quṭrī*) had been familiar for decades. Furthermore, there were not enough qualified technical people to formulate the laws and regulations necessary to manage an efficient and competitive financial sector.

In addition, the structural barriers remaining from the long record of corruption at the highest levels of the regime hindered implementation of the necessary reforms.[52] In the absence of a turnover of elites within the party for two decades, networks of corruption were allowed to develop and to establish a kind of security cum economic alliance that monopolized trade deals and killed confidence in the legal, financial and economic reforms. Foreign investments served the interests of those who benefited most from the regime and, without competition and transparency, the economic sector could not develop.[53]

In fact, Bashar al-Asad did not want to destroy, at least not immediately, the foundations of the regime that had allowed him to rise so meteorologically; he appeared to want to keep in with the regime's former idols and stalwarts. Then, gradually and through two government changes and the tenth regional conference (*almout ʿamar al-quṭrī*) (June 2005), he managed to replace all these former icons, including his deputies ʿAbd al-Ḥalīm Khaddām, Zuhayr Mashāriqah and other members of the regional leadership (*al-Qiyādah al-Quṭrī*), with new men who were close to him and who had worked with him in the Syrian Computer Society. Moreover, a number of Syrian ministers were brought in who had managerial and scientific experience in international institutions such as the World Bank and United Nations.

Bashar al-Asad held onto many of the features of the regime he had inherited from his father, especially the hierarchical structure that guaranteed his dominance. His role as president granted him absolute authority over all other state institutions, so no one could challenge him politically or personally. The imbalance of power in favour of military and security institutions posed the only possible threat to his supremacy. However, there was no immediate danger because it would take a long time to rebuild the sorts of loyalties that might take advantage of his weaker position and, in any case, Bashar al-Asad had gradually been strengthening his position in the pyramidal structure by reinforcing the protective mechanisms that operated in his favour through the government, party and security services. Thus, it was always the president who made the final decision, as it had been in the era of his father. The president continued to control the three faces of the pyramid.

The image of Bashar al-Asad as a reformist was severely shaken by the repression that was exercised against the so-called 'Damascus Spring' movement. The members of this group articulated their abhorrence for the government in a number of political forums, which were somehow allowed to flourish without punishment or control and the voices from within these forums started to demand comprehensive political reforms. These included the termination of martial law, which had been in force since 1963; the release of all political prisoners; the formation of political parties; and enactment of a modern information law that would allow publication of private newspapers and magazines. Above all, they demanded substantial modifications to the Syrian constitution.[54]

The leadership that al-Asad supported took a strong stand against the 'Damascus Spring' movement, accusing its activists of a number of misdemeanours and eventually culminating in a series of arrests, including many of the movement's most influential leaders. This clampdown caused widespread disillusionment with President Bashar al-Asad, whom many people had looked upon as a possible reformer of Syrian political life; he started to talk about adopting the Chinese model of reform where economic modernization is given priority over political reform.[55]

Because of the Syrian regime's known sensitivity to words used by the media, a quirk that dated back to Hafez al-Asad's time, Bashar al-Asad had reservations about the use of the term 'reform'. There was also a sense in which the Syrian regime under the 'eternal leader Hafez al-Asad' (as the official media called him) had been faultless, so there was no need for reform after his death. Much the same logic prevailed when Kim Jong-il succeeded his father as leader of North Korea. The general attitude was that the regime should carry out 'development and modernization' along the lines of what the eternal leader had previously built, modernizing existing frameworks in line with the period's requirements and technologies. Therefore, Bashar al-Asad has repeatedly refused to talk about 'reform' and has always answered his critics by saying, 'the terms we use in Syria are development and modernization'.[56]

Al-Asad mentioned in one of his interviews that a problem lay in the fact that the enormous number of decrees and legislations[57] issued in the early years of his regime had not been implemented, and he wondered why.[58] Perhaps he was referring indirectly here to the huge bureaucracy he had worked to enhance rather than undermine because of the protection it offered him. If al-Asad found that the party's bureaucratic cadres, or even more importantly the regional leadership (*al-Qiyādah al-Quṭrī*), were responding reluctantly to or deliberately delaying implementing his economic reforms, then from his position at the top of the pyramid, he should have been able to overcome these obstacles routinely, which is what happened after the Ba'th Party's tenth regional conference (*almout 'amar al-quṭrī*) (June 2005) when so many of the country's leaders were changed. There was nothing to stop him making any changes he wanted, including all senior leaders within the state's government institutions, the two vice presidents, any of the party's regional leaders, including the regional assistant secretary. In fact, not even his close associates from within the so-called Syrian Computer Society were immune.[59]

The conference took a decision to initiate economic reform without any political reform. This was demonstrated in a number of steps such as allowing private banks, a securities market and private insurance companies, in the hope of emulating the Chinese pattern of reform. But it was difficult to accomplish economic reform in Syria without a minimum level of political *détente* to help create a suitable investment environment. Unlike China, Syria has a small production cycle. Moreover, the decision for economic reform in China originated in a political decision from the Communist Party that still has influence in contrast with the Syrian Ba'th Party, which has no effect on political life. Any decision the party takes is a response to the president's wish to maintain his regime's stability rather than a response to the country's internal needs. Furthermore, the Syrian regime started to take the shape of a family regime (al-Asad family) rather than a totalitarian partisan regime, which is the case of the Chinese Communist Party.[60]

In China, economic reform has been associated with a management 'revolution'; China today has the largest number of technocrats in the world in administrative positions; it is also a country with excessively precise well-qualified managers (as described by *Newsweek*). Most of the 24 members of the Communist Party's political bureau hold technical certificates from prestigious universities, such as Beijing Petroleum Institute or the Harbin Institute of Military Engineering. Also, all nine members of the political bureau's standing committee are engineering specialists; former President Hu Jintao graduated from Tsinghua University in Beijing and worked on the Three Gorges Dam Construction Plan, which is the largest building project in the world.[61]

Compare that with the new Ba'th Party's regional leadership (*al-Qiyādah al-Quṭrī*), where only four of its members hold postgraduate degrees at the doctoral level and two of these obtained their degrees from East European universities, one from Romania and the other from the Ukraine. That gives us a fairly good indication of what sorts of 'reform ideas' the Ba'th Party's leaders are promoting.

The conference called this new economic 'reform policy' the 'social market economy'. Its aim was to maintain social stability while at the same time moving towards the market economy, thus easing the burden on the state's budget of having to subsidize basic commodities, which costs the state hundreds of millions of dollars annually.[62]

The way in which the party's tenth regional conference (*almout 'amar al-quṭrī*) was managed, and the position of President Bashar within it, reflected the extent to which partisan traditions had collapsed within the Ba'th Party, which is now centred on the personality of the leader-president who derives his ideology from his own statements and speeches. The party no longer plays its historic role of mobilizing the masses or promoting the ideological cohesion that binds them together. As the Syrians often say, 'the borders between the Ba'th Party as a political organization and the security forces are jellylike and unclear.' The opportunism that characterizes the majority of junior and middle-rank party members hoping to secure senior positions is a dominant feature of all the party's branches in the governorates and, paradoxically, they are always subject to criticism inside the party through the regular organizational reports submitted to the national conferences, especially the most recent ones.[63]

We can therefore say that the Syrian regime's political and organizational foundations established during President Hafez al-Asad's 'golden age' of the third republic can still explain the decision-making mechanisms of an era that is no more than the natural extension and continuation of the previous one. Any differences are differences of degree not substance. Reviewing events from an historical perspective rather than from a purely contemporary one, it becomes clear that any differences between President Bashar Asad and his father stem from psychological personal differences between them rather than differences in the political system.

Political Institutions in the Era of Bashar al-Asad

Bashar al-Asad has maintained the bureaucratic institutions he inherited from his father. The National Progressive Front, established essentially to consolidate the foundations of the regime President Hafez al-Asad built and to broaden its political support beyond the Ba'th Party's confines, remained in place, though al-Asad attempted to integrate some other marginal parties into it. These parties were no different from other socialist and nationalist movements, such as the Syrian National Social Party or the Arab Socialist Movement, which changed its name to the National Action Party. In addition, the Socialist Union Party was split into two parties both of which became members of the NPF: these were the Arab Socialist Union (Ṣafwān Qudsī) and the Arab Democratic Union (Ghassān Aḥmad 'Uthmān).[64] These parties suffered a fate more dangerous even than the horizontal and vertical splitting characteristic of NPF parties, namely the 'bequeathing' of the party leadership by inheritance rather than election. After the death of Ahmed al-As'ad , secretary-general of the Social Democratic Unionist Party, for example, his son Firas al-As'ad was appointed as the new secretary-general.[65] When 'Abd al-'Azīz 'Uthmān, the secretary-general of the Arab Socialist Movement, died in 1995, his son Ghassān 'Uthmān succeeded him.[66] Before that, when Khālid Bakdāsh, founder of the Syrian Communist Party, died, his wife Wiṣāl Bakdāsh and his son 'Ammār Bakdāsh succeeded him in the secretariat, and so it goes on.

Given this practice the concept of 'party' seems very far from these parties; they are more 'cliques' or family institutions with political interests. Syrian people, therefore, make jokes about their numbers and names. Since its establishment, the NPF has excluded liberal and Islamic currents from political representation, making it exclusive to the nationalist-leftist tendency, which gradually changed its ethos from public service to acquiring perquisites.[67] These marginal parties get a number of seats in the cabinet and parliament. However, they put forward their candidates to the president, who decides who is going to be a minister or an MP from among the names they nominate.

The central leadership of the NPF has no real effect on decision-making; its meetings are merely 'educative', in other words the president explains his policy solely to get it ratified. In his last decade of office, President Hafez al-Asad rarely attended the NPF's meetings and often delegated his deputy Zuhayr Mashāriqah to inform the 'allies' of political developments. President Bashar al-Asad, however, regularly attended NPF meetings and would give NPF parties the go-ahead to open offices in the governorates, act in universities and issue their own newspapers[68] on condition that the number of copies distributed did not exceed the number of subscribers in each party.

When at its tenth regional conference (*almout 'amar al-quṭrī*) in 2005 the Ba'th Party acknowledged the need to enact a law to regulate political life in Syria, President Bashar al-Asad announced more than once that the right time had not yet come[69] for it because regional and international pressures were operating against Syria, particularly since the assassination of Lebanese Prime Minister Rafīq Ḥarīrī in February 2005.

The Syrian parliament, or People's Assembly, had had a historic and pivotal role in political life during the French mandate and in the post-independence period; it is the oldest parliament in the Arab region, but it was dissolved when the Ba'th Party came to power in 1963, and no parliamentary elections to the People's Assembly were carried out until the arrival of President Hafez al-Asad to power in 1970, when he appointed the MPs in February 1971.

Elections were carried out for the first time using the Ba'thist manner of appointment in 1973. After that, once the NPF parties had decided to share the seats among themselves, they were held once every four years. Even when President Hafez al-Asad increased the overall number of seats in parliament and the number of independent members to 83, the Ba'th Party and its allies in the NPF maintained a two-thirds majority. It is worth highlighting here that independent candidates have very limited chance of success if they are not in full agreement with the regime.

The parliament had no role in political life during the third republic; its role was confined to approving the laws the government proposed. It has never withdrawn confidence from any government, or objected or defeated any draft law a government had issued. Therefore, it is not surprising that participation in parliamentary elections remained low, usually not exceeding 15 per cent in all elections.[70] In fact, President Hafez al-Asad would not require the parliament to be anything more than a kind of official rubber stamp giving legitimacy to the claim that Syria had a republican presidential parliamentary system.

Therefore, the parliament did not exercise its monitoring functions over the government, or supervise the management of important political matters; its role did not go beyond adminstrative and service functions. According to the Syrian constitution, the president chooses the prime minister and ministers, and the cabinet delivers the constitutional oath before the president; the People's Assembly has no power to affirm or withdraw confidence in the government. Therefore, the Baʿthist and independent MPs kept repeating a boring type of ritual of discussing, then ratifying, the laws the government proposed.

President Bashar al-Asad has not introduced any changes to the laws governing election to the People's Assembly or any amendments to its role and performance. Moreover, two serving MPs (Riyāḍ Sayf and Maʾmoun al-Humṣī) were arrested in 2001 because of their opinions and political standpoints; Sayf had uncovered a corruption deal relating to contracts for mobile phone companies, and this, in addition to his political activity in the 'Damascus Spring', put him in prison for five years.[71] All that gave a very negative impression of the regime's willingness to allow MPs to play any real role in monitoring and calling the government to account. For this reason, the percentage of the population participating in the parliamentary election held on 2 March 2003 during President Bashar al-Asad's regime was the lowest on record; unofficial statistics claim that it did not exceed 10 per cent, though official statistics put the figure at 63 per cent.[72]

Opposition parties represented in the so-called National Democratic collation boycotted the elections on the grounds that they lacked even minimum standards of democracy, honesty and legitimacy. The Ba'th Party won 137 of the 167 assigned seats to the NPF, as it was known in advance that it would. The remaining 83 seats went to independent candidates, especially to businessmen allied with the regime.

These facts illustrate the weak, or rather non-existent impact of the Syrian parliament on political or economic decision-making. The president can dissolve the People's Assembly and since 1970 the Syrian government has derived no legitimacy from it, for it cannot present a vote of 'no confidence' to the government or to any minister. Neither has parliament ever suggested draft laws for discussion; laws are referred to it from the government. Furthermore, the People's Assembly has no role in foreign policy-making; it cannot discuss sensitive and essential issues, such as Syrian–Lebanese or Syrian–Iraqi relationships, and thus its role remains no more than a formality.

Between 2003 and 2009 the Syrian government did refer some laws to the People's Assembly for discussion, and the official media tried to focus on its role, especially during the discussion of the Rent Law and other laws relating to sensitive social matters. Where other laws were concerned, however, the parliament could not, or rather was not allowed to, intervene to make any amendments to them. This happened with the Law of Publications (enacted in 2001), the Labour Law and other laws that were issued during its 2003–07 legislative term.

The second parliamentary elections during Bashar al-Asad's term (22 April 2007) resulted in the number of seats for the Ba'th Party and its NPF being increased to 170, and all those 'won' as if unopposed and without any electoral competition. None of them, even those with the lowest number of votes, has failed to be elected since 1974 – they all end up at the forefront of the winners.[73] The allied business people kept their seats, which turned the process into meaningless 'elections without voters'[74] and made Syrians reluctant to participate at all, or even to show interest in the proceedings.

Election law has not been amended as promised. The elections were held under the same old election law, with only a tiny formal amendment made that related to the volume of funds disbursed for the electoral campaign. This has nothing to do with the essence of the election process, which is supposed to lead to democratic, transparent and honest elections. Apart from the inadequacy of election law, there are weaknesses relating to the constituencies. Each governorate is treated as one constituency, which makes it impossible for any independent person or any party other than the Ba'th Party, to enter parliament. For example, it is impossible to conduct an election campaign in a governorate like Rural Damascus, which is equal in size to the whole of Lebanon. There cannot possibly be any real popular representation; it is a static representation that fails to reflect the voters' opinions because the area of the governorate is too large for voters genuinely to choose a real representative. The issue of supervising the election process is a critical one; there is no guarantee that elections will be transparent and honest because there is no mechanism for the judicial supervision of them.

All this explains the very low turnout in elections.[75] The very low level of participation in elections reflects the loss of confidence not only in the electoral process and its impact on decision-making, but in the political regime and its ability to reflect the legitimate interests of the largest number of Syrians.[76] As is so often said among the populace, 'participation and non-participation leads to the same result'.

Article 144 of the constitution affirms the competence of the Supreme Constitutional Court (whose members the president appoints) to settle disputes arising from the electoral process. The court is entrusted with investigating the validity of elections relating to the People's Assembly (Article 144). However, none of the reports filed on the parliamentary elections has been taken seriously, and sometimes verdicts revoking some MPs' membership have been ignored.

In May 2007 the parliamentary elections were followed by a referendum on a second presidential term in which al-Asad gained 97.62 per cent of the votes, the same percentage his father had obtained in the past. A lavish propaganda and advertising campaign preceded the referendum, which was something the Syrians had been unused to during the era of his father, Hafez al-Asad. Although al-Asad was the only candidate, large posters were distributed on which was displayed a single phrase: 'We love you.'

The scheduled date of the referendum was brought forward because of external pressures, especially the reports of the international committee charged with investigating the assassination of former Lebanese prime minister, Rafīq Hariri. Some Syrians had been accused of being involved in the assassination, which cast suspicion on the Syrian government of complicity in the affair. All this strengthened among the Syrians the image of Bashar al-Asad as the inheritor of the regime rather than as a reformist, particularly after the widely-publicized news about the major commercial transactions that his cousin Rāmī Makhlūf had undertaken on his behalf. Makhlūf not only had the monopoly of the two mobile phone companies, but he also controlled the free trade zones on the Syrian land borders and ran more than 200 agencies belonging to foreign companies operating in Syria.

3

Damascus Spring: The Rise of the Opposition in Syria

Syrian society exhibits characteristics similar to those of other societies ruled by totalitarian regimes. Take, for example, the richness of oral – and almost total lack of written – political culture. Analyses and predictions depend more on rumours than on written or oral information. Events are used to confirm rumours to the extent that one Western specialist on Syria remarked that 'rumours in Syria become a fact within days or months'.[1]

Expressions of this rich oral culture are usually confined to family visits or encounters with friends, for voicing political views in public can have dire security and political consequences. Consequently, political comments are often sidetracked into comedy, and the formerly taboo political jokes for which Syrians are famous began to be heard in public in the 1990s.

The economic, political, cultural and social pressures in the society at that time were such that some of these concerns were aired in official public forums, like the Syrian Society of Economic Sciences, which used to meet once a week on a Tuesday. This society discussed the Syrian government's economic policy, and what made its discussion so ardent was the attendance of Bashar al-Asad before he became Syria's president in 2000. A number of the participants thought that these meetings were 'covered or protected', to use a Syrian popular expression,[2] so a larger space was made available for community discussions. Some of these unofficial seminars took place at the Abu Zlam Forum for Modern Studies in the al-Baramka area of Damascus, as well as at the Dumar Cultural Forum. The forums gained greater dynamism when their members felt the need for serious debate on proscribed political issues. They worked efficiently to gain the participation of other social sectors to express their opinions in a free and responsible manner.

Numerous factors played a part in the authorities tolerating, rather than repressing, as in the past, this climate of debate and discussion. The reopening of peace talks between Syria and Israel in December 1999, after Ehud Barak became prime minister of Israel, provoked extensive discussions on the topic of normalizing relations with Israel and the attitudes of the intelligentsia and Syrian society at large to a peace agreement.[3] With the failure of these negotiations, internal talks about corruption and reform in Syria resurfaced and took a dramatic turn with the expulsion of Prime Minister Mahmoud al-Zu'bi, followed by his dismissal from the party and subsequent suicide in May 2000. This prompted a limited round of talks, for out of the silence people were beginning to speak about the need for political and economic reform to ensure a better future for Syria.

The seventh legislative elections to the People's Assembly in 1999, which preceded these events, witnessed many daring requests from figures such as Riyāḍ Sayf and Dr ʿĀrif Dalīlah, who had been elected to represent Damascus. They asked for adjustment of the electoral law as well as the activation of the role of the People's Assembly. In a speech during the opening of the sixth legislative council, President Hafez al-Asad criticized corruption and government bureaucracy, and instead championed development and modernization. This speech gave Syrians an 'additional amount of prohibited freedom' with which openly to address criticisms of the 'symbols of corruption'.[4]

Bashar al-Asad became president of the Syrian Arab Republic through recourse to an adjustment of the constitution and a 'popular' referendum. His inauguration address on 17 July 2000 emphasized the importance of respecting the opinion of the 'Other'. This permitted a modest space for freedom of expression and, naturally, intellectuals were the first to grasp this opportunity. The promotion of the concept of 'civil society' as an introduction to democratic reform happened during the periodic meetings a number of leftist intellectuals organized shortly before Hafez al-Asad's death. These discussions addressed the need to reactivate civil society after its long suspension by the authorities. With the presence of industrialist and representative Riyāḍ Sayf in the final sessions, the idea was floated of establishing the 'Association of Civil Society Friends'.[5] The participants wrote two drafts arguing that:

> Civil society, as we see it, is a group of social committees, parties, organizations, associations and free media which are non-governmental; its essence is democratic choice, and democracy cannot be achieved without the awakening of society with its systems and organizations creating an atmosphere of critical dialogue between society and government for the good of the homeland. Activation of the organizations of civil society is the sole path to building a real state for everyone and to creating an effective social movement.[6]

They went on to call for the 'establishment of the Association of Civil Society Friends' in the hope of producing something that could contribute towards building a developed democratic society.

Later, on 27 September 2000, came the first communiqué of a group of Syrian intellectuals known as the 'Communiqué of the 99 Intellectuals'. It urged the authorities to cancel:

> the state of emergency and martial laws applied in Syria since 1963, a general amnesty for all political prisoners, the return of all exiles, the establishment of a state of law, a grant of general freedom, and the recognition of political and intellectual plurality, as well as freedom of association, freedom of the press, and the free expression of opinion.[7]

It was signed by a number of influential Syrian intellectuals, such as Antoine Maqdisi, Burhan Ghalion, Sadeq Jalal al-ʿAzem, Ṭayyib Tīzīnī and a considerable number of cineastes and well-known lawyers. The event attracted the attention of international and Arab media, who described it as 'the first cry for freedom' to come from inside Syria.[8]

This memorandum, which came as a long-awaited awakening for

Syrian intellectuals, signalled the recovery of their symbolic authority in the collective imagination. The communiqué described the intelligentsia as the group best suited to express the popular consciousness that would lead to freedom and justice. The authorities' response to the memorandum was very positive by Syrian standards. None of the members who signed the memorandum was subjected to pressure from the security apparatuses, which was unusual in Syria given the extent of infiltration into citizens' lives. On the contrary, the authorities and President Bashar al-Asad personally responded by releasing 600 political prisoners in October 2000, and the official newspapers were the first to publish the news on their front pages.[9] This was the first official recognition of the existence of 'political prisoners', as opposed to 'criminals', which the authorities had always insisted on calling them, often continuing to detain them long after they had served their sentences.

These events stimulated the growth of social and political movements, especially among intellectuals, who found in them an opportunity to exert more pressure to bring about political reforms that would ensure real legal protection and not protection *based on the green light principle or the policy of turning a blind eye.*[10] As Ibrāhīm Ḥumaydī explained, forums and meetings began to mushroom, such as the Cultural Forum for Human Rights and Jamal al-Atāsī's Forum for Democratic Dialogue on 13 January 2001.[11] A number of Syrian intellectuals rallied by forming the Establishing Committee Board for the Revival of Civil Society, comprised initially of 20 members. This shrank to 14 members who met regularly and collected the necessary signatures for the 'Manifesto of the Thousand', which analysed critically the period between the Baʿth Party's rise to power in Syria on 8 March 1963, and Hafez al-Asad's ascendancy to the presidency in November 1970.[12] The 'Manifesto of the Thousand' made waves, as witnessed by the reactionary declarations of a number of Syrian officials such as minister of defence Muṣṭafá Ṭalās,[13] minister of communication Muḥammad ʿUmrān, and others.[14] Harsh criticism appeared on the front pages of the regime's official newspapers[15] and in journals published in Beirut that are considered Syrian government mouthpieces, such as *al-Muharrer al-Arabi*.[16]

The stirrings that led to the 'Manifesto of the Thousand' influenced society directly, making the authorities stricter. More and more public declarations by intellectuals calling for freedom and recognition of political plurality were reflected directly in discussions between ordinary Syrians. The Establishing Committee gained a symbolic presence as the voice of Syrian intellectuals. At this time, Riyāḍ Sayf introduced a new approach by launching a Forum for National Dialogue composed of 14 members.[17] Some of these members combined their activities in the Establishing Committee Board for the Revival of Civil Society with their participation in the Committee of the Forum for National Dialogue.

The positive atmosphere encouraged Riyāḍ Sayf to bring forward the announcement of a new party called the Movement for Social Peace at the Forum for National Dialogue on 31 January 2001, calling for its political existence outside the NPF. Sulaymān Qaddāḥ, former regional secretary of the Ba'th Party, had led him to believe that a new law would be announced on 14 February 2001 allowing for the expansion of the NPF through creating similar-minded nationalist parties. This would have constituted a public relations coup by the authorities, while proscribing political activity outside the NPF.

Sayf prematurely wrote a memorandum entitled *Movement for Social Peace: Principles for Dialogue* that failed to provide a political formula that could coexist with the contemporary political reality.[18] Neither the authorities nor the Syrian nationalist opposition accepted his defence of minority rights. The prevailing Arab nationalist mentality remained the main political frame of reference within which Syrians thought. Sayf's Movement for Social Peace thus triggered a negative reaction among Syrian politicians after its announcement on 31 January 2001.[19] Vice President 'Abd al-Ḥalīm Khaddām saw it as a call to divide Syria, and this accelerated the repression of these forums.[20]

It appears that the regime had calculated that such steps would be taken and planned accordingly. It had given a measure of internal and external legitimacy to the fluid transition of power in a 'republic' from father to son by justifying it as a project for combating corruption, updating legislation and opening up space for participation.

This is apparent if we observe the way that power was transferred – through lining up new policies by the political, military and security elite.[21]

The Damascus Spring would have been impossible without the presence of two elements causing a socio-political movement at a historical moment. First is a change in political leadership while maintaining a totalitarian system based on a strictly hierarchal order in which the president is considered the sole executive director of the system and its institutions. The other is the willingness of a society – known historically for its diplomacy, vitality, culture and participation – to revive itself through overcoming barriers to have its voice heard and taken into account. These two elements had coincided on a number of occasions in Syria's past, transpiring in parallel and coherent ways before tyranny finally triumphed over the society, thus returning it to the old silence that it had known during the last two decades of the twentieth century. The political elites wanted to introduce legal and economic reforms to improve Syria's external image without opening space for political alternatives. But while the new opposition front seemed at first to be short-sighted and piecemeal in its demands, it gradually became more mature and visionary.

The authorities announced conditions to regulate – or more precisely, to stifle – the activities of these forums. People in charge of organizing such gatherings were ordered to provide the names of lecturers and participants, as well as to submit the conference papers 15 days in advance for official authorization.[22] This meant that the Ministry of the Interior's security wing was effectively bringing these activities to a halt. This coincided with a statement from the regional Baʿth Party's leadership (*al-Qiyādah al-Quṭrī*) in which Syrian intellectuals who participated in these activities were accused of collaboration with an external agent.[23] Furthermore, some Baʿth Party members organized visits to Syrian districts to warn people against the concept of 'civil society.'[24] In the face of these obstacles, most forums announced the suspension of their activities. One exception was Jamal al-Atāsī's Forum for Democratic Dialogue, which represented the Nasserite Arab nationalist tendency that was ideologically similar to the Baʿth Party.[25] The transformation of the Forum for National Dialogue after the crackdowns led MP Sayf to describe the forum before its permanent closure as nothing but a 'chattering guesthouse'.[26] The end of the Damascus Spring followed shortly thereafter.[27]

Despite this situation, the intellectuals carried on with their activities through those of their representative committees that had gained real legitimacy. On 25 February 2001, the Establishing Committee for the Revival of Civil Society issued another document named *Consensuses*,[28] while Jamal al-Atāsī's forum continued its activities by giving a lecture on the 'Culture of Fear'.[29] The Forum for National Dialogue – despite Deputy Riyāḍ Sayf's summons for interrogation because of his document on the Movement for Social Peace – carried on with its meetings and decided to continue with legal registration and to resume its activities regardless of the authorities' wishes.[30]

The repression of the forums seemed to suggest that the reforms had never seriously been intended, but that the authorities had simply used a temporary relaxation to renew Syria's seriously damaged image at home and abroad. Syria's deteriorating image had activated earnest discussions among both the authorities and intellectuals. The former engaged in clandestine discussions on how best to control intellectuals and activists, meanwhile giving priority to economic – not political – reform. The intellectuals in the committees and forums, on the other hand, were more open in their discussions and writings about the authorities' attitude to the entire civil mobilization. Where would it lead? How were they going to protect the achievements of the Damascus Spring?

Economic liberalization was partial, limited and did not bring about any comprehensive reform. Opening private banks, modifying some laws and drafting plans to introduce unemployment benefits amounted to a patchwork policy on a threadbare economy. Discussions about their utility are still ongoing. To justify the rapid political crackdown and reluctance to approve serious economic reforms, the authorities took a few timid steps towards creating fractionally more political openness. For example, although the authorities were aware of the weak representation and near obscurity of the NPF parties, they were allowed to open offices in the provinces and to issue their own journals.

The final crushing of the Damascus Spring came – ironically – on 11 September 2001 with the arrest of the movement's best-known activists. This sent a message to activists in particular, and to the society at large, about the importance of maintaining the status quo that had characterized the Syrian regime since the late 1970s. This step backwards brought home the futility of trying to effect meaningful change in the current regime, especially given that the Damascus Spring actually rehabilitated the image of the regime within and outside the country. The regime emerged with no incentive to break with its former domestic policy based on fear, oppression and a monopoly on truth and patriotism.

The arrests began with the detention of Deputy Maʾmūn al-Humṣī in August 2001 and his subsequent decision to go on hunger strike.[31] They arrested Riyāḍ al-Turk, general secretary of the political bureau of the Syrian Communist Party, in September 2001 after he had appeared on an Al-Jazeera television programme called 'Without Borders'.[32] Activities resumed at the Forum for National Dialogue with a lecture on 6 September 2001 at which Burhan Ghalion, who had flown in from Paris, was guest speaker. At the beginning of his speech titled 'Future of Reforms and Change in Syria: Towards a New National Contract', he suggested starting a new chapter in Syrian socio-political life.[33] After five hours, the 500 participants – of whom I was one – felt a new and vital bond with each other as Syrians, irrespective of our ethnic or ideological differences. The notion crystallized when the lecturer recommended creating a national pact between the authorities and different political factions on the one hand, and between society and opposition forces on the other. The Syrian authorities reacted by arresting Deputy Riyāḍ Sayf in September 2001,[34] thereby infuriating the Forum for National Dialogue, which promised to carry on with its activities.[35]

The authorities quickly arrested four members of the Forum for National Dialogue – ʿĀrif Dalīlah (former dean of the faculty of economics), Walīd al-Bunnī, Kamāl al-Lubwānī, Ḥasan Saʿdūn and Ḥabīb

Ṣāliḥ from the Cultural Forum in Ṭarṭūs.[36] After publicly condemning the arrests and blatantly carrying on with their political activities, two other activists were detained on 11 September 2001. They were Ḥabīb ʿĪsá (lawyer and spokesperson for Jamal al-Atāsī's Forum for Democratic Dialogue) and Fawwāz Tal-lū (a member of the Committee of the Forum for National Dialogue).[37] These arrests coincided with the 11 September attacks in New York, which facilitated the quiet round-up of Syrian intellectuals and activists while the world's attention was diverted elsewhere. After 11 September, intellectuals remained inactive for a while to ponder what political moves to make in the light of this international event of such mammoth significance. While these detentions marked the official end of the Damascus Spring, Syrian intellectuals and activists gambled on, hoping to create a new climate for justice and civil liberty in Syria after decades of living in a civic vacuum. Unfortunately, this bet failed because of the political regime's intolerance of openness or change, and its insistence on monopolizing all political, social and media matters.

The social mobilization – despite serious limitations – produced a new political atmosphere in Syria. Regardless of their ideological differences, activists and intellectuals agreed to reject clandestine operations in favour of transparency and consciously to link their openness to the pursuit of peace as a first step towards democracy. This link became a central theme in the numerous statements produced during that period. We can observe this change in the Syrian Muslim Brotherhood and also in the political bureau of the Communist Party, which announced its new name – the Popular Democratic Party – after its sixth anniversary conference. These parties moved, in rhetoric and the public imagination, from dogmatic, ideologically-centred entities to proponents of the democratic process.

The Muslim Brotherhood announced in May 2001 its 'National Honour Pact for Political Work', stating its dedication to dialogue, a 'democratic political framework', 'abandoning violence' and to work towards 'protecting human rights, and those of individual citizens'.[38] The pact referred to the so-called 'modern state' or a:

> contractual state in which agreement is established between the leader and the led. It was claimed that the mode of a contractual state is one of Islam's gifts to human civilization. A 'modern state' is an institutional state, based on ensuring separation of power and the independence of authorities at all levels of society. In a modern state there is no place for one individual, one party or one power to rule exclusively or to manipulate the state's facilities. In a modern state, justice prevails and social security rather than state security is the priority. The concept of a 'state of emergency' would not be a normal part of the law.

The pact adds that the:

> modern state is based on free and just elections as a principle of power alternation between all citizens. It is a pluralist state, where visions, interpretations and attitudes vary. Opposing political factions as well as civil society play the role of observer and detector, so that the state does not fall into a cycle of tyranny and corruption.

In the pact, the Muslim Brotherhood stated its compliance with 'the mechanisms and means of democratic work, ensuring equal rights for all to benefit from the state's possibilities, to enable them to clarify their attitude, to achieve their visions and propose their programs'. Furthermore, they abandoned violence as a political method, stating that 'security measurements for conflict resolution between (state and society) and the state of violence are an introduction to corruption'. Here, we note a remarkable shift in the political mentality of the most prominent Islamic movement in Syria – the same party famous for its violent uprising and crackdown in the 1980s.

The Syrian Muslim Brotherhood's acceptance of the concept of democracy and of peaceful changeovers of power was similar to the programme proposed by the Popular Democratic Party, which adopted democracy as its policy programme. The programme announced at its sixth conference stated that 'the popular party struggles for a national democratic order, based on the principles of freedom, equality and social justice'. It concluded that:

> the experiences of the past 40 years indicated a failure of the prevailing security state, established through autocracy and the idea of one ruling party, and the *Qa'ed* (the leader), which brought Syrian society backwards in all aspects of political, economic, social and cultural life, disrupting its national infrastructure, implicating it in internal, Arab and international crises. The overcoming of such a state requires the return to democracy.[39]

Despite the repetition of old leftist arguments about democracy, the programme recognized that:

> there are no democracies that are different in their essence, designed according to each nation; there is one democracy. It is a system of modern and universal values and principles based on the doctrine of liberty, ruled by the population. It is a state of institutions and alternation of power through free and periodic elections. The population chooses the government, observing and questioning power, always ready to reconsider it. It is a system based on the reign of justice, where all obey without any discrimination or exception, a law that guarantees both fundamental and pluralistic freedoms.

According to the programme, this stipulates the:

> rebuilding of the constitutional state that is structured on a democratic constitution as a principle of a parliamentary system, ensuring equal rights for all citizens and lining up their duties, where injustice and monopoly vanish, their re-establishment precluded. A rectification should be presented by a liberally elected committee and should be subject to a public referendum. This constitution should establish the inde-

> pendence of each authority, and the executive authority should comply with a freely elected legislative power. It should be a constitution that guarantees the independence of law, the rule of justice and the equality of citizens before the law.

We are at a unique stage in Syria's history. Before, politics consisted of calculating personal interests and conflict along ideological lines. For the first time, the idea of democracy prevailed, at least within the opposition's consciousness. The movement not only spurred the intellectuals but challenged the opposition political parties to choose a peaceful political methodology, despite their vastly different visions of society.

This build up of democracy in Syrians' political awareness came at a high price, for lengthy deliberations about the concept, the efficacy of its application and its applicability to Arab culture preceded it. Democracy was clearly apparent in a number of civil and cultural movements that emerged – private forums such as the Forum for National Dialogue (which closed down in September 2001) and Jamal al-Atāsī's Forum for Democratic Dialogue (which closed in June 2005). Activists and intellectuals in the Committee for the Revival of Civil Society spread themselves through Syrian districts to maintain a political and intellectual dynamism. At this time, human rights groups gained prominence in Syrian consciousness.

Because of the paucity of available platforms in the Syrian media, the internet remains the sole place where democratic debates take place. The internet is a democratic leveller, where different streams and ideologies interact freely. Even Syria's youth are becoming aware of democratic alternatives, they being the ones who naturally would be the first to benefit from this facility.[40]

The feat of attaining a democratic consciousness during and immediately after the Damascus Spring clearly differs from the kind of political awareness that was present in Syria during most of its contemporary history. Post-independence Syrian history can be characterized as an expression of the political, social and economic movements that prevailed during the pre-independence period. There was no disconnection or gap between generations that might mark a distinct historical era, despite different circumstantial details. On the other hand, the Damascus Spring stood out as a mutation in a history of continuous inactivity. While it is true that contemporary Syrian history has witnessed the arrival and departure of various opposition movements, these were never able to reconcile themselves with the society at large. Their political discourse – grounded as it was in dogmatic authoritarianism – resembled that of the authorities, with no difference in political method. They aimed simply to supplant the leadership with their own people. The sacrifices offered by previous opposition movements during their conflict should not be denied. Despite a similarity in discourse, there is no comparing the principled actions of much of the opposition with the moral corruption of the authorities. However, the Damascus Spring demonstrated a real separation from previous opposition movements in its discourse, slogans, objectives and practice. The movement championed pluralistic politics, freedom of expression and uncompromising liberal democracy. This was not a mere show of modesty, but a real belief that before striving for power, they needed to work towards the recuperation of civil society.

The Damascus Spring witnessed individual and collective initiatives coming from various cultural, economic and social sectors, which was another trait that distinguished the period from previous opposition movements. Activism emerged from below, for the majority of the activists were intellectuals and not politicians. Political parties participated in the movement at a later stage, but the activists and intellectuals were the most principled in demanding change. Also, the Damascus Spring belonged to Syrian society at large, not only to a factional or ideological group within it, thus ensuring that it spread to new sectors, despite the heavy security measures imposed after renewed repression. The Damascus Spring remained the property of the multitude, even though parties or groups were banned from associating with it.

How do we read the future of this democratic movement? How much value did the Damascus Spring add to the accumulation of a political consciousness in Syria? What is the magnitude of the reform impulse that could now be created? The nature of socio-political movements in Syria differs from movements in other Arab countries, due to the particular political regime involved. Each system deals with opposition differently. Ultimately, it depends on the margin of freedom of expression allowed in each country. The Syrian regime's domination of the vital aspects of society such as parties, trade unions and the media – as well as the ban on forming organizations and independent radio or television channels – makes the issue of democratic struggle difficult and risky work.

Activists, intellectuals and some unlicensed opposition political parties have held demonstrations in front of the court of justice and the state security court, but such protests are always ferociously crushed, in some cases with the demonstrators arrested and imprisoned. Therefore, the question of the future of this movement and its possible spheres of influence is a legitimate one, and open to various possibilities. We observe the determination of activists to express their opposition by all means allowed, regardless of the consequences. At the same time, we also see that the officials insist on repressing and banning such protests for fear that they might spiral out of its control.

We cannot separate the changes that are taking place in Syria from those that are happening in the region and further afield. The increased pressure that the United States put on authoritarian Arab regimes during the George W. Bush administration, with all its talk about 'reforming the system', meant that the question of democracy in Syria became a rather sensitive one. Activists insist on regarding democratic reform as an exclusively domestic and national concern. On the other hand, the regime carries on associating any domestic opposition with external pressure, a fact that has ignited debates among Syrians about an 'inside/outside' dualism.

Limitations placed on these movements translate into an incapacity to coalesce into a real threat to the regime. Demonstrations composed of tens of participants, and electronic declarations and critiques published in Arab newspapers are critical but insufficient means of transforming the democratic movement in Syria into an effective force. The mission remains difficult unless the security presence becomes less hermetic. Then, perhaps new sectors of Syrian society will be persuaded to participate – sectors that are currently not involved in the process through fear of jeopardizing their interests, especially the youth and businessmen. The movement would be able to expand, to influence and act internally. Without this critical internal mass, the regime will maintain its iron-clad control, waiting for a regional and international move against it to impose change on its performance, policies and, possibly, its structural framework.

4

Bashar al-Asad and Foreign Policy

Foreign Policy Decision-making

The Syrian constitution, issued in 1973 during President Hafez al-Asad's term and still in effect, confirms that the president of the republic is responsible for foreign policy, while the prime minister, despite being nominally responsibility for it, does not play much part in its formulation. In Article 94 the constitution states that the president of the republic lays down the foreign policy of the state and supervises its implementation through consultation with the Council of Ministers; the role of the legislative power, according to Article 71 of the constitution, does not go beyond discussing the minister's policy and ratifying international treaties and agreements related to state security.[1]

Theoretically, the Ministry of Foreign Affairs and not the Council of Ministers is in charge of formulating Syrian foreign policy, which is based on close coordination with the president of the republic. The Ministry of Foreign Affairs collects and analyses the information, drafts the foreign policy and presents it to the minister for foreign affairs who, in turn, submits it to Asad who makes the final decision. Through coordination with various related Syrian institutions, the Ministry of Foreign Affairs puts a certain policy or resolution into effect.[2]

The minister of foreign affairs takes main responsibility for routine foreign-policy issues, for the unchanging aspects of Syrian foreign policy such as decisions on voting in the United Nations. If the decision has a military or security element, however, the minister's role may be reduced. Here the president, as the general leader of the armed forces, and some assisting institutions such as the Ministry of

Defence, the intelligence organizations and general staff, assume the greater role.[3] In the case of war, for example, it is necessary to get the consent of the People's Assembly, and here it is the president who makes the main decision.

President Hafez al-Asad personally took charge of all foreign-policy decisions during the direct Syrian–Israeli negotiations (1991–2000) following the Madrid conference, particularly while the United States was exerting pressure on him to engage in general diplomatic initiatives to encourage Israeli public opinion and to prepare it for a potential peace agreement. Some people called al-Asad's negotiating style 'word by word diplomacy',[4] for he would check each word of the Syrian officials' releases, reserving for himself any position he would like to declare or publicize. He sometimes handed over initiatives or statements to the minister of foreign affairs, Farouk al-Shar'a, and charged him with the responsibility of putting them into effect. Al-Asad conducted any negotiations with a high degree of control, and directed his negotiators in such a way that they performed their tasks effectively. The fact that they were answerable to him alone gave them confidence and at the same time protected them from the intervention of the other military and security institutions.

After President Hafez al-Asad's death, his foreign minister, Farouk al-Shar'a, played a significant role in directing foreign policy, for his good relations with President Bashar al-Asad and with other security institutions had helped secure a calm atmosphere for the transition of power. Farouk al-Shar'a showed his true colours during the build up to the United States' war with Iraq and during the crisis in relations with Lebanon. At press conferences he seemed unrestrained, making several announcements that angered a number of his colleagues, particularly with regard to his position on resolution 1559, which he described as a 'stupid resolution'.[5] His influence on formulating foreign policy, however, increased with his promotion from minister of foreign affairs to vice president, a change traditionally regarded as both a 'promotion and a paralysis'. But the legislative decree issued in 2006, which charged him with supervising information gathering and foreign policy, made it possible for him to practise wider authority.

This reflects the reality of the work of formulating Syrian foreign policy, which is based on people rather than being crystallized in policies. Despite the office of the president's deputy being legally and constitutionally prescribed, Farouk al-Shar'a's position had been marginal under Hafez al-Asad and he played no effective part in decision-making, but with the acquisition of authority from the new president of the republic, he was able, as the president's deputy, to perform a role for which the position *per se* would not otherwise have given him authority.

This was also the position of Walīd al-Mu'allem, who was appointed minister of foreign affairs at the beginning of 2006 after having been nominated as a deputy for the foreign minister in 2003. By this appointment, he would not be subject to the 'functional retirement' usually applied in state institutions.[6]

The main purpose of appointing al-Mu'allem as foreign minister was to improve the image of Syrian foreign policy abroad, for he was already well known to the United States and to the European Union's institutions. Al-Mu'allem was known for his moderation, especially when he had served as Syrian ambassador to the United States for the ten years of the honeymoon period of Syrian–American relations from 1990 to 2000. His position in the Syrian political hierarchy, however, was relatively weak.[7] This takes us back to the problem of position, power and influence: position does not necessarily give power, as it usually would in other parts of the world, because in Syria power and influence are linked to the trust given to a particular person, first of all by the president and secondly by the security organizations. Many factors determine how much power and influence an individual enjoys – for example, membership of the Ba'th Party, loyalty to particular interest groups or participation in influential networks. Furthermore, administrative corruption is not only permissible or overlooked; its practice is sometimes actually encouraged because it is needed to build up and protect the network of influence.

The role of the NPF central leadership, or for that matter the regional leadership (*al-Qiyādah al-Quṭrī*), in making foreign-policy decisions has been completely whittled away, in fact reduced to providing legality and factional support for the president's decisions. This was clearly evident from the statements issued during the withdrawal from Lebanon in March 2005.[8] The same more or less applies to the Syrian People's Assembly, which is sometimes called upon to act out a 'popular drama' for the purposes of giving a previously taken political decision the appearance of popular support for domestic and foreign consumption. Al-Asad resorted to this ploy when he decided to withdraw the Syrian forces working in Lebanon. He announced his decision during a public address to the People's Assembly,[9] which had played the same role when previous vice-president, ʿAbd al-Ḥalīm Khaddām, had declared that he was dissociating himself from the Syrian regime and would settle in Paris.[10]

The unspoken aspect of Syrian foreign policy is in the role played by military and security organizations in making foreign-policy decisions. It is generally not mentioned in the media, though all the political players, observers and even foreign diplomats are aware of it; some even assume that the military and security organizations in fact make the final decisions. This is particularly true when a decision of great significance is concerned, involving the states surrounding Syria, or when a decision is associated with a security dimension within Syria. For example, the increasing numbers of Palestinian refugees living in Syria, or the influx of Iraqi refugees after the invasion of Iraq in 2003 created some security problems. Their numbers have greatly increased, especially since the increase of violence caused by civil war since 2005, and now exceed 1.2 million.

In such cases, the political decision is often preceded by very high-level security discussions in which the final decision is that of the president with priority given to the security aspect at the expense of suggestions made by the Ministry of Foreign Affairs.

Under President Hafez al-Asad, Syrian military intelligence played a crucial role in developing the Syrian–Lebanese relationship, as well as Syria's relationship with the Palestinian organizations. Ghazi Kanʾan, head of the Syrian security apparatus in Lebanon, was responsible for pursuing Syria's relationship with the different Lebanese parties. He took on this responsibility despite the presence of the Common Syrian–Lebanese High Council[11] and even though he theoretically belonged to a subdivision of military intelligence, so was not very senior in the hierarchy. He considered himself to be directly responsible to President Hafez al-Asad who, in turn, dealt with him on this basis and gave him the necessary authority.

When Bashar al-Asad assumed power as the new president, he conducted his relations with Lebanon through the same military-security channels his father had used, despite the increasing number of Lebanese voices opposing the Syrian military presence in their country and its interference in Lebanese internal affairs. Later on Rustum Ghazālah replaced Ghazi Kanʾan, but in addition to lacking Kanʾan's experience and sophistication, Ghazālah behaved rudely towards many Lebanese officials, which meant that a number of Lebanese and Syrians complained about him to President Bashar al-Asad. With mounting international pressures on Syria and more and more Lebanese people calling for the Syrian army to withdraw from Lebanon, al-Asad decided to entrust Walīd al-Muʿallem, then the deputy of the Syrian Ministry of Foreign Affairs, with the task of modifying the relationship in the light of political rather than security considerations. His visit, however, was not welcomed by the Lebanese,[12] since it had not been so long ago that the assassination of the previous Lebanese prime minister, Rafiq al-Hariri, on 14 February 2005, had brought the Syrian–Lebanese relationship to a state of crisis.

Even after the evacuation of the Syrian forces from Lebanon in March 2005, a parliamentary election was held in Lebanon in which the political parties opposing the Syrian presence predominated. During the time of Fuʾād al-Sinyūrah's first government, it was the Syrian president in consultation with Syrian military intelligence, and not the Syrian Ministry of Foreign Affairs, who was responsible for Syria's generally good relationship with the Lebanese parties, includeing Hezbollah and the Amal movement.

Quite apart from the accusation of complicity in the assassination of the Lebanese ex-prime minister Rafiq al-Hariri, Syria's entanglement in the complexities of the struggle with Israel may have added additional strain to this relationship. The strategic vision of Syrian security was based on the principle of a tactical balance with Israel, but since the beginning of the 1980s Lebanon had been regarded as no more than a Syrian appendage that had to be fortified and securely-controlled. It was this that later changed Lebanon into an arena for Syrian interference in all its security, military, political and even domestic municipal affairs.

Things were not very different with the Palestinian organizations, particularly those based in Syria, such as Hamas, the Islamic Jihad, the Popular Front for Liberating Palestine and the Democratic Front. The relationship of these organizations was with Syrian military intelligence, which coordinated anything relating to political or security issues. Here, the final decision was certainly with the president, but the Syrian Ministry of Foreign Affairs endorsed it; information passed through the subdivision of military intelligence charged with reporting decisions and transmitting the viewpoints of these Palestinian organizations to the president. This was the only channel through which President Hafez al-Asad dealt with the Lebanese Hezbollah and the Palestinian organizations in Syria, all of which the United States branded as 'terrorist' organizations. Thus, despite the close relationship between the Lebanese Hezbollah and the Palestinian organizations in Syria, President Hafez al-Asad did not meet, at least publicly, any of their leaders. On coming to power, President Bashar al-Asad maintained contact with Hezbollah and the Palestinian organizations through the military-security channel, but he seemed to be bolder about holding public meetings with, for example, Ḥasan Nasr Allah, secretary-general of the Lebanese Hezbollah, Khaled Mash'al, head of the political bureau of Hamas, or Ramaḍān 'Abd Allāh Shallah, secretary-general of the Islamic Jihad movement. His meetings with the Palestinian organizations were fairly regular, especially once the strategic relationship with Hezbollah had been consolidated in the wake of the Israeli war against Lebanon in July 2006, and the stability of the relationship with Hamas (which had come to power after elections in 2005) had been established.

With regard to foreign policy, when Bashar al-Asad commenced his rule he took the oath with a speech that evoked the admiration of everybody. In it he declared his adherence to the peace process saying: 'we are in a hurry to realize peace but we are not ready to renounce the land and we do not accept any limitation to our sovereignty. That is to stay we are in a hurry for peace because it is our choice.'[13]

His arrival to power, however, was in the context of extremely sensitive regional situations, which made his policies seem confused and incoherent. With Barak's agreement on 28 September 2000 to allow Sharon, the leader of the Likud opposition, to visit the site of the Holy Mosque, a Palestinian Intifada (uprising) broke out as retaliation for what was considered a deliberate Israeli provocation. The Intifada started with stone throwing and demonstrations that were generally non-violent, albeit angry, revealing the extent of the suffering and the deliberate marginalization of Palestinian human rights, which had been going on for decades. But Israeli policemen fired on the Palestinian crowds, killing seven people and wounding many more. Georges Malbrunot's well-documented narrative of the Palestinian Intifada entitled *From Stones to Guns*[14] confirms that the Palestinian leadership had not been planning the Intifada as the Israeli analysts claimed, and that the Intifada had only resorted to weapons after several weeks and then only as a response to the Israeli army's suppression. In the words of Malbrunot: 'Between 28 September 2000 and 2 January 2001 the Israeli army killed 204 Palestinians out of whom 73 were under seventeen and 24 were members of the Palestinian security division.' The Palestinian leadership was then driven to pursue a new policy. As one of the leaders said: 'We were unable to bear the loss of ten children every day, it is a high human price and we had to adopt a new strategy.'[15]

The 'Al-Aqsa Intifada (Uprising)', as it came to be called, aroused unprecedented Arab popular and official support, which the previous Intifada had not attained. In transmitting news of the events, Arab television and radio stations played a prominent role in stirring up Arab support and feelings of sympathy for the Palestinians. The Syrian position was clear with regard to its official support. Though still keeping their distance from Yaser Arafat, the Syrian authorities showed spontaneous eagerness to support the Palestinians and their second Intifada. For example, in an unofficial interview in the

Jordanian newspaper *al-Majd* al-Asad said: 'We, first of all, aim to support the popular Intifada, which we see as a courageous demonstration of resistance that must not be neglected or left without support.'[16] Following the outbreak of the Intifada, Bashar al-Asad criticized the attempt to 'crystallize a nationalist project under the wing of peace', especially since there was no American sponsor and Israel had not observed its international commitments. On 21 October 2001, at the Arab interim summit in Cairo convened specifically to support the Intifada, he suggested that Arabs had to reconsider their policy of 'peace as a strategic option'[17] and that it was necessary to sever all relations with Israel, including all relations with states that had established economic and diplomatic relation with it.

This led to cold relations with Egypt, which had continually adopted a 'give them the benefit of the doubt' policy, which the official Syrian press widely criticized. Asad's position at the Islamic summit held in Doha on 11 November was similar to the previous one, and the summit officially agreed to sever relations with Israel.[18] At this point the Lebanese opposition escalated its demands for the withdrawal of the Syrian army from Lebanon. It was this that drove al-Asad to take a number of steps towards consolidating his position at both the regional and central levels. Foremost among these was his decision in late November 2000 to redeploy the Syrian army in Lebanon.[19] The intensification of the Intifada, along with Arab support for it, encouraged Hezbollah to press heavily on the other front, carrying out a number of operations on Sheb'a Farms with a view to returning the area to Lebanese sovereignty. This led to Syrian–American tensions because the United States and Israel held Syria responsible for these operations. This was what the American ambassador passed on to Damascus in a warning letter, and Israel accused Bashar al-Asad of 'not merely allowing such operations but of also encouraging them',[20] thus accusing Bashar al-Asad of considering the liberation of south Lebanon as a 'worthy example to be followed for liberating other Arab occupied territories'.

With the official declaration of Bush's success in the American elections in December 2000, and the election of Sharon as prime minister of Israel in February 2001, the Middle East seemed to be reaching a new stage, particularly after the events of 11 September 2001 when all regional as well as international relationships would be turned upside down.

The world after 11 September 2001 became obsessed with security and the struggle against terrorism. The election of Sharon also had a direct influence on Syrian official political discourse, even on the speeches of Asad, who continually questioned the possibility of peace with a 'society unprepared for peace, a society that elected Sharon'.

In his first prolonged press interview with the newspaper *al-Sharq al-Awsat* on 7 February 2001, after he had been elected president, al-Asad seemed to be more intransigent with regard to the peace process than his father. President Hafez al-Asad had limited his idea of a 'comprehensive peace plan' to Syria and Lebanon, because both the Palestinians and the Jordanians, Syria's partners in the Madrid peace conference, had concluded separate agreements. President Hafez al-Asad, therefore, would be satisfied with an accord that would satisfy Syrian and Lebanese interests.

His son Bashar, on the other hand, declared that agreement on the Golan Heights and Lebanon alone would not constitute a comprehensive peace plan; there must be 'a balanced Lebanese, Palestinian and Syrian axis'. He confirmed the nationalist basis of the Syrian viewpoint regarding the peace process saying, 'signing an accord with Syria would not be enough to solve the problem and attain the purpose of coordinating other policies.'[21] Bashar al-Asad also wanted peace but he wanted an agreement with all Arab countries that would demonstrate real support for the Palestinian Intifada and so he agreed to the establishment of 'the Syrian Arab Popular Committee for supporting the Intifada and resisting the Zionist project'. Its main objective was to offer tangible support for the Intifada from all Syrian governorates.

At the same time Bashar al-Asad continued to consolidate the strategic partnership with Iran, visiting it in January 2002,[22] and continued with the gradual process of openness towards Iraq by receiving the Iraqi vice-president in Damascus and strengthening economic and commercial relations between the two countries.[23] In his speech at the periodical Arab summit in Amman on 27 April 2001,

Bashar al-Asad vehemently attacked the Israeli populace, claiming that there was no difference between the right and the left in Israeli society. 'For us, as Arabs, all the Israelis are rightist', he said and criticized previous Israeli governments, from Rabin to Barak, accusing them of introducing false, illusionary propositions with regard to peace. Sharon, he declared, was regarded in the world in general and in Israel itself as 'a man of massacres, a man of killing, a man who hates the Arabs'. He asked, 'Do they expect us to be convinced that the people who elected such a man are peace-loving?' He sounded even angrier when he said: 'The peace process started with Shamir and ended with Sharon. They and all those who came between are all the same; there is no difference between the first and the last or those who came between. The whole of Israeli society is racist, more racist than the Nazis.' He concluded by saying:

> The strong uprising in the Arab street witnessed today is the result of different factors, the most important of which is the Palestinian Intifada. Without that, it would have been difficult to attain that surge, and it is our duty to safeguard its energy so that it does not turn into a daily routine with no impact on us. It is necessary to support this Intifada through different means such as supplying direct material support and initiating an international campaign to affirm its legality.[24]

At the Amman summit he arranged an informal meeting with President Yaser Arafat. By taking this step he hoped to open a different type of Syrian–Palestinian relationship, a relationship that might be able to forget the discords of the past.

When Hezbollah carried out a number of operations against Israel to liberate what was left of Lebanese territories under Israeli occupation, Sharon did not hesitate to charge Syria with the responsibility for these operations, accusing it of encouraging them.[25] In retaliation, he bombed a Syrian military camp at Ḍahr al-Baydar in Lebanon in April 2001.[26] Farouk al-Sharʾa, the minister of foreign affairs, expressed the Syrian mood when he said: 'Damascus will not give Sharon the satisfaction of escalating the conflict.'[27] Accordingly, he kept his silence.

This, however, increased the hostility of the Syrian president's speech. He repeated in the press conference that he held with the Spanish prime minister in Madrid that Israeli society was more racist than Zionist.[28] This resulted in a wave of political criticism and personal calumniation of President Bashar al-Asad in the Western media, which accused him of being anti-Semitic. This hostility was intensified by the speech he delivered at the end of Pope John Paul's visit to Damascus. The speech was misunderstood as comparing the prophet's sufferings at the hands of the Jews with the sufferings of the Palestinians.

Bashar al-Asad was, therefore, subjected to a campaign that represented him as an enemy of peace and a warmonger. This put him in an embarrassing position with respect to his visits to Europe, especially his expected visit to France. He succeeded in modifying his speeches to some extent, announcing in an interview for the second channel of French television that peace was still the strategic option for Syria and that Syria would be ready to acknowledge Israel 'when Israel is ready to offer real peace'. In keeping with this acknowledgement, there would be 'ordinary natural relations like any other relations between two states or two peoples in the region'. He reasserted that returning the Golan Heights to Syrian sovereignty in accordance with international resolutions would ensure the attainment of a peace agreement.

He tried to explain his comments during the pope's visit to Damascus by pointing out that there is a difference between comparison and parallelism, saying that 'Israeli racism is manifested in acts of killing whether during the Intifada or throughout the existence of Israel.' In his speech before the pope, he concentrated on 'the principles of the three religions of the book, which stress justice, peace and love'.[29] Despite the continual Israeli provocation such as bombing a Syrian radar station in the Beqa᾿a, which killed a number of Syrian soldiers, Syria had refrained from retaliation in order to deny Israel an opportunity to wage a new regional war. However, there was instant retaliation from Hezbollah, which immediately destroyed an Israeli radar station.[30]

In an interview with the German newspaper, *Der Spiegel*, before his visit to Germany, Asad reiterated that while Sharon clearly and openly sought war, peace was a Syrian ideology and not just a political strategy. Syria, therefore, would not be drawn into war but would not run away if war were imposed on it.[31] In another interview, he said: 'We will remain firm and resist aggression even if we estimate that the enemy will destroy a lot of our public utilities; we can remain stronger more than they imagine and rebuild whatever might be destroyed. And we have the means to do extreme harm to the enemy.'[32] Such warlike posturing seemed to calm down when the events in America on 11 September 2001 overshadowed the region and the world. The Intifada and *fidāʾīyīn* (commandos) moderated their tone a little and President Bush seemed resolute in his talk with Sharon when he said that he did not want anything to distract him from his real battle, which was now the war against terrorism.

The events of 11 September, however, seriously affected Syrian–US relations. Despite Syria having got a temporary seat in the Security Council without opposition from the United States,[33] the new American policy, determined by President Bush on the basis of a simplistic opposition (he who is not with us is with terrorism), put Syria on the spot for its support of Hezbollah and Palestinian organizations such as Hamas and the Islamic Jihad defined by the Americans as terrorist organizations. Thus knee jerk reactions dominated most declarations by American officials starting with Richard Armitage, assistant secretary of state, who did not exclude military action against Syria if it failed to respond to American and Western demands.[34]

Damascus, however, strongly protested against Armitage's declarations and sent for the US ambassador in Damascus to notify him of the objection to these pronouncements. As a result, President Bush made a statement saying: 'The Syrians talked to us about how they can help in the war against terrorism, and we take this seriously and will give them a chance to do it.'[35] Still, the Syrian position, which called for defining terrorism by looking into its causes and differentiating it from legitimate resistance, could not easily be publicized internationally in the face of the American administration's refusal to respond to any questions of this kind beyond discussing the means of fighting terrorism. (Presumably, questions of causes and legitimacy could lead to labyrinthine discussions that would dilute the urgency of responding to terror.)

Thus, Damascus found itself obliged to deal with the American logic, offering its assistance in fighting terrorism. It started to investigate the Syrian bank accounts of people suspected of being associated with terrorist organizations,[36] but insisted on adhering to the differentiation between terrorism and resistance. At a press conference held in Damascus for the British prime minister Tony Blair, President Bashar al-Asad declared that Damascus was 'the most able to determine the nature of the organizations existing in Syria',[37] a point that al-Asad repeated in his meetings with many successive Congress delegations visiting Syria.[38] This point was also made in the context of the Syrian answer to Security Council resolution 1373 with regard to fighting terrorism.[39] With the increase in violent Israeli actions mounted against Palestinians in the West Bank and Gaza Strip in retaliation for the suicide operations carried out by Palestinians inside Israel, popular anger at American support for Sharon increased and took an institutionally organized form. Committees were formed to boycott American goods and to demonstrate daily against Israel and the United States; the demonstrations usually culminated in burning the flags of the two states. The official newspapers were filled with sharp-tongued criticism of American policy. Syrian officials then circulated this criticism, especially al-Sharʾa's speech at the first conference of the leaders of the NPF parties.[40]

On the other hand, Syria did provide the United States with intelligence about Al Qaeda, thus saving the lives of many Americans, as more than one American official acknowledged.[41] But, despite this cooperation, the United States did not take Syrian interests into consideration; rather, Syria was completely neglected. No American high official visited it except the Secretary of State Colin Powell, who made a sudden unplanned visit just for the purpose of getting Syrian commitments to calm the situation in south Lebanon. In a speech expressing his viewpoint on peace on 24 June 2002, Bush completely bypassed the Syrian right to retrieve the Golan Heights. Moreover, he asked Syria to 'choose the right side in the war against terrorism by closing terrorist camps and expelling terrorist organizations'. He added that 'leaders who want to participate in the peace process have to demonstrate unconditional support for peace through their actions.'[42] The speech received wide Israeli approval,[43] but clear Syrian official coldness,[44] which changed later into open criticism by Farouk al-Shar'a, the foreign minister at that time.

Most important, however, was Bush's understanding of 'peace', which his mission to fight terrorism defined and which completely sidestepped the Arab peace initiative the Beirut Arab summit had ratified in March 2002 in the wake of the 11 September events. The terms of the initiative, which had originally come from Saudi Arabia and which the Saudi crown prince had proposed with a view to improving US–Saudi relations, were the normalization of relations in return for Israel's withdrawal from all Arab territories occupied in 1967. Following this initiative, Saudi Arabia, which had distanced itself from the normalization argument, now became more interested in it than other Arab states. In fact, Syria had originally floated the idea of normalization as a step towards reaching a just peace agreement, but the Saudis hijacked it and it came to be seen as their initiative. The American journalist Thomas Friedman, who had joined the Saudi crown prince for supper, suddenly announced the idea without consultation with any Arab party.

Bashar al-Asad, as he mentioned in a press interview, was accidentally informed of it during a visit to Italy in February 2002.[45] His position towards it was indecisive, particularly since some of its items were ambiguous. Visiting Saudi Arabia a few days after the announcement, however, he played a significant role in widening its provisos, particularly with regard to the rights of refugees to return to their homes.[46] This annoyed Friedman, who had heralded the idea[47] that was now considered to be the first integrated Arab initiative related to the peace process. It was supposed to support the peace movement in Israel and give it priority over the radical 'rightist' trend that had brought Sharon to power.[48] Most public opinion polls in Israel at that time, however, continued to put Sharon in first place despite the severe economic downturn following the Palestinian suicide operations carried out in Israeli cities.[49]

After the Arab summit in Beirut on 27 and 28 March 2002, the Saudi initiative became an Arab initiative and all Arab countries adopted it.[50] This was met with Western and Israeli approval because it was the first time that the Arabs had introduced a comprehensive peace initiative in their struggle with Israel.[51] Sharon's response, however, came quickly and decisively. He invaded the West Bank, laying siege to the Palestinian president Yaser Arafat in his headquarters in Ramallah, reducing a number of Palestinian cities and camps to piles of rubble, and carrying out massacres in Jenin and in the old town of Nablus. This deprived the Arab peace initiative of any significance or use, and it lost its value in the eyes of the Arab communities.

After the intervention against the Taliban in Afghanistan in October 2001, the United States started making preparations to wage war against Iraq. The US–British occupation of Iraq in April 2003 totally changed the whole Middle East profile. For Syria, the most important effect of this war was its severance of relations with the United States. Despite the USA continuing to praise Syria for its important role in fighting terrorism and particularly for the considerable assistance it offered to the CIA with respect to exchanging intelligence information about Al Qaeda and other terrorist organizations in the wake of the events of 11 September 2001,[52] Syria became, after the war on Iraq, one of the states most threatened with punishment in the speeches of American officials.

Pressure was put on the US Congress to introduce a draft Syrian Accountability Act and accusing it of complicity in the suicide bombings carried out in Israel. At first Congress rejected the draft law,[53] a position the State Department and CIA supported, but the Pentagon refused to relax its policy of inflexibility towards Syria. This reflected a clear split in the administration over how to deal with Syria. When George Bush decided to invade Iraq and set in motion the economic, legal and military preparations for it, he adopted an inflexible position toward Syria, and the hawks of his administration like Donald Rumsfeld, defence secretary, his assistant Secretary of State Paul Wolfowitz, the engineer of the war on Iraq, and John Bolton, their assistant started the propaganda campaign against Syria that threw a series of indictments against it, starting with its regional relationships and ending with accusations that it was developing chemical and biological weapons.[54]

This change in American policy put Damascus in an impossibly difficult position. Syria was against the military invasion of Iraq and voicing its opposition in the Security Council was awkward, for it was a temporary member there at the time of the preparations for war against Iraq. Once the administration had definitely decided to attack Iraq militarily and started to prepare the international stage politically and diplomatically, the position of Damascus became even more difficult, leaving it with no option but to support Security Council resolution 1441, but justifying its position by saying that it would safeguard Iraq from an international blow.[55]

Syria stepped up its official consultations with Iraq and al-Asad received more than one senior Iraqi official, as well as a letter from the Iraqi president Saddam Hussein, which ʿAlī Ḥasan al-Majīd, a member of the Revolutionary Leadership Council in Iraq, delivered to him personally.[56] Al-Asad saw the attack on Iraq as 'a cover for the Israeli crimes and the encirclement of the Intifada and resistance' and, at the Arab summit at Sharm al-Shaykh in March 2003, he appealed to the Arab leaders to refrain from offering facilities that would allow the United States to destroy Iraq.[57]

Eventually, the United States waged its war on Iraq, ostensibly under the pretext of looking for weapons of mass destruction, which were never found, but in effect for the purposes of changing the regime. This declaration of war without a UN resolution evoked strong opposition from the peoples and officials of the Arab world in particular and from the wider international community in general. The Syrian position was no different, but what distinguished it from the others was that it was counting on the ability of the Iraqi regime to thwart the American intervention. Even after the war had started, Bashar al-Asad expressed this view in a famous interview with the Lebanese newspaper *As-Safir* on 27 March 2003, when he charged the Arab states with the responsibility of opposing the war and said: 'Even if the American scheme succeeds – and we doubt whether it will – there will be a popular Arab resistance which has already started.'[58] This provoked the Americans, who took it as a hostile action against them and who then accused Syria of providing the Iraqi army with military assistance and of allowing the transfer of weapons through its territories.[59]

The Syrian prediction proved wrong and the Iraqi regime fell dramatically on 9 April 2003, after which Syria entered the frame, possibly – according to some influential neo-conservative voices in Washington – as the next domino to fall. American accusations against Syria increased to the extent of threatening regime change, which looked ever more likely after Saddam Hussein's fall in Iraq. Washington started by asking Syria to extradite Saddam's supporters and not provide them with shelter. President Bush then personally accused Syria of having chemical weapons[60] and of carrying out new experiments on weapons of mass destruction. These indictments were added to the earlier list about supporting Hezbollah and the Palestinian organizations. Damascus, however, distanced itself from these accusations on the grounds that they were merely repetitions of the Israeli ones. America was reminded that Syria had been antagonistic to the former Iraqi regime and in the Security Council had introduced a plan to rid the Middle East region as a whole of weapons of mass destruction, a fact that the United States had no doubt completely overlooked.[61]

This evoked Syrian fears that Washington wanted to repeat the experiment it had inflicted on Iraq and that Syria was going to be the next country in line. With the dominance of the neo-conservatives in the American administration there was much talk in the government and in the various research centres that America should go to war against Syria because 'the Syrian regime does not respond to any other language'.[62]

In the face of these threats, the Syrian regime felt obliged to defend its position without jeopardizing its interests. This required turning a blind eye to the US attack on Baghdad without closing the door to a dialogue with Washington. Washington, however, was not interested in a dialogue. Instead, it presented Syria with a list of demands to which it had either to comply or to face punishment. Colin Powell famously visited Damascus on 3 May 2003 heavily armed with a never-ending list of demands that did nothing to address Syria's concerns, whether related to retrieving the Golan area or to securing its interests in Lebanon.[63] As the American officials saw it, Damascus did not deserve a reward because it supported terrorism. Consequently, the Israeli prime minister turned down a Syrian offer (made through mediators) to resume negotiations because he did not want to 'create circumstances that would decrease American pressure on Syria'.[64]

Damascus tried to decrease these pressures by asking Palestinian groups in Syria either to leave voluntarily or at least to stop their general activities to prevent America using them as a pretext for exerting pressure on Syria.[65] At the same time, Damascus took a positive step towards the United States by absenting itself from the Security Council session in which resolution 1483 on Iraq was being voted on (though recording its support for the resolution).[66] The majority of party leaders, including the minister of foreign affairs, had been firmly against the resolution that would legalize the American occupation of Iraq. For this reason, the Syrian ambassador to the United Nations abstained from voting. Unwilling to antagonize the United States and recognizing that violating the global consensus would do nothing to improve the country's international image, President Bashar al-Asad asked the foreign minister to notify the party leaders that the president wanted them to ratify Syria's acceptance of the resolution. He made this known without even attending the meeting with the regional leadership. The next day, Syria informed the Security Council that its vote was to be 'yes'.[67] This suggested that Syrian diplomats were confused about Syria's foreign policy and that a split had surfaced among Syria's political decision makers.[68] This confusion was also apparent in Syria's position on the so-called 'road map'. Since the 'road map' did not address Syrian interests, al-Asad had said, 'We will not interfere in what the Palestinians decide',[69] but at the opening of the thirtieth meeting of foreign ministers at the Islamic Conference, al-Shar'a interpreted his remark as meaning that 'Syria neither opposed nor supported the road map.'[70]

At that time Washington considered that Syria was behaving as if 'it had not understood the lesson perfectly' and so started to step up its political and sometimes military provocation against it. US forces stationed on the border between Syria and Iraq attacked an Iraqi convoy on the Syrian side, which resulted in the wounding of five Syrian soldiers who had been under temporary arrest.[71] This was a clear message to Damascus that the United States would control the Syrian–Iraqi border if Damascus failed to monitor it adequately. This was a direct challenge to Syrian sovereignty.

In its foreign policy the United States became more ideological and less pragmatic in its thinking, pursuing its Middle East policy at the expense of Syrian interests. Syrian diplomacy, therefore, declined in importance. Jordan, for example, had a role that exceeded that of Syria even although Damascus had played a very much more central role in the region over the course of the previous three decades. Jordan's political closeness to the United States enabled it to play a role that extended well beyond its borders, while Syria and Lebanon were excluded from the Sharm al-Shaykh summit in June 2003. Only so-called 'moderate' Arab states such as Saudi Arabia, Egypt, Bahrain, Jordan and the newly-appointed Palestinian prime minister Mahmoud Abbas (Abu Mazen) attended.[72] The aim of the summit was to give a real impetus to the 'road map' on the assumption that the Palestinians would perform the part it imposed on them.

The increase of resistance in Iraq, and the absence of a clear vision in American thinking about what the situation would be after the fall of Saddam Hussein's regime, gave Syria a fairly wide security margin in which to operate. It used this in an endeavour to extend its political influence into the Iraqi heartland by holding meetings with a large number of factional and independent Iraqi personalities and officials. It was eager to convince Washington that it had a role in Iraq and that if the United States wanted to secure stability in Iraq it would needed to talk openly about it to Damascus.

The US State Department had asked Congress to suspend the Syrian Accountability Act. This was to ensure that Syria would not stand in the way of US political involvement and that the exchange of information regarding terrorist organizations in the region would not be cut off.[73] According to Colin Powell, however, the State Department changed its position on this law after 'its disappointment' at the Syrian position.

In truth, Syria's lack of support for the war against Iraq is what determined America's policy towards it.[74] The United States had asked for everything without making any promises to do anything in return to protect Syria's interests. The clearest evidence of this is the way the USA ignored Syria's views on the matter of the road map. US and European assurances have failed to convince Syria that it is being included in the second round of the road map, for Damascus now realizes with complete certainty that the US administration has no serious intention of resuming the peace process in the Middle East.[75]

In October 2003 Israel raided a deserted camp housing the general leadership of the Popular Front for Liberating Palestine at Ain al-Saheb near Damascus.[76] This was a clear violation of the agreement between Syria and Israel signed in 1974 for the disengagement of forces. There was no loss of life or even material damage, but the Israeli message was clear: Israel has the right to pursue any Palestinian organization it regards as 'terrorist' wherever it is. According to the Israelis, Damascus had played a part in supporting the suicide bombings carried out inside Israel, so Syria had therefore to be punished for each of these operations. America's support of this raid was a great blow to Damascus, whose diplomacy had failed to obtain an international resolution condemning Israel for violating Syrian air space.[77]

While Syria declared that it would practise as much restraint as possible to deny Sharon an excuse to escalate the conflict, it at the same time threatened to attack Israeli settlements in the Golan area.[78] Damascus then tried to retaliate through Hezbollah in southern Lebanon, for that would be less burdensome for it. A clear message came from the United States, however, when Congress ratified the 'Syrian Accountability Act' and regained 'Lebanon sovereignty' without any objection from the American administration,[79] which had previously opposed this law.

Discussing this law in the US Congress was tantamount to carrying out a campaign against Syria and its view of US policy, particularly towards Iraq. US demands were increased to include retrieving money the former Iraqi regime had deposited in Syrian banks.[80] The Senate ratified the law with an overwhelming majority[81] and President Bush did not hesitate to sign the law that, in its final draft after many amendments, provided for political and economic sanctions against Syria, including banning all American exports to Syria apart from food and medicines, freezing the funds of certain Syrian personalities and organizations, and placing reserves on the American banks' transactions with Syria.

In an attempt to reduce these pressures, President Bashar al-Asad tried, in his interview with the *New York Times*, to issue a peace initiative calling for the resumption of negotiations with Israel at the point at which they had stopped.[82] The Israeli answer, however, came in the form of a plan to increase settlements in the Golan area by 50 per cent and double the number of settlers over a period of three years.[83] Sharon asked Damascus to stop its support for Hezbollah if it seriously wished to resume negotiations with Israel,[84] while Moshe Katsaf, the former Israeli president, invited Bashar al-Asad to visit Israel to confirm his seriousness about peace. Damascus responded that this speech was an evasion of peace and that Katsaf's call could not be considered serious.[85] The American administration seemed completely uninterested in the Syrian initiative, suggesting that Syria should follow the Libyan example in its voluntary relinquishment of weapons of mass destruction.[86]

Again Syria tried to ease the burden of pressures by opening other doors, making a final attempt to promote the Syrian–European partnership agreement for use as a political cover against American hegemony. However, it confronted European inflexibility over the question of weapons of mass destruction, so the initialization of the agreement was postponed until October 2004.

The Syrian policy makers tried to predict the result of the American presidential elections in November 2004, hoping that there would be a change from the Bush administration with its inflexible policy towards Syria. However, Senator John Kerry, the Democrat candidate, was no less strict in dealing with Syria than Bush, since he declared that he would not postpone the sanctions against Syria.[87] After ratifying the Syrian Accountability Act, the US Congress took further steps in this direction by endorsing a law calling on Syria to withdraw its forces from Lebanon immediately and stop its support for Hezbollah.[88] In fact, this law was a response to Security Council Resolution 1559, which was a call to respect Lebanese sovereignty. This was tantamount to a blow directed against Damascus after its support for the extension of President Émile Lahoud's term of office in the wake of a constitutional amendment,[89] which evoked a lot of arguments and protests within and outside Lebanon.

Syrian–Lebanese Relationships: Discomfort in the Brotherhood

To understand the complications of Syrian–Lebanese relations it is necessary to go back a little into history to look at the various social, economic and political interpenetrations of former relations between the two countries.

Syria emerged from the October 1973 war declaring that the period of internal and regional strife that had lasted from Husni al-Zaʾim's first coup in 1949 to Hafez al-Asad's assumption of power in 1970 was over. President Asad's popularity, which exceeded that of any previous Syrian president, had helped transform Syria from a piece of land over which everyone competed to a player whose goodwill everyone sought. In the wake of the October war, Syria moved from being an inward-looking area to a force to be reckoned with among the surrounding regions competing for its resources.[90] This is the main thesis of Israeli researcher Moshe Maʿoz who summarizes Syria's transformation as follows:

> Under the leadership of Hafez al-Asad, Syria changed from a weak and fragile country to a state which seemed strong and stable, and to be a regional force in the Middle East. Syria, which had been for decades a victim of the expansionist policies of its Arab neighbours and the Israelis became under al-Asad's leadership one of the region's most influential and effective forces.

He dubbed al-Asad 'the Sphinx of Damascus'.[91]

The October 1973 war brought al-Asad to the centre of Arab and international attention, particularly during Kissinger's rounds of shuttle diplomacy. This so increased his presence and symbolic importance that he was successfully able to invest it in consolidating his regime and ensuring its stability. After regaining al-Qunayṭirah, 'liberated' through the forces' disengagement agreement, he personally went there to raise the flag and establish Syrian sovereignty over it – a symbolic act the Syrians continually imitated. The official regime had come to regard al-Asad as 'the hero of the two *Tishreens* (October and November)', thus vindicating his role in the corrective movement, namely the coup that brought him to power in November 1970. He went to war in 1973 hoping to liberate the Golan Heights but he could only 'regain' al-Qunayṭirah.

The new regional role that Syria would play in the future started with a rare visit to Lebanon on 7 January 1975 for a meeting with President Sulaymān Faranjīyah. They met in Chtaura on the Syrian–Lebanese border to confirm Syria's full support for maintaining Lebanon's sovereignty and safeguarding its lands. Just three months later, on 13 April 1975, the Lebanese civil war erupted.[92] Thus, Lebanon came into a new period of changing conflicts and shifting alliances that put a complete end to state control, transforming the country into a number of disparate districts ruled by armed gangs that ran their fiefdoms according to their own political and sectarian rules. Syria intervened early on with a view to stopping the fighting between the conflicting parties.

Maintaining Lebanese unity had been part of the strategy that Asad supported to keep the balance in the Arab–Israeli struggle, especially given the sensitivity of Lebanon's geographical location in relation to both Syria and Israel. Although al-Asad decided to intervene in Lebanon for strategic reasons related to consolidating the eastern front, there had been no Syrian military intervention before the beginning of the civil war because al-Asad had first wanted to settle the conflict between the parties in a political way. At that time, the foreign minister, ʿAbd al-Ḥalīm Khaddām, made so many visits that the Lebanese dubbed him 'the governor'. Al-Asad had wanted 'a political settlement' of the war between the Maronite Christian party and the Lebanese national movement and this was realized when Damascus supported the launching of the Lebanese 'constitutional document' on 14 February 1976.[93]

At the same time, the Israelis continued to escalate their operations against Lebanon with a view to kindling the sectarian divisions. Each Israeli operation against the Palestinians in Lebanon produced two conflicting positions – the Christian one, which held that the state ought to punish the Palestinians to prevent them repeating their operations from Lebanese territory, and the leftist Muslim one, led by the late Kamal Jumblatt,[94] which called on the Lebanese army to intervene to defend and protect the Palestinians. Israeli attacks intensified in retaliation for the *fidāʾīyīn* (commando) operations the Palestinians carried out inside Israel.

These repeated Palestinian attacks were leading the region to the brink of a new war. Kissinger, the American secretary of state, warned against this eventuality and considered it might be necessary to resume military operations to put an end to the attacks, thus cutting off the supply routes, which Washington believed originated in Damascus. Through Richard Murphy, the American ambassador in Damascus, the United States notified al-Asad that Israel might find it necessary to encroach into Lebanese territory to put an end to the Palestinian operations. Al-Asad feared that Israel might indeed interfere militarily in Lebanon, in particular because the newly elected Israeli prime minister was Yitzhak Rabin, the 'hero' of the June 1967 war.

Despite that, al-Asad hesitated to step into Lebanon, especially in light of the American warnings the US ambassador transmitted, the most urgent of which was on 16 October 1975 when he openly cautioned: 'Israel considers any armed foreign (Syrian) interference in Lebanon an extremely dangerous threat.'

The international aspects tended to involve only the United States because the Soviet Union's position was limited to giving moral support to Jumblatt in the face of the Syrian intervention against him in Lebanon. Al-Asad, however, saw this as a fleeting cloud he could easily remove from the Damascus–Moscow sky, which is what he tried to do at his first meeting with Brezhnev in Moscow. Thus, oddly enough, American and Syrian interests accorded over the need for Syrian intervention in Lebanon to protect the Christians. To maintain Syrian interests in Lebanon, the United States ensured that Israel would not intervene and Syria, in turn, ensured the survival of the Maronite Christians who were loyal to Israel.

The two parties agreed to Israel's so-called 'red line' policy, a tacit agreement to limit Syria's military profile in Lebanon. However, Syria did not formally acknowledge it and did not ratify its contents. According to a letter that Yigal Alon sent to Kissinger who, in turn, transmitted it to Damascus, the agreement stipulated that Syrian deployment in the air and sea had to be so limited that it did not go beyond the line of Sidon–Jazzīn (the red line), and that the Syrian forces were not to introduce surface to air missiles to the south of the Damascus–Beirut road. In return, Israel would acknowledge Syrian interests in parts of Lebanon.[95]

Al-Asad's road to intervention in Lebanon was anything but smooth because, after the failure of 'the constitutional document', he gambled on Ilyās Sarkīs being elected president of the republic in May 1976, even before the end of Faranjīyah's regime. Eventually, al-Asad decided to release his military forces into Lebanon to protect the Christian strongholds. On the eve of this decision the regional leadership in Syria witnessed a fiery meeting and hand-to-hand fighting between the opponents and advocates of intervention in Lebanon. A military squad commander preferred to relinquish the squad leadership rather than lead it into Lebanon.[96] Finally, the leadership decided to intervene in Lebanon on the grounds that it was their 'national duty' to preserve Lebanese unity and safeguard its territories from foreign interference.

On 1 May 1976, having withdrawn most of the armed forces from the cease-fire line in the Golan Heights and distributed them between Lebanon and the fragile Syrian–Iraqi border, al-Asad sent an armed force of 4000 soldiers and 250 armoured vehicles into Lebanon. These forces were soon able to break the blockade surrounding the Christians in the city of Zaḥlah in the Beqa'a valley.[97] However, this intervention (which was expected to be limited at the beginning) expanded little by little in the Lebanese territories and, at the end of June 1976, it took a tragic turn. Syrian forces were laying siege to Palestinian and leftist strongholds in and around Sidon's sea port in the south and the Syrian tanks got stuck in an ambush prepared by the Palestinian forces. Brutal killings were carried out, which not only caused pain to al-Asad but also led to an everlasting personal enmity between him and Yaser Arafat, the head of the Palestine Liberation Organization. The battle of Sidon, however, was not the end as much as the beginning of the real Syrian involvement in the Lebanese civil war. Syria was no longer the regional guardian of Lebanon, but an interested party in the war. The brutality of the war increased with the battle of Tell al-Zaʾater in which Kamīl Shamʿūn's troops (*al-numūr* or the Tigers led by his son Danie) laid siege to 30,000 Shiʾites and Palestinian refugees until the camp finally fell on 12 August 1976, bringing down the curtain on a brutal massacre of about 3000 civilians mostly slaughtered at the hands of the Lebanese Tigers.[98]

The Syrian intervention in Lebanon to support the Christian party at the expense of the Palestinian party brought forth a storm of protest. The popularity that al-Asad had enjoyed since the October 1973 war as the leader who took care of Arab interests and worked hard to maintain Arab solidarity in the face of the 'Zionist enemy' had come to an end. The 1973 war had brought him the popularity in the Arab world to which he had always aspired, for he was eager to take his place in the Arab popular memory as the glorious successor of Gamal Abdul Nasser. No domestic, international or Arab protests deterred al-Asad from his decision to intervene, which he took to be his 'national duty'. Later he would use this term to justify his intervention during the reconciliation conference in Riad on 16 October 1976, when Syrian forces were acknowledged as 'the Arab deterrent force'. This was seen as a diplomatic victory for al-Asad who also got financial support from Saudi Arabia and Kuwait after having been cut off when the Syrian troops entered Lebanon.

Asad's position with regard to the Arabs was reinforced after the Cairo conference on 25 October 1976 when once and for all the League of Arab States ratified the body of the Arab deterrent forces consisting of 30,000 soldiers from a number of Arab countries such as Saudi Arabia, Kuwait, Libya, Tunisia and Sudan, but with the highest number coming from Syria.[99]

Syria's move towards becoming a dominant force in the regional game had, therefore, started with Lebanon, but was reinforced when al-Asad recognized the significance of the international changes following the first Gulf war in 1990. He understood that the changes in the Soviet Union, his main ally, had made any strategic balance with Israel impossible, so he cautiously adapted to the new American strategy in the area. He did not, however, neglect the development of his military forces, which needed to be strong enough to deter Israel from taking risks and undertaking adventures likely to have dire consequences. What reinforced the Syrian power of deterrence was keeping Syrian forces on Lebanese soil and deploying them in strategic positions to defend Lebanon's western and southwestern borders in case of any sudden Israeli attack. Thus, al-Asad had changed his strategy towards Israel from one of trying to maintain a 'strategic balance' to validating the 'power of military deterrence'. For this he depended on North Korea with which Syria had military and political relations. This, however, did not prevent al-Asad from making use of the Gulf war to secure financial and political gains once he had established with certainty that the United States was the only power able to put pressure on Israel to work towards a comprehensive and just solution to the Arab–Israeli conflict. He responded to the American wish to build an international alliance against Iraq because he expected America's gratitude to translate into fulfilling US promises to Syria, and to other conflicting parties in the Middle East, thus allowing him to maintain his interests in Lebanon.

Thereafter, al-Asad used Lebanon to redraw the regional map. After the Sharm al-Shaykh summit in 1996, for example, he turned to Lebanon, which was where for 20 years he had overcome numerous regional and international challenges, to ruin American attempts to rearrange the area without Syria. These attempts on the part of the United States started with the Geneva conference in 1973, then went on to Reagan's initiative in 1982, Schultz's plan in 1987 and finally ended up with the settlements of 1993.[100]

By that time (1993) Yitzhak Rabin's government had started an unprecedented military escalation in south Lebanon. The Israeli forces launched an attack they called Operation Settling of Accounts (also known as Operation Accountability). It lasted seven days and the Israelis saw it as retribution for Hezbollah's successive attacks on the occupied Lebanese strip. Israel regarded the area as its own 'security strip', while the Lebanese and Syrians considered it 'the insecure region'. The attacks were spread over many areas in the south, the Beqa'a, the north and the outskirts of Beirut. The operation resulted in 130 casualties and 500 wounded. It covered 120 villages in which 10,000 houses were destroyed and 300,000 people displaced. A similar number of civil and public establishments such as schools, bridges, roads and water supplies were destroyed. On the Israeli side, according to an Israeli army spokesman, only 26 soldiers were killed and 67 wounded.[101] A verbal agreement, which came to be known as the July agreement, brought the operation to an end. It stipulated that Hezbollah had to stop launching Katyusha rockets in return for an undertaking that Israel would not bombard Lebanese civilians and populated villages. The agreement was concluded after an American mediation between Syria and Lebanon on one side and Israel on the other.[102] At that time the Syrians, particularly President Hafez al-Asad, were resolute about Hezbollah's right to resist Israeli occupation of its country and insisted that the sanctions had to apply only to attacks against civilians on both sides.

Rabin realized that if he really wanted Syria to agree to this accord he would have to accept these stipulations. He therefore informed Dennis Ross, US envoy for the peace process in the Middle East, of his consent to the conditions as long as Syria agreed. Once al-Asad had declared his agreement the July 1993 accord came into effect.

The Israelis looked on the accord as a victory because it made the Syrians responsible for accepting a ceasefire and maintaining the conditions that would make its realization possible. According to Auri Saghi, then head of the Military Intelligence Department, the Israelis also believed that it would introduce new rules to the dialogue with Syria and Lebanon that would drive the peace process forward.[103] It was also an opportunity for Rabin to praise the Syrians for adhering to their commitments, whether written or verbal. Al-Asad, however, was of a completely different opinion and considered the agreement very one sided.

His view was that the Katyusha rockets had been used only in response to Israeli aggression and that when that stopped so too would the Katyusha rockets. The rockets were not the cause, as the Israelis would have the world believe, but rather the pretext.[104] Farouk al-Shar'a, the Syrian foreign minister at the time, was frank: 'According to us', he said, 'the last Israeli aggression against Lebanon may destroy the peace process as a whole, and we are not ready to continue negotiations under the threat of Israeli guns.'[105] At first Lebanese officials were confused and declared that the Lebanese army was deployed in the south, but they came back after a meeting with al-Asad on 16 August 1993 to say that there were no Lebanese forces in the south and that their previous declaration had been the result of 'confusion, extemporization and hastiness'. They hoped that al-Asad could save them from their confusion and point them in the right direction.[106] Al-Asad would not allow the Israeli military force to interfere with his strategic interests in southern Lebanon. He insisted on the right of the southerners to resist, which, in the wake of this unwritten accord, acquired the legality of defending the Lebanese occupied territories. He used this rationale continuously to exhaust the Israeli army in the borderline area, which lost 99 soldiers between the start of the Israeli occupation in 1985 and July 1993.[107] Although the Israeli losses were small in comparison with the Lebanese ones, they were sufficient to make the Israelis feel insecure, particularly given how unpopular the continued occupation of southern Lebanon was in Israel.

The Israelis had always held Syria responsible for the escalation of Hezbollah's operations in the south. They sometimes thought that al-Asad had personally agreed to these operations, so the tension in southern Lebanon was often brought up at Syrian–Israeli talks. The Syrians, however, refused to talk about it because they regarded it as the business of the Lebanese delegation.[108] Despite ongoing negotiations, the front in southern Lebanon never calmed down; in fact, it sometimes escalated so dangerously that it threatened a permanent Syrian–Israeli rift. As a pragmatic politician, al-Asad did not believe in negotiations alone as a substitute for military force; rather, he believed that a combination of diplomacy and military force, especially when he could show that there was Arab and international support for Syria, would be an indispensable resource in the confrontation with Israel, especially since diplomacy had previously allowed Israel to slip away from the consequences of its repeated aggressions against the Arabs.[109] The Israelis therefore received painful blows in southern Lebanon at the same time as the Syrians were talking to them about peace. Moreover, al-Asad was skilful in integrating diplomacy and pressure. He thought that withdrawal from the occupied territories ought not to be subject to negotiations since it had been demanded in a series of UN resolutions. He did not resort to negotiations until he realized that regaining these territories through war had become impossible. (He considered that the Hezbollah attacks constituted a legal resistance to occupation.)

In March 1996 Hezbollah launched an attack against the 'secure area' in the south, whereupon, in April 1996, Israel launched its Operation Grapes of Wrath in southern Lebanon aimed, once and for all, to put an end to these attacks. The United States tried to persuade both Syria and Israel to calm things down on the grounds that escalation of the conflict would be against the interests of all parties. Martin Indyk, the US ambassador in Israel, delivered Israeli Prime Minister Peres a letter in which he asked Israel to abstain from any military action in southern Lebanon.[110] Al-Asad, on his part, was not interested in escalation despite the international isolation in which he found himself after the Sharm al-Shaykh summit, the main objective of which had been to 'condemn terrorism' in the wake of the Hamas attacks inside Israel. Syria had abstained from participating in this move. Then the Americans felt that it was their duty to bring al-Asad out of his isolation because his stance might turn things upside down, but Israel started its Grapes of Wrath operation in southern Lebanon, which lasted from 11 to 26 April 1996. This operation had a number of objectives.

First, it was intended to improve Peres's electoral chances, especially now that the public opinion polls had started to give him a lower rating than Netanyahu, his opponent in the Likud Party. Second, it aimed to modify the July 1993 accord to bring it more in line with Israeli interests by insisting on an end to the operations carried out by Hezbollah against 'the secure area' in southern Lebanon. Third, it was an attempt by Israel to make a bilateral Israeli–

Lebanese peace plan (bypassing Syria) that would ensure that the Lebanese army would be redeployed in the areas that Hezbollah occupied at that time.[111]

Israeli military aircraft then carried out continuous air raids against the region of Sur (Tyre), and in the following days these raids were extended to include the southern suburb of Beirut. By the end of this operation the air raids had targeted 159 villages, 7201 residential units and a number of hospitals, schools and power plants, as a result of which 153 civilians, 5 Syrian soldiers and 13 fighters from Hezbollah were killed and 359 civilians and 9 soldiers were injured, including the victims of the Qānā massacre.[112] This raid, which took place on 18 April, played a decisive role in putting an early end to the operation. Israeli aircraft bombed a UN building in which 150 Lebanese civilians, mostly women and children, had taken refuge – 11 people died and 129 were injured in the fire that subsequently destroyed the building. Despite this massacre, Israeli aircraft carried on with their attacks, which were being shown on Israeli television. Peres appeared on the air to announce that the UN building had been bombed by mistake and that the Israeli Defence Force had not known that it contained civilians.[113] In discussing the situation later, the leaders of the Israeli Defence Force defended the bombing on the grounds that all the military attacks had been exceedingly precise and had hit their targets. It was unfortunate that there had been civilian casualties, but they argued that even if they had photographed the camp a few hours before the attack they would have been unable to see the refugees because they had been in two covered enclosures.[114]

The Israeli military operation in southern Lebanon had thus changed from a clear and successful victory to a muddy impasse from which Peres did not know how to extricate himself, particularly after the massacre at Qānā.[115] He had lost all the Arab and international support he had gained at the Sharm al-Shaykh summit. Having imposed conditions for the resumption of negotiations with al-Asad, the boot was now on the other foot and Peres struggled to lighten the burden of the conditions that al-Asad, who had returned centre stage after the attempt to isolate him at Sharm al-Shaykh, now imposed. Foreign ministers from the United States, France, Russia,

Italy, Spain and Ireland started to knock at his door to persuade him to agree to an immediate ceasefire. Peres, now resentful, angry and feeling that al-Asad had gone too far in humiliating him, told one of his visitors that there was 'no need for haste'.[116]

After a series of meetings between al-Asad and Peres, with US Secretary of State Warren Christopher mediating, on 26 April the two sides agreed to a text for a ceasefire. This new accord stipulated that the armed groups in Lebanon would not carry out attacks with Katyusha rockets or any other weapon on Israeli soil, while Israel and its allies agreed not to target (with any weapon) civilian or civil institutions in Lebanon. Furthermore, both parties made a firm pledge not under any circumstances to target civilians and agreed that it was impermissible to launch attacks from populated civilian areas or any industrial or electrical facilities. Finally, the accord confirmed that in case of non-compliance with the agreement, there would be no option but to deny either party the right to self-defence.[117]

A supervisory group was formed with representatives from the United States, France, Syria and Israel charged with supervising the application of the accord as well as receiving complaints. With the agreement of the parties mentioned in the accord, the text was drawn up in English. It is clear that this accord gave the Lebanese rights that they had not had in the accord of July 1993, since it did not mention any restrictions imposed on the activity of resistance to the Israeli military presence in Lebanon apart from the humanitarian restrictions imposed on Israel itself. The document clearly recognized the legality of resistance to occupation. It also provided for a mechanism for supervising and observing its implementation. Negotiations on the framing of this mechanism had started in Washington on 10 May but the agreement reached its final form on 3 July 1996 after the formation of Netanyahu's government.

Syrian–Lebanese Relations after 2000

With the Israeli withdrawal from southern Lebanon in May 2000, a few days before al-Asad's death, Syrian–Lebanese relations reached a new point. On 24 May Israel withdrew from all of southern Lebanon apart from Sheb'a Farms, which the Security Council considered to be

Syrian,[118] whereas the Syrians insisted belonged to Lebanon.[119] The arrival of information to Barak about the critical state of al-Asad's health,[120] confirming that he would need to take stimulants during the Geneva summit with President Clinton to be held in March 2000, accelerated the Israeli withdrawal from Lebanon. Barak decided to withdraw earlier from Lebanon, even before the appointed date of July 2000, for he feared that if al-Asad died things might spiral out of control, especially since no one really knew who al-Asad's successor would be. Everyone expected that his son Bashar would take over, but no one knew for sure. Barak therefore decided to withdraw while al-Asad was still alive because he was the most reliable guarantor that no aggression would take place on the Lebanese front to bring the region to the brink of a war for which nobody was prepared.

Following al-Asad's death and the assumption of power by President Bashar al-Asad, Syrian–Lebanese relations became a topic of serious discussion in Lebanon, particularly in the light of internal pressure calling for the withdrawal of Syrian troops from Lebanon in compliance with the Ta'if Agreement. The international changes, however, which included the bombing of the twin towers in New York on 11 September, the advent of a new US administration with a wholly new international and regional agenda, and the war on Iraq, were of course even more significant. In addition, UN resolution 1559 calling for respect for Lebanese sovereignty came as a blow to Damascus, especially given that it had supported a constitutional amendment to ensure the extension of President Lahoud's term of office[121] that had evoked a lot of arguments and protests inside Lebanon.

Before the UN resolution, Syria had redeployed its forces in Lebanon four times, but what was new this time was the French position towards it. Syria found itself in a difficult situation in Lebanon. Syria's severest loss from this resolution was that it introduced tensions into its strategic relations with France, which had reached a high level of agreement with considerable coordination and integration of policies. The French position in the Security Council (in fact France had actually instigated resolution 1559) brought Syrian–French relations back to an earlier stage characterized by apprehension, suspense and caution. Syria was now completely isolated, despite having initialled the partnership accord with the European Union at the beginning of October 2004.

With the assassination of former Lebanese Prime Minister Rafiq al-Hariri, Syria entered a new and different period, not only regarding Syrian relations with Lebanon but also with respect to its regional and international relations. The Lebanese opposition, which had encouraged the 'independence uprising', now considered it was time to reformulate these relations, but this time with a formula other than 'the one path' or 'one people in two states' logic.

The international community placed resolution 1559 high on its list of priorities immediately after al-Hariri's assassination, though it had been voted on before the assassination and had been acceptable to both the Americans and Europeans. The latter saw nothing in Syrian–Lebanese relations apart from a Syrian 'occupation' based on domination and the control of intelligence and security. Because of its firm control of the security situation in Lebanon, Syria was accused of assassinating al-Hariri, or at least being indirectly responsible for it.[122]

In the parliamentary elections, the opposition took most seats in the Lebanese parliament and assumed the reins of power. Damascus, however, had to take full responsibility for the deterioration of its relations with Lebanon because it had failed to pay attention to the need to establish the relationship on a new footing that superseded the depiction of Lebanon as 'the soft flank'. The accumulation of mistakes on the part of Damascus had ensured that everything would blow up in its face.

Damascus had repeatedly insisted that agreements and contracts should regulate relations between the two sides and that these should be determined by the institutions of the two states. However, the short-sightedness of Syrian policy making, which was based more on personalities than on a solid foundation of real strategic policies, was made evident in its attempt to try to prolong the regime of President Émile Lahoud and to put pressure on him through the Lebanese parliament. Actually, the Syrians had no real reason either to legalize this step or to make it acceptable to international opinion.[123]

The Syrian announcement of a complete withdrawal of intelligence facilities and troops before the end of April 2005 put an end to the Syrian regional role that had originated in Lebanon in 1976.

During his press conference with UN Envoy Terje Rød-Larsen, Syrian Foreign Minister al-Sharʾa stated that, through its complete withdrawal from Lebanon, Damascus had carried out its part of resolution 1559; the other parts of the resolution were entirely the responsibility of the Lebanese. Al-Asad had announced this in his speech to the People's Assembly on 5 March of the previous year when he declared: 'By the end of this withdrawal, Syria will have fulfilled its obligations according to the al-Taʾif accord and the requirements of resolution 1559.' Al-Asad asked Rød-Larsen to set up an international commission of inquiry to verify Syria's complete implementation of its obligation under resolution 1559, lest some international bodies use it as a pretext for trying to prolong the crisis by showing that Syria was procrastinating in the execution of its obligations. Damascus faced intense international pressure to implement its part of resolution 1559, contained along with other options in clause seven. All possible sticks were used but without any evidence of a carrot, so President Hafez al-Asad's hope of striking a bargain was no longer realistic or realizable. US President George Bush's administration insisted that Damascus carry out its obligations to Iraq, Lebanon and Palestine without offering anything in return. At the same time, Damascus remained unconvinced that withdrawal would end American pressures on it. And this proved to be the case. The United States waited until the obligation of withdrawal had been conclusively satisfied and then exerted pressure for the fulfilment of another obligation, namely that Syria use the presence of its intelligence services to help disarm Hezbollah.

Then the Security Council issued a new resolution, 1636, under the pretext that Syria had insufficiently cooperated with the Security Council in the international commission of inquiry into the assassination of Rafiq al-Hariri. The resolution was drawn up on the basis of clause seven of the charter of the United Nations, which made international sanctions applicable if there were any defiance of internationally constituted bodies. In his second report, Detlev Mehlis, the previous head of the international commission charged with inquiring into the assassination of Rafiq al-Hariri, stated that Syria had failed to cooperate with the international commission of inquiry. This opened the door to several options, the worst being international sanctions after a former UN resolution and another one (1644) had been confirmed. The Security Council issued a new resolution, 1680, backed by 13 states while Russia and China abstained from voting. This resolution called for delineating the common borders between Syria and Lebanon 'particularly in the areas where the borders are indefinite or debatable [a reference to Sheb'a Farms], and the establishment of relations and complete diplomatic representation'. The council also requested the Syrian government to take procedures similar to those taken by the Lebanese government 'against transporting weapons to Lebanese territories'. Damascus responded vehemently. The Syrian Ministry of Foreign Affairs described the resolution as 'an unprecedented procedure' and 'interference in the internal and bilateral affairs of sovereign states, who are members of the United Nations. It is a provocative move which will only make the situation more complicated'.[124]

Syrian Foreign Minister Walīd al-Mu'allem warned: 'Increasing the tension in the area will not serve Lebanese interests.' Delineating the borders, starting from the north, and establishing diplomatic relations between the two countries require 'a suitable positive atmosphere' between them. He said that some American–French efforts were being made with some forces and personalities in Lebanon, but he expected nothing to come of them because the ability of both Washington and Paris 'is too limited to affect the Syrian–Lebanese relationship'.[125] At the same time, the Beirut–Damascus declaration, to which a number of Syrian and Lebanese intellectuals subscribed, called upon the two states to revise Syrian–Lebanese relations radically, starting with Syria's final recognition of Lebanon's independence and ending with the delineation of the borders and diplomatic reciprocity between the two countries. The response of the Syrian authorities was to arrest a number of intellectuals and activists who had taken part in issuing the declaration, and to accuse them of 'arousing racial and sectarian instincts, and circulating false news which causes damage to the state's prestige'. They were sentenced to three years' imprisonment.[126]

According to Walīd al-Muʿallem, Syria's view was that the time was not ripe to establish diplomatic relations with Lebanon. He also said:

> We think that if there had been embassies in the two countries in such a negative atmosphere, the ambassadors would have been withdrawn or the embassies would have been closed. In principle, we have no problem with regard to opening the two embassies, but we must wait for a suitable moment.[127]

According to al-Muʿallem, there was resentment in Damascus because some Lebanese, including members of the government, had 'anticipated the investigations and charged Syria with the crime of killing al-Hariri'. He said, 'Some Lebanese have launched an unfair propaganda campaign against Syria, while what is needed is simply an improvement in the current atmosphere between the two countries.'[128] Thus, Damascus saw Beirut as the instigator of the changes it was experiencing. Syrians no longer feared Iraq, which in any case was in the throes of a civil war, but rather Beirut, which until recently had been its closest ally.

In a rare written speech presented to the People's Assembly (parliament) in which he dealt with Syrian foreign policy, al-Muʿallem said: 'Syria is subject to the Americans because of its national position, its objection to the war on Iraq and its resistance to foreign interference and predominance.' However, he went on, 'the American project is critical and unsuccessful because of the courageous resistance of the Iraqi people and because of the exposure of the false justifications that were invented for the purpose of invading this country. The project of the larger Middle East got caught in the Iraqi mud.'

The Syrian minister added:

> In the light of this American failure, and for the purpose of increasing pressures on Syria and the attempt to intensify the blockade against it, the American–French coordination of action with regard to Lebanon came into being ... [despite] the differences in American and French interests and objectives in some aspects and their concurrence in others.

He also mentioned:

> The points of concurrence that resulted in the Security Council resolution 1559 ... [were] and ... [are] still used as a tool for international pressures against Syria on the one hand and for bare-faced interference in Lebanon on the other. To these the crime of assassinating Rafiq al-Hariri, the Lebanese ex-prime minister, was added and the accusation was immediately directed towards Syria without any evidence in spite of the fact that Syria was the main victim of this assassination. This confirms that the crime was part of a conspiracy against Syria and Lebanon and, therefore, against the region as a whole.[129]

This speech reflects the thinking of the Syrian Ministry of Foreign Affairs about the change in the regional balance of power, especially since America's heavy involvement in Iraq. Then, the war of July 2006 between Israel and Hezbollah brought many changes to the international and regional balance of power.

Syria after the Lebanon War: Reviving its Regional Role

The war came as a surprise to Syria, which had not expected the Israelis to react as strongly as they did to the kidnapping of two Israeli soldiers, but, according to a Syrian official, the changes in the rules of the game would eventually benefit Syria.

At first, Farouk al-Sharʾa, who represented the official Syrian position, charged Israel with the responsibility for escalating the war, saying: 'the resistance will continue as long as the occupation continues.' The official newspapers spoke highly of the Hezbollah operation that led to the two Israeli soldiers' capture.[130]

The indecisiveness of the Israeli position towards Syria at the beginning of the war led to a state of lying in wait for American and Israeli declarations regarding possible Israeli aggression against sites in Syria. While the Israeli government had previously targeted Syria, Olmert's government focused on Hezbollah in his declaration of war, and Damascus was not mentioned. Even when Olmert was asked about Syria, he said, 'Syria is a country with a government of a terrorist nature. Suitable preparations have to be carried out for responding to the behaviour of the Syrian government.'

Israel's failure to resolve its position on Syria at the beginning of the war meant having to lie in wait for announcements, either from America or Israel, on possible Israeli aggression against sites in Syria.

This was quite different from the American position: Frederick Jones, the US National Security Council spokesperson, said, 'We charge Syria and Iran who [*sic*] support Hezbollah with the responsibility for the attack and the violence which followed it,' just as Secretary of State Condoleezza Rice said, 'Syria has special responsibility for making use of its role in a positive way,' and George Bush said, 'Syria has to be brought to account for its misdeeds.'[131]

From the declarations of its leaders and coverage on the Israeli media, it appeared as if Israel was trying to 'calm down the fears' of Syria. It even went so far as to issue a reassuring statement that calling for thousands of reserve forces was not for the purpose of attacking Syria.

The military and later the political leadership reiterated the message that Israel had no intention of attacking Syria and that calling for reserves was associated solely with the war in Lebanon and was for no other objective.[132] Within the space of 24 hours the Minister of Defence Amir Peretz twice repeated that Israel had no intention of attacking Syria, but then somewhat countered the reassurance by saying that 'the Israeli army has to be prepared for any scenario'. He added that Israel was doing its best to keep the Syrian front as it was 'and we convey this message hoping that it will be understood and that Hezbollah will not draw Syria into the war'. In spite of this, Israel accused Hezbollah of using Russian weapons that had been intended for Syria.

The newspaper *Ma'arif* reported that security officials had claimed that Tel Aviv had shown Moscow some documents containing evidence that Hezbollah had used Russian weapons originally intended for the Syrian army. The newspaper alleged that 'photos of rockets along with rocket containers and covers were shown to the Russians, including flying certificates issued in Russia confirming that these rockets were made in Russia especially for the Syrian army'. The

Israeli army said that Hezbollah fighters were using a new prototype of anti-tank rockets – 'Mitis-M' and 'Corneit' – which had been delivered to Syria in the 1990s.[133]

Syria later confirmed that any Israeli attack against it would meet an immediate Syrian response. Muḥsin Bilāl, the Syrian minister of information, said in the first official response from Damascus since the Israeli wide-ranging attack against Lebanon, 'Any Israeli attack against Syria will be directly and strictly encountered by a Syrian response limited neither in time nor in methods.' He also said: 'If we are exposed to any aggression we will undertake such reprisals as the Israeli aggression deserves. Syria supports the Lebanese national resistance in its struggle against Israeli aggression' and, he added, 'the resistance will be victorious.'[134] On a popular level, Syria witnessed a massive immigration of Lebanese refugees, which gradually increased with the escalation of the Israeli military actions in Lebanon, particularly after attacks on the Rafiq al-Hariri international airport. During the war Syria hosted about 400,000 Lebanese refugees; the Syrians received them into their homes and many non-governmental organizations and charitable bodies took responsibility for finding them accommodation and work.[135]

The Syrian–Arab Disagreement during the War

On the eve of the Arab foreign ministers' meeting in Beirut in August 2006, convened for the purpose of establishing a unified Arab position on the Israeli war against Lebanon, Syrian Foreign Minister Walīd al-Muʿallem came to Beirut. This was the first visit of a Syrian official since the Syrian withdrawal from Lebanon in April 2005. His visit and the statements he delivered provoked a storm of protest. These started with an organized demonstration in front of the government building in Byblos, which prevented Fawwāz Ṣallūkh, the Lebanese foreign minister, from receiving him there, so the reception took place at the Libyan embassy. The most vituperative response to his visit came from Walīd Jumblatt, who accused him of 'bidding for the last drop of blood of the Lebanese people'. He said, 'Had not good manners and polite social behaviour prevailed, he would have been stoned and driven out of the country.' This was because on his way to the ministerial meeting al-Mu'allem had said that Syria would immediately 'respond to any Israeli aggression' against it. Answering a question about the possibility of an outbreak of a regional war he said: 'Welcome to the regional war; we are ready for it and we do not hide our preparations.' Then he added: 'I am ready to be a soldier under the leadership of Ḥasan Nasr Allah.'[136]

Then he declared that Syria supported the seven points the Lebanese government had laid down to stop the war, so long as the Lebanese agreed with them and provided that the Lebanese accord encompassed 'all active groups in Lebanon of which Hezbollah is a fundamental part having led the battle beside the Lebanese people and the brave Lebanese army'.

He described the first draft of the American–French Security Council resolution[137] to stop the war as a 'recipe for the continuity of war and as a recipe for a possible breakout of civil war in Lebanon'. At the same time, he declared that his country was 'ready to delineate the borders between Syria and Lebanon from the north to the south', and agreed that 'the Sheb'a Farms are Lebanese and Israel has to withdraw from them and from any stretch of Lebanese territory.' This was the position Bashar al-Asad had expressed when he described the American–French resolution as a 'recipe' for conflict, warning that there would be increased instability if the Security Council sanctioned the American–French resolution on Lebanon without the agreement of all the political forces in the country. What aroused the fears of Damascus was the idea of deploying international forces in the south and disarming Hezbollah. If this happened, they would 'lose Hezbollah's powers of deterrence in the border areas and cause Damascus to lose a fundamental political alliance'.[138] Condoleezza Rice's talk of a 'new' Middle East, aroused Syrian suspicions that new regional arrangements were being made without Syria's knowledge and without any regard for its interests. Syria, therefore, was clear in its rejection of the resolution in its first draft. Preoccupied by a desire to preserve the capability of Hezbollah intact, or at least what was left of it, Syria was prompted later on to accept resolution 1701.

Putting an End to the War

After the Israeli war against Lebanon had been waging for a whole month amid weeks of wearisome negotiations, the Security Council unanimously adopted resolution 1701. It called for an end to hostilities between Israel and Hezbollah as a preliminary step towards a permanent ceasefire, as well as an Israeli withdrawal from Lebanese territory accompanied by the simultaneous deployment in the south of the Lebanese army supported by the United Nations Interim Force in Lebanon (UNIFIL). It was decided that the size of this force should be increased to 15,000 and that it should be given more equipment and greater capability. The resolution also put the issue of the Sheb'a Farms onto the agenda of the secretary general of the United Nations Kofi Annan for a whole month.[139]

In the face of Lebanese objections, the resolution allowed Israel to carry out defensive military operations while postponing the decision about the Sheb'a Farms to a subsequent date. The resolution did not comply with the Israeli call to establish a multinational force distinct from UNIFIL, which had been based in Lebanon since 1978. Furthermore, it did not contain a call for the release of the Lebanese captives arrested by Israel, or for immediate withdrawal of the Israeli forces, but it did stress the need for the unconditional release of the two Israeli soldiers whom Hezbollah had captured on 12 July 2006. This issue was not included in the list of steps required for a permanent ceasefire.

Fundamentally, the resolution had two elements – the instant cessation of the fighting that started on 12 July; and a series of steps that would lead to a permanent ceasefire and a wide-ranging solution. These steps included establishing an area between the Blue Line and the Litani River that would be free of any armed elements, weapons or equipment apart from those that belonged to the Lebanese government and UNIFIL. The resolution was adopted in a session of the Security Council attended by Secretary General of the United Nations Kofi Annan, US Secretary of State Condoleezza Rice, French Foreign Minister Philippe Douste-Blazy, British Foreign Minister Margaret Beckett and al-Shaykh Ḥamad bin Jāsim bin Jabr Āl Thānī , the foreign minister of Qatar whose country represented the Arab group on the

Security Council. This resolution reflected exceptional international concern about the outcome of this war and its regional consequences.

In fact, the resolution permitted the use of a UN peace-keeping force of a maximum of 15,000 men to support the deployment of the Lebanese army in the south while Israel withdrew beyond the Blue Line. As mentioned, the resolution called for a 'complete cessation of military action', but it failed to determine whether this would happen immediately. It asked Israel to withdraw its forces from southern Lebanon 'as soon as possible', simultaneously with the deployment of the Lebanese army and the extended force of the United Nations. On Lebanon's insistence, the United States and Britain agreed to omit the reference to the seventh clause of the United Nations charter, which authorizes the deployment of a strong force using arms for purposes other than self-defence. The resolution did, however, say that the United Nations forces could 'take all measures deemed necessary for their operations'. The task of the international force was 'supervising the ceasefire and accompanying and supporting the Lebanese forces during their deployment in southern Lebanon, including along the Blue Line, simultaneously with the Israeli withdrawal from Lebanon'. The task also included 'coordinating this deployment with the governments of both Lebanon and Israel'.

In compliance with the wish of the United States, the draft resolution imposed a ban on all military weapons and equipment 'for any individuals or entity in Lebanon' save for those permitted by the Lebanese government or UN force charged with supervising the prevention of military actions. The resolution also called on both Lebanon and Israel to work for a long-term solution, which would include the establishment of a buffer zone in the south unoccupied by any militia. The resolution did not, however, commission the international force to disarm Hezbollah.[140]

Following Security Council resolution 1701, Damascus officially commented saying:

> We acknowledge the Lebanese national consensus as well as its reservations expressed in the Lebanese official position. In the light of the historical achievements realized by the Lebanese

> national resistance and the heroic steadfastness of the Lebanese people, and after this long time of deliberations, Damascus had hoped that the Security Council would issue a balanced resolution which would have respected the interests of Lebanon as a whole and met its just demands to liberate all occupied territories and maintain its national security, sovereignty and independence.

It also declared that Syria had been 'informed about the contents of the resolution such as the requirement to put an end to military actions and the importance of realizing a comprehensive just peace in the Middle East on the basis of the Security Council's two resolutions 242 and 338'. Only adherence to these last two resolutions would make it possible to deal with the roots of the conflict in the area and to bring about security and stability.[141]

But something took place that Israel never expected. Before the voting on the resolution, Israeli Prime Minister Ehud Olmert played a double game by exploiting differences of timing, declaring his acceptance of the resolution on the one hand, but ordering the Israeli army to start the ground attack, which the small ministerial council for security and political affairs had approved a few days previously, on the other. The resolution was generally regarded as the best possible development and the best chance of stopping the aggression that had caused the deaths of more than 1000 Lebanese, most of them civilians, and had destroyed the Lebanese infrastructure. Yet, Olmert decided to attack southern Lebanon with a view to destroying all Hezbollah bases as far as the southern bank of the Litani River. The Israeli army suffered an overwhelming defeat, both in terms of casualties among the Israeli soldiers and the destruction of Israeli vehicles in the areas of Bint Jubayl and Aita al-Shaab. This showed that Hezbollah and its fighting capabilities in the face of the Israeli army was no myth, and forced a reassessment of its power in the region. Though limited, this 'victory' brought about by courageous defence and killing a large number of Israeli soldiers on the battlefield, gave huge support to the Syrian position and enabled it to consider the option of resistance at a suitable opportunity in the Golan area.

Syria's Return to Active Diplomacy

It can be said that one of the most important benefits Syria derived from the Israeli war against Lebanon was its return as a player in international, regional and Arab diplomacy. At the beginning of the war[142] Damascus became involved in extensive diplomatic activity, thus resuming its regional role after its isolation in the wake of the assassination of Rafiq al-Hariri. As the Spanish foreign minister Miguel Ángel Moratinos, who was considered to be a friend of Syria, put it: 'Syria, which is seriously isolated, has to be incorporated into the international game.'[143]

The Western (and later the Arabian) media circulated the view that isolating Syria had been counter productive because it prompted the latter to consolidate its relations with Iran and to become less flexible. Thomas Friedman, an American commentator who visited Damascus during the war, suggested in the *New York Times* that dialogue with Damascus should be resumed to keep it away from Tehran, thus encouraging the attempt to 'drive a wedge' between Syria and Iran.[144]

The presence of the UNIFIL force, which was drawn from a number of European countries but mainly from France and Italy, considerably enhanced the Syrian role because all the states participating in it wanted to encourage direct dialogue to guarantee the security of their soldiers. This almost completely ended Syria's isolation, particularly in relation to Europe. When the president of the European Commission invited al-Mu'allem to Helsinki, it was the first visit of a Syrian foreign minister since the establishment of the EU. This visit was taken as a sign that the isolation policy that the European Union had adopted after the assassination of the former Lebanese prime minister had now ended. Three states in particular strongly supported dialogue with Syria – Spain, Italy and Germany – and this essentially for the purpose of securing stability in southern Lebanon. Damascus, therefore, tried to make use of this friendlier climate to justify separating investigations into the assassination of Hariri from other political matters. A partnership agreement with the European Union (initialled at the end of 2004) had been delayed pending the results of the investigation, but Damascus now put pressure on the European Union to sign the agreement without waiting for the results of the international commission of inquiry.

The Syrian Exploitation of the War

President al-Asad's postwar speech to the fourth conference of the Journalists' Union in Damascus, in which he severely criticized most Arab rulers, accusing them of being 'half men', was surely Syria at its most controversial. Deviating from the written text on several occasions, the Syrian president launched into a brutal attack on the Lebanese forces for wishing to disarm the resistance, accusing them of attempting to 'create divisions in Lebanon', but he emphasized that they had failed and that 'their fall is not far off', given that the forces of 17 May (in fact meaning 14 March) are 'an Israeli product'. As al-Asad put it:

> Now one of their future tasks, after the failure of the war, is to safeguard the internal situation in Israel and the present government, either through creating sedition in Lebanon, and, therefore, transferring the battles from the Israeli interior to that of Lebanon, or through the possibility of realizing disarmament of the resistance, but I bring good news to them that they failed, and the fall does not seem to us to be far away.[145]

The speech elicited widespread Arab and international responses. The first of these was the cancellation of the German foreign minister's planned visit to Damascus, thereby creating an estrangement between Damascus on the one hand and Egypt, Saudi Arabia and Jordan on the other. On the Arab level, al-Mu'allem did not take part in the Arab foreign ministers' meeting in Cairo, which welcomed the Lebanese army's deployment in the south and stressed the need to give Lebanon all possible means of support in its political and economic reconstruction and to assist it in establishing control over its territories as a whole. They also advocated the application of resolution 1701.[146]

In keeping with that political escalation, al-Asad turned down a European suggestion to deploy an international force between Syria and Lebanon on the grounds that it would cause enmity.[147] Al-Asad then increased the intensity of his campaign against the 14 March forces in Lebanon saying that he thought that Lebanon would fall into the 'abyss'.[148]

With the deterioration of the internal situation in Lebanon after the war, especially the strengthening of the alliance between the Shi'ite opposition and Major General Imad Aoun, many questions about Syria's role in Lebanon resurfaced. Of particular concern were the Hezbollah coup and its armed attack on Beirut on 23 March 2008, when the party took hold of the city streets in response, so it was said, to the Lebanese government dismantling its own communication system. This created the threat of real civil war based on the sectarian Shi'ite–Sunni conflict. This problem was not overcome until the Doha accord, which led to the election of a new president, Major General Michel Sulaymān, and gave to Hezbollah, along with the opposition allied with it, the role of balancing third power in the Lebanese government.

Syria's Foreign-policy Challenges

Regarding its foreign policy, especially the Syrian–Lebanese relationship, Syria is now at a crossroads. Ever since the accusations of complicity in the assassination of Rafiq al-Hariri were first voiced, Syria has faced mounting international pressure to change the nature of its relationship with Lebanon by complying with a number of conditions. These include delineating the borders between the two countries, recognizing Lebanese sovereignty and exchanging ambassadors. And, as mentioned, the Security Council issued a special international resolution to the international court for the purpose of conducting the trial of those involved in the assassination of al-Hariri, which had started in early 2009. This court was formed on the basis of the seventh clause of the UN constitution, which allows the use of force, after agreement among the five permanent-member states in the Security Council, especially Russia and China. (The Shi'ite opposition, which Hezbollah and the Amal movement represented, had refused to ratify an agreement relating to the court based on the sixth clause of the United Nations charter because the court was not consistent with the institutional and constitutional procedures applied in Lebanon.)

One of the most crucial if not the main challenge that Syria will have to face is how it should respond to the outcome of the international tribunal. International pressure against Syria is likely to increase considerably, as will the threat of international isolation, which decreased – at least on the European level – after the war of July 2006 and on the American level after the arrival of the Obama administration, with its policy of enagement.

The second major challenge Syria faces is how to balance its relations with Iran (and to a lesser extent Hezbollah) on the one hand, and its historical role within the Saudi–Egyptian–Syrian axis on the other. This latter axis, which had determined Middle East policy for decades, was subject to disruption by the loss of its Syrian link after the assassination of Rafiq al-Hariri. Saudi Arabia took this as a blow directed against it personally. The outbreak of war in July 2006 followed by al-Asad's speech in which he accused the leaders of Saudi Arabia, Egypt and Jordan of being 'half men', drove a deep wedge in relations between Syria and Saudi Arabia, and between Syria and Egypt. Despite Egypt having disregarded the consequences of the speech, Syrian–Egyptian relations never quite recovered their old intimacy, but continued to be muddied by the many, sometimes hidden, disagreements that surfaced from time to time.

Syria had previously gone through a similar experience when it chose to maintain its relationship with Iran at the expense of that with Saddam Hussein, whom the Gulf States and most Arab countries supported. This decision had serious repercussions for Syria. It led to an economic blockade; severance of the aid the Gulf States had been giving it since the October 1973 war; and the blocking of its political decisions at the 1990 Arab summit held in Baghdad, even although Syria did not attend the summit because of the ongoing conflict between Hafez al-Azad and Iraqi President Saddam Hussein. Saddam Hussein's invasion of Kuwait in August 1990, however, presented Syria with an excellent opportunity to improve its uneasy relations with the Gulf States, the Arab states and the United States when it took part in the international alliance led by the United States to eject Iraqi forces from Kuwait.

Together with the Arab Gulf States and Egypt, Syria formulated what was called the declaration of Damascus, which enabled it to receive abundant economic aid from the Gulf States. At the same time Damascus availed itself of the opportunity to improve its relations with the United States to the extent that the period between 1991 and 2000 was described as a 'honeymoon' with regard to the Syrian–American relationship.

Today, however, Saddam Hussein – who was executed on 30 December 2006 – is no longer around to bring Syria out of its isolation. Since his execution, regional negotiations have been based on the priorities of the American administration. The Lebanese question seemed to pose a real obstacle, although there do seem to be attractive regional options for both sides. Iraq came under suspicion because of the different approaches Syria made to the Iraqi parties after the fall of Saddam Hussein's regime, although Iraq's problems seem to be bigger than those of either Syria or the United States. The solution to the civil war in Iraq will depend mainly on whether Iraqi national forces are able to unite against foreign interference, but at present that at least seems to be a very long way away.

Iraq is the third foreign-policy challenge Syria faces. How can Syria formulate a Syrian foreign policy when it does not recognize the occupation as legitimate? And how can it deal with an Iraqi government put into place under the protection of occupying troops? Syrian policy might have to be pragmatic without necessarily being based on legality. This is what happened at the beginning of the US–British military occupation of Iraq when Syria – then a member of the Security Council – cast a vote recognizing the military presence. In other words, it supported the political process that started with a transitional governmental council, moved on to a provisional government and then finally became an elected government. However, Syria refused to deal with all the Iraqi governments that followed the occupation because it did not want to acknowledge their legitimacy.

With the United States having reached an impasse in Iraq, with the worsening of Syria's relationship with the Lebanese government, and with the consolidation of political, military, economic and security relations with Iran, the Syrian government found the time to be ripe to resume diplomatic relations with Iraq. The agreement of the two sides to reopen their embassies in Damascus and Baghdad respectively reflected a fundamental political change in the Syrian position towards a 'government under occupation'. Finding that this step would be important in the context of the strategic exchange, Syria abstained from using legal language and gave priority instead to the logic of political pragmatism. It is therefore important for Damascus clearly to determine its options towards Iraq and to carry on a role that will help put an end to civil war being an indispensable pre-condition for attaining political stability and security and for removing foreign forces from the country.

The fourth and last challenge for Syrian foreign policy is the need to re-establish its bases while keeping sight of its national options while respecting its own and others' intrinsic wishes. This raises the vital and pressing question of democracy. In a former time it had been possible to formulate the country's foreign policy irrespective of what Syrian citizens wanted or decided, though of course having to bear in mind that foreign policy choices have an effect on domestic interests. Syrian domestic interests, however, were often used as a pretext for pursuing the regime's external interests.[149] Thus, how can Syria re-establish its foreign policy within the bounds of the theory of strategic regression?

The war against Lebanon was a strategic opportunity for Syria to reconsider its foreign and regional policy in the light of its objective of regaining the occupied territories in the Golan Heights and re-establishing the internal situation on a sound basis.

In his book *The Rise and Fall of Great Powers*, the political theorist Paul Kennedy was the first person to introduce an integrated theory about the consequences of the critical differences between the rate of economic growth and the cost of military engagements. He claimed that the fall of the ancient Roman Empire and of the British and other empires came about because of too great a disparity between the increase in military expenditure and the decline in material resources or economic activity.

Syria is clearly not an empire, and one of the defects in its foreign policy might be that some of its officials have viewed it as such. But Kennedy's theory is still applicable. In other words, political and economic development at the domestic level may be insufficient to carry the burden of an expanded foreign policy. Over the last few decades, Syrian foreign interests have expanded enormously. At the centre it has been necessary to establish relationships with the neighbouring regional states, especially over questions associated with Lebanon and Palestine. At the same time, it has attempted to widen the circle of active diplomacy with Saudi Arabia, Egypt and Iran. It has also had to deal with the consequences of the Israeli occupation of parts of Syrian territory in the Golan Heights. All this diplomatic and military activity has been accompanied by internal political and economic stagnation, which means that Syria needs to reconsider how to balance its internal and external interests.

At this point there is no way out of the impasse except through what I call 'strategic retraction'. This is the gradual withdrawal from some commitments (while trying to avoid any adverse regional and international repercussions) with a view to establishing domestic politics on a new footing. It would not entail isolation, which would in any case be impossible in a constantly changing regional milieu; rather, it would mean engaging in internal political discussions in the hope of finding a new approach to political life. Once the local politics has been consolidated, foreign policy can then be resumed along new lines. An American political proverb states that 'policy is local' because unless it has local support it will come to nothing. 'Strategic withdrawal' would create an opportunity to reflect on the implications of regional policy for pursuing domestic interests, given that the objective of any policy should be to fulfil the developmental interests and expectations of the society. It would be necessary, however, to combine strategic withdrawal with internal political reforms of a progressive nature. Establishing a sound political life based on strong national political parties that support the country's external agenda would give the policy strength and continuity. If it is clear to everyone that a policy is formulated to promote the interests of Syrian society, then it would immediately acquire internal and external credibility.

To achieve a balance between progress at home and a curtailment of interests abroad requires a wise, cautious and efficient administration that is prepared to countenance change if that will lead to a better future for all the society's different groups and factions.

5

The Challenge of Political Islam: Muslim Brotherhood and Democracy

Political Islam has been a prominent part of political life in Syria since independence. Islamic movements expanded significantly, especially in the 1960s and 1980s when unprecedented waves of violence broke out between the security forces and the most eminent Islamic movement, the Muslim Brotherhood. More recently, there has been a return to public manifestations of devotion within Syrian society and an increasingly powerful awareness of an Islamic movement outside it. After having formed a number of alliances with the Syrian opposition both inside and outside Syria, the Muslim Brotherhood has put itself forward as an alternative focus of loyalty. This movement adopts Islamic authority as a fundamental determinant of its political, economic and social vision, even although its need to adapt to modern political concepts such as democracy, human rights and civil society has meant that it has had to undergo some fairly deep transformations.

The development of the relationship in Syria between secular society and Islamic movements, and the latter's role in shaping the political landscape, including the process of democratic transformation, is an ongoing and extremely important issue, especially given the huge popularity of these movements in society. Thus, it is necessary to study the history of these Syrian Islamic movements and, more specifically, their future role in political life.

But, from a sociological point of view, we have first of all to make a distinction between the public expression of religious devotion in society on the one hand and active support of Islamic movements on the other. We might otherwise fall into the trap of exaggerating the role of Islamic movements or of seeing society in terms of generalized stereotypes.

The Early Relationship between Religion and State in Syria

The relationship between the Syrian state and Islam, represented by its governmental and non-governmental organizations or in the discourses of those who believe in its role in public life, goes back to before Syrian independence in 1946. During the period of reform in the Ottoman Empire known as the Tanzimat, many religious scholars from Damascus were allowed to establish charitable societies with openly propagandist as well as charitable programmes, and these societies also played a political role.

These societies came into being as an expression of the desire of religious scholars to recover their influence in the wake of the Ottoman state having introduced regulations that accorded value to non-religious knowledge, thus undermining their moral power. There had been a rise in the authority of reformers who thought it necessary to borrow political, economic and social concepts from Europe to establish and build a modern state, and who saw the scholastic tradition as an obstacle standing in the way of the reforms the Ottoman state adopted at the end of 1860. These reforms found expression in the design of public schools in the Ottoman Empire that laid emphasis on teaching the skills and knowledge of modern professionals such as bureaucrats, lawyers, doctors and army officers. With the increasing number of these schools, the number of educated Ottomans attached to the values of the secular regulations grew so that they imposed their interests and general points of view in a way that harmed the power as well as the position of the religious scholars.[1]

Sheik Taher al-Jazae'ri, who died in 1920, established the first charitable society. This society was particularly active in promoting education, opening schools based on philosophical principles geared towards reforming society through education and enabling the individuals to live according to the ideals and values of Islam.[2] Since then, the religious institutions existing in Syria have been greatly affected by the nature of their relationships with different government institutions, which of course vary depending on what political party is in power.

Later, especially during the French mandate (1920–46), the number of associations increased greatly. The creation of the Jamʿīyat al-Gharrāʾ with Muḥammad Hāshim al-Khaṭīb al-Ḥusaynī as its president was in effect a protest against French educational policies. It struggled for the right to teach Islamic religion and to establish private religious schools in which teaching would be carried out by religious scholars.[3]

Later on the society played a significant political role, particularly after the end of the mandate and during the successive elections when it had a notable influence on the collective awareness of people in Damascus and on their social behaviour and traditions. In fact, the British Ministry of Foreign Affairs described it in one of its reports in 1942 as the 'Syrian Party' that 'organizes protests against the government for issuing licences to places where people engage in immoral practices such as unveiling women, or attending movies and nightclubs, and for allowing the secularization of teaching courses'.[4]

These religious societies, which subsequently multiplied, were established by prominent figures in Damascus society who mostly belonged to the scholarly class. The Islamic Guidance Society was formed in 1931 with Kāmil al-Qaṣṣār as its most significant figure. The weekly magazine *Islamic Urbanization* was launched in 1932 to represent the views of the minor bourgeoisie, such as imams, doctors and lawyers. Its leaders included a number of figures from high-class traditional Damascene families, including Ahmad Muzhar al-ʿAsma and Muḥammad Bahjah al-Bīṭār.[5]

The magazine did much to assist the National Bloc, which played a central role in achieving independence for Syria in 1946, by provided it with a number of influential figures. It later did the same for the Syrian Muslim Brotherhood, to which it introduced a number of important characters such as Omar Bahaa Addeen al-Amiri in

Aleppo and Muhammad al-Mubārak in Damascus. *Islamic Urbanization*[6] was widely read in Egypt in particular and in the Arab Levant in general. Its contributors belonged to a broad spectrum of intellectuals and writers who were highly regarded in Syrian society at that time.[7]

Along with these societies, there were many others such as the Islamic Cooperation Society, the Islamic Orientation Association, the Association of Islamic Charitable Works, and the Ethics and Benevolence Society.[8] Whereas the activities of these societies during the period of the French mandate were confined to and/or focused mainly on educational, charitable and intellectual matters, they later became increasingly political. Of particular importance here was the work of the Muslim Brotherhood, one of the largest of the political Islamic movements and one that still affects Syria's political landscape.

The increase in religious societies enhanced the amount of political and educational influence that these societies were able to wield in areas formerly controlled by aristocratic landowning families with Western educations. On reviewing the occupations of Syrian MPs way back between the years 1919 and 1954, there would usually be only one or two religious scholars at any given time in the Syrian parliament, which was a clear indication that their numbers were decreasing at a time when the overall number of parliamentary representatives was increasing.[9]

This encouraged the establishment of the Scholars' Society in 1937, which to all intents and purposes was a scholars' union dedicated to rendering services to Islam by increasing the scholars' influence on political, social and educational life in general. The founder of the society, Kāmil al-Qaṣṣāb, was one of the more influential figures in the Arabic National Movement. In 1938 the society started an organization to plan and then to establish a high school for al-Sharīʿah scholarship. A Sharīʿah college was established in 1942.[10]

The Scholars' Society – perhaps because of al-Qaṣṣāb's leadership – was, however, unable to play a sufficiently authoritative role for the scholars and so the Scholars' League, to which the Muslim Brotherhood affiliated, was established in 1946, along with the Islamic

Urbanization Society, the Jamʿīyat al-Gharrāʾ and the Islamic Guidance Society. In the 1947 elections Kāmil al-Qaṣṣāb nominated himself on a list other than that of the Scholars' League.[11]

The political influence of these societies was clearly tested in the 1943 election. They backed Shukrī al-Quwatlī, then leader of the Nationalist Movement and later president of the country. His electoral list included an outstanding figure from the Jamʿīyat al-Gharrāʾ leadership – Sheik ʿAbd al-Ḥamīd al-Ṭabbāʿ, a merchant from the Shagour Quarter and much loved religious leader. He became the clear favourite on al-Quwatlī's list.[12]

This alliance, however, did not last long. Only one year later, in late May 1944, a clash occurred that effectively brought cooperation to an end between the governing class and the Islamic societies. It started with a protest march against a scheduled dance performance, but culminated in a number of loud demonstrations in Damascus that lasted for several days, during which life in the city came to a standstill and four people died. The participation of Muslim women in a concert organized by Nuqṭat al-Ḥalīb (Milk Drop), a female group run by some upper-class women in Damascus, deeply offended the Islamic societies, which saw it as a challenge to Islamic values.[13] These events marked the beginning of the political role of Islamic societies, especially of the Jamʿīyat al-Gharrāʾ, in demonstrating their power and influence within Syrian society. These societies did not openly enter the realm of politics, but pretended rather that their goal was merely to defend Islam and protect the society's religious values. The fusion of these Islamic societies into one movement later, in 1945, led to the establishment of the Muslim Brotherhood as the greatest Islamic political movement in Syria.

The Establishment of the Muslim Brotherhood in Syria

A Muslim youth group in Homs, which a man called Abu al-Souʾd Abdul Salam had set up in 1936, joined forces with a society in Aleppo called Dār al-Arqam, which Omar Bahaa Addeen al-Amiri had also established in 1936. In 1937, this joint organization, now called the Muslim Brotherhood, held two conferences in Homs and a third in Damascus in 1938.[14] It is unclear whether any Islamic societies in the capital, Damascus, affiliated to it in these early days, for the Muhammad Youth Society that ʿAbd al-Wahhāb al-Azraq set up in 1941 was no more than a high school students' union, whereas the Scholars' Society and the Jamʿīyat al-Gharrāʾ already wielded quite a lot of influence inside Damascus. This may explain the weakness of representation from Damascus in the group's executive committee throughout its history and even among its junior staff in comparison, for example, with the representation from Aleppo and Hama. This was to be a continuing pattern in the history of the Muslim Brotherhood from its establishment until now.

In the summer of 1946, these two youth groups reorganized and united under the name Muslim Brotherhood. Muṣṭafá al-Sibāʿī was elected general guide and Omar Bahaa Addeen al-Amiri his deputy. Although the new name, Muslim Brotherhood, might suggest it was a subsidiary of the Muslim Brotherhood in Egypt, the Syrian Muslim Brotherhood enjoyed a high level of organizational independence from its headquarters in Egypt. There are two explanations for this situation. First, its Egyptian leader, Ḥasan al-Bannā, who had established a decentralized pattern of political work, was preoccupied with the Egyptian situation.[15]

Second, differences between the political and social environments of Syria and Egypt forced each country to develop its own distinct political theory, organizational structure and legal processes. The political, religious, racial and sectarian diversity present in Syria was not characteristic of Egypt at that time. In Syria, parties, parliament and the press are freer than their counterparts in Egypt. The central office of the Muslim Brotherhood is in Egypt and each of the countries associated with it is represented by two members elected to the central executive. Syria is represented by the general guide al-Sibaʾe and his deputy, al-Amiri. But, despite the overall intellectual supervision based in Egypt, the Syrian Muslim Brotherhood developed a political discourse independent of the official Egyptian line.

Unlike other associations, the Muslim Brotherhood's activities were not confined to missionary work and education. The structure and organization[16] of the group clearly show that, in addition to its other tasks, political work was central to its mission. The movement started al-Farā, a semi-military organization based on training young men in how to use arms under the supervision of the army. The Muslim Brotherhood also ran a private government recognized school at which teaching was free. In addition, the Muslim Brotherhood participated in teaching in government schools in Damascus, which gave them increasing influence in society.

Despite Muṣṭafá al-Sibāʿī's[17] charismatic influence on the movement, it still retained a form of group leadership that continually promoted its activities and expanded its influence in different Syrian provinces.

Since 1949 Syria has experienced a number of coups, which has led to confusion in the Syrian political system and has had a serious impact on the stability of political life. Starting with Husni al-Zaʾim's coup in March 1949, which lasted only 137 days, the relatively rapid succession of coups has served to weaken the country's constitutional, political and legislative institutions.[18]

This coincided with a rise in ideological and doctrinaire political parties in Syria, which found fertile ground in which to flourish after the establishment of the Israeli state in May 1948. The rise of Israeli military threats on the Syrian borders and the increase of American authority through military alliances created an underlying threat to Syrian influence in the region and to its stability. The general outcome was the creation of a fruitful environment for the development of leftist, nationalist and religious trends. Through the formation of the so-called Islamic Socialist Front in 1949, the Muslim Brotherhood managed to get four of its deputies elected to the parliament.

The first conflict between political institutions, especially in parliament, arose over negotiations about the contents of the 1950 constitution. Various texts setting out the relationship between religion and the state were presented. The Muslim Brotherhood insisted that the constitution should state unequivocally that 'the state religion is Islam', regardless of how this affected the Christian and Jewish minorities and the susceptibilities of other minorities such as the Druze, Alawite and Ismaelite sects living in Syria. During this period there were violent disputes between all the diverse political movements over the wording[19] of the constitution and how this affected the positions of the various minorities.

On 6 April 1950 the constitutional committee, with a majority of 13 to 10, ratified Article 3 of Section 1 in the draft constitution, which included the statement that the state's religion is Islam. Although the Muslim Brotherhood was the only political organization in Syria to demand that Islam should be entered as the state religion, the voting clearly indicated that, in this conflict at least, it was expressing the view of a large proportion of the people.[20]

Following the opposition of most other parliamentary blocs, heated arguments went on in the parliament until Muṣṭafá al-Sibāʿī suggested the following amendment to Article 3:

- The president's religion is Islam;
- Islamic jurisprudence is the main source of legislation;
- freedom of belief shall be maintained;
- the state will respect all holy religions and guarantee each the freedom to practise their rituals so long as this does not commit a breach of public order; and
- the personal laws of religious sects will be preserved and observed.[21]

This amendment was indeed ratified on 26 July 1950 in a way that reflected the Muslim Brotherhood's political pragmatism in matters to do with negotiations and political alliances. Al-Sibāʿī defended the 'Islamic element' in the 'secular constitution', for he saw it as an example of what the constitutions of Islamic states should be.[22]

The 'constitution crisis' brought to a head the extent of the Islamic influence among the political elite and within different classes of Syrian society. At the same time, it also showed that, despite the centrality of religion to their interests, the Muslim Brotherhood nevertheless acted as a purely political movement. It neither considered itself the only legal representative of Islam nor monopolized the right to speak on behalf of Islam. Rather, it went through pragmatic political manoeuvres with respect to matters that the Islamic Sharīʿah considered to be legally and jurisprudentially beyond debate, particularly with regard to the constitution.

In general, this shows that the Muslim Brotherhood became very influential in Syria, but it was not the only influential movement, or even the leading one. In a report of 2 February 1955, the *New York Times* mentioned that the number of Muslim Brotherhood members ranged from 10,000 to 12,000, but it also indicated that, through its various associated organizations, it could carry out a wide selection of missions.[23] Later, during the frequent changes of regime, the Muslim Brotherhood played an even bigger part in the political game, which no doubt impinged on its cohesiveness and level of activity. It suffered many setbacks, especially after Husni al-Zaʾim, who led the first military coup in March 1949, disbanded the political parties. Al-Shīshaklī did the same thing and again it created alliances and divisions among the Muslim Brotherhood that threatened the movement's continuity as a political force and its commitment to political work. This was not helped by a clash between the main group in Egypt and the Egyptian president, Gamal Abdul Nasser, which arose over the president's office sending an order instructing the group to keep out of the inner political arena.[24]

When the Muslim Brotherhood returned to parliament following the resumption of democracy after the fall of Adeeb al-Shīshaklī in 1954, their presence was so weakened that not even al-Sibāʿī could be guaranteed a seat in parliament. He was defeated again in the May 1957 by-election in which he stood against the Baʿthist Riad al-Mālikī. After his defeat, al-Sibāʿī started to suffer from hemiplegia, which greatly affected his vitality.[25]

At that time, the Muslim Brotherhood faced two options – either back Syrian–Egyptian unity, which an overwhelming majority of the Syrian public wanted but which meant wholeheartedly supporting President Nasser; or express their hostility to Abdul Nasser who had condoned the torture of Muslim Brotherhood, especially in the wake of the al-Manshia incident in 1954.

Thanks to his unique personality, al-Sibāʿī could cleverly navigate his way around the crisis. He fully committed himself to the idea of unity and published his famous book *Islamic Socialism*[26] in 1959. In this he tried to find a legal justification for the agrarian reform law passed by Abdul Nasser and for the principle of nationalization applied later.

Politically, he supported Abdul Nasser's nationalist stand, especially during the triple attack on Egypt in 1956, from which Nasser emerged a national hero. Nasser, in fact, inflamed the imagination of the Syrian politicians and threw them into a real predicament with respect to the problem of supporting him openly. At the same time, the Syrian regime was undergoing complete 'political deterioration' to which there was no solution other than integration with Egypt, despite Nasser's stipulation that all political parties in Syria would have to be dissolved. This had a disastrous effect on all the political parties, especially after the separation from Egypt in 1961.

On Syria's return to democracy after the separation, the Muslim Brotherhood won ten seats in the parliamentary elections that were held in the same year.[27] Its parliamentary bloc led by ʿIṣām al-ʿAṭṭār was known as the Cooperative Islamic Bloc and it managed to maintain some sort of balance between its relationship with Nasser and its adaptation to the reality of the separation.[28]

With the Baʿth Party's accession to power in 1963, the Muslim Brotherhood entered a completely new phase. This was most clearly manifested in the so-called Hama Rebellion of April 1964, lasting 29 days and led by Hama local leaders of the Muslim Brotherhood headed by Marwān Ḥadīd and Saʿīd Ḥawwá. A number of supporters of the Muslim Brotherhood mounted a sit-in in al-Sultan mosque and engaged in battle with the army units that eventually decided to break into the mosque to put a violent end to the protest. This led to early tensions between the Baʿth Party and the Muslim Brotherhood, some of whom agreed with the Damascus leaders in their refusal to endorse the rebellion, seeing it as a turning away from their decisions, and others of whom supported those local leaders in Hama who held the view that the leadership had agreed to the rebellion and had authorized the Hama leadership to do what it deemed right.[29]

The Hama Rebellion was an early sign of the rise of a jihadist trend within the Muslim Brotherhood, which was inconsistent with its peaceful and democratic ideals. This trend, dubbed Muhammad's Battalions (*Kata'ib*), would later generate the Muslim Brotherhood's militant vanguard that initiated the tragic events of Hama in 1982. The transformation can only be explained by looking at the changes of the opposing side. Establishing the 'third republic' had involved the monopolization of political authority, the imposition of a state of emergency and the ending of political plurality and an independent press.[30]

These measures made political engagement useless, and motivated many political movements to resort to violence as a means of solving disputes. Islamic Trend was possibly the movement most attracted to the possibility of violence because of the reservoir of religious and legal writing that enables radical movements to interpret enough texts in such a way as to justify resorting to arms. At this time, conflict was also breaking out between competing regional and national Ba'th elements, concealing the conflict between the countryside and the city, as well as a sectarian and class clash, demonstrated clearly by more than one event. In 1966, for example, the 23 February movement, after holding off its rivals and punishing them cruelly and violently, gained power over the party and the regime. It adopted a strong left-wing discourse that terrified conservative Syrian society, which seemed to be supporting President Hafez al-Asad's movement against Salah Jda'ed, hoping to get rid of the radical left-wing rhetoric prevailing within the Ba'th Party leadership at the time.

Double Religious Containment Policy

On assuming power in 1970, and throughout the many years of his rule, al-Asad managed to centralize power in such a way as his instructions and decisions, not to mention the force of his own personality, assumed paramount importance in the administration of state affairs.

Following his coming to power in November 1970, he toured most of the Syrian governorates and tried to meet a number of the people who had congratulated him on his victory. He was sufficiently sophisticated to realize the importance of winning over the religious lobby, which would find it easy to cast doubt on his legitimacy because of his Alawite background. He therefore tried, within the confines of his secular nationalist beliefs, to get closer to the religious scholars. To achieve this, in 1973 he made large personal donations to religious schools in the governorate of Hama and to Islamic charitable societies in Homs. In 1974, he raised the salaries of employees in religious institutions. This increase benefited 1138 imams, 252 teachers of religion, 610 preachers and 280 reciters of the Quran. In 1976, and again in 1980, he increased their financial benefits; also in 1976, under his sponsorship, 5.4 million Syrian pounds were ring-fenced for building new mosques.[31] Until his death in 2000, he would celebrate Iftar on a certain day of Ramadan with the highest ranking Islamic scholars.

As mentioned above, as an Alawite in a predominantly Sunni country, al-Asad felt hesitant about taking on the position of president of the republic and at first contented himself with the post of prime minister, assigning the presidency to an unknown Sunni schoolteacher called Aḥmad al-Khaṭīb. Later, however, he changed his mind and, on 21 March 1971, a plebiscite confirmed his seven-year appointment as president.[32]

Climax of Armed Conflict

The first clash between the Syrian authorities and the religious movement came when the new Syrian constitution was published on 31 January 1973. Protests broke out, especially in Hama, because the clauses stating that the president of the republic should be Muslim had been dropped from the proposed draft of the constitution. This clause had been present in the constitution of 1950 and was maintained again in later constitutions.

Complaining began to increase in Hama and Homs, and the influential Sheikh Ḥasan Ḥabanakah led a campaign in the Midan area of Damascus. Al-Asad ordered the People's Assembly to add an article stipulating that 'the religion of the President of the Republic is Islam',[33] but he declared at the same time that true Islam should be far removed from 'narrow-mindedness and awful extremism, as Islam is a religion of love, progress, social justice and equality'.[34]

The question raised later on was, 'is an Alawite a Muslim?' Some 80 Alawite religious figures made a formal statement in which they declared that their book is the Quran and they are Shiite Muslims adopting the al-Ethna Ashari creed.[35] Imam Mūsá al-Ṣadr, the head of the Islamic Shiite Council in Lebanon, issued a legal opinion that

Alawites belong to the Shiite Muslims.[36] Despite all the protests demanding the inclusion of 'Islam as the state's religion', al-Asad held the view that no Syrian constitution before 1973 had made that stipulation, and he insisted on maintaining his position, which a referendum carried out on 12 March 1973 had supported.

Al-Asad realized that the Muslim Brotherhood had more power in some governorates than others. Its position in the capital, Damascus, was weakest because of the range of different political, cultural and economic influences to which its inhabitants were exposed. For this reason, al-Asad thought it expedient to attract the religious scholars of Damascus to his side. He thus set out to win over the moderates and build a network of economic interests between those scholars and the Damascus tradesmen who were considered the principal providers of charitable and religious donations, as well as the supervisors of the works carried out by the scholars. The tradesmen began supporting al-Asad, especially since the economic policies that he pursued were more liberal than those of previous periods of Ba'th rule, which suited their interests and those of the large property owners in the capital.

The Ba'th Party resisted the nomination of the Medanite sheikh of Damascus Ḥasan Ḥabanakah[37] to the position of mufti of the republic, but strongly supported the appointment of Aḥmad Kuftārū to that position in 1965. Kuftārū belonged to a Kurdish family that had lived in Damascus for a long time and his father had attained a distinguished religious status. Since the 1940s he had been well known for his efforts to promote 'harmonious relations between Muslims and Christians'. Through pressure on the High Islamic Council, the Ba'th Party succeeded in ensuring the position for Kuftārū.[38]

Al-Asad appointed Kuftārū to the first People's Assembly in 1971. He also won over other Islamic scholars, mostly graduates of the religious schools and institutes led by the Islamic charitable Jam'īyat al-Gharrā'. These establishments gradually began to cooperate with the authorities to ensure that their small religious concerns could continue. In return, they gave al-Asad complete backing and support. Sheikh Kuftārū considered that al-Asad's re-election whenever there was a leadership referendum should be seen as a 'religious duty and a national obligation'.[39]

Al-Asad was thereby able to neutralize a large section of the 'religious trend', whose only real concern was its personal safety, the protection of its interests and its ability to fulfil its religious duties freely. At the same time he worked towards taking advantage of the many deep divisions that began to occur in the ranks of the Muslim Brotherhood, dividing them into three groups. The first of these groups was the Combatant Vanguard established by Marwān Ḥadīd, which attracted the younger elements and adopted a radical line justifying violence on the basis of a legal fatwa that charged the existing regime with 'infidelity'. The second was the faction that came to be known as the Group of Damascus under the leadership of ʿIṣām al-ʿAṭṭār, who could not return to Syria and so remained in Lebanon until he left for Germany. And finally there was the wing led by Sheikh ʿAbd al-Fattāḥ Abū Ghuddah in Aleppo that would secure for itself recognition by the Muslim Brotherhood's International Council in 1972.[40]

Marwān Ḥadīd, who studied agricultural engineering at the Egyptian university of Ain Shams and graduated in 1962, was influenced by the writings of the late Sayyid Quṭb, who adopted a very radical approach, describing Muslim societies as 'pre-Islamic' and accusing their leaders of infidelity because they failed to follow 'the Rule of Allah'. It is from his work that the term *al-ḥākimīyah* (governorship)[41] was derived, which a number of extremist Islamic movements adopted to justify their rebellions against existing regimes.[42]

At the same time Syria was suffering from a serious economic crisis. It had received generous financial aid in the wake of the October war in 1973, but this had by now almost completely whittled away. By 1979, workers in the public sector – the fastest growing sector in Syria – had to endure losses in real income despite having had wage increases in 1975 and 1978. This increased the public's general anger with the regime and led to political and social disturbances between 1975 and 1980.[43] In fact, there had been public protests two years earlier, which had led to the fall of ʿAbd al-Raḥmān Khulayfāwī's government on 7 March 1976. After his first stint as prime minister, Khulayfāwī had returned to his former position when

Maḥmūd al-Ayyūbī took charge of the second government in al-Asad's regime on 22 December 1972. However, nothing changed the reality of the economic situation, which started to show clear signs of corruption, bribery and pillage.

The 'nouveaux riches', as they were known, began to multiply in a way that affected the nature of social relations in Syria and the balanced growth mechanisms that al-Asad had considered to be well established. In 1963 there were 55 (Syrian currency) millionaires in Syria; in 1973 there were 1000 and by 1976 the number had risen to 2500, 10 per cent of whom owned more than 100 million Syrian pounds (at that time the exchange rate was five Syrian pounds to the US dollars). Many of these millionaires had acquired their wealth by theft, which had become possible through government projects and such illegal procedures as money laundering. This led to the formation of alliances between businessmen and the regime's high-ranking political and military officials. Theirs was an unholy alliance influenced only by personal profit, with no consideration whatsoever given to the public interest.[44]

This prompted al-Asad to set up courts of economic security through a decree passed on 8 July 1977 and to form an 'investigating committee into illegal earnings' on 17 August. The committee's mission was to root out embezzlement, misuse of position, bribery and illegal earnings. It had powers to investigate, detain or arrest where necessary and to seize property suspected of being obtained illegally. It could also prosecute and pass judgement. Its authority extended to the right to investigate people of high position, civil and military employees and anyone who worked in a public service.[45] This committee, however, faltered and failed in its mission when it found itself in direct conflict with figures close to the regime, such as Rifaʾat al-Asad who was clearly culpable.[46]

At that time, al-Asad badly needed the security services to repulse 'terrorist attacks' – as the authorities called them – waged by members of the Muslim Brotherhood. These actions, based on sectarian divisions, increased in severity after Captain Ibrāhīm al-Yūsuf led a massacre on the artillery school in Aleppo on 16 June 1979,[47] which resulted in the extermination of dozens of military students belonging to the Alawite sect. The Syrian authorities' reaction was strong and violent, especially after the discovery of an attempt to assassinate President Hafez al-Asad in June 1980, whereupon the military defence units, led by Rifa'at al-Asad, shot dead more than 700 Muslim Brother prisoners in their cells in Tadmor (Palmyra) prison.[48]

Marwān Ḥadīd and Sa'īd Ḥawwá, who are looked upon as the most productive ideological theorists in the extremist wing of the Muslim Brotherhood and who led the Hama Rebellion in 1964, were the spiritual fathers of the group's military wing. After Ḥadīd was arrested, tortured and then released, he applied his ideas even more fervently than before and in 1975 he established what became known as the 'fighting group of Hezbollah'. Researchers and specialists in the field are still debating about the closeness of this group's association with the Muslim Brotherhood, its parent organization, and the extent to which the group obeys its decisions, despite the majority of its members having left the Muslim Brotherhood.

At the time of the ratification of the constitution, Ḥadīd began to instigate opposition to the existing regime and to call for the use of arms against it. He also campaigned against some members of the Muslim Brotherhood in Hama who had stood as candidates for the parliamentary elections of 1973. This led the leaders of the group to criticize him publicly and to dissociate themselves not only from his actions, but also from his political and juridical opinions. On 30 June 1975, the Syrian security forces managed to arrest Ḥadīd. He was tortured in prison so severely that he died from his injuries in the prison's hospital in 1976, which gave his group an additional excuse to increase its violent operations. The confrontation between the fighting group and the Syrian security forces escalated out of control, starting with the assassination of Major Muḥammad Jarrāḥ, chief of the general intelligence branch in Hama, in early 1976 and eventually culminating in the artillery incident in 1979.

A general strike by doctors, lawyers, and engineers calling for basic freedoms, political liberty, the rule of law and respect for human rights, preceded these above-mentioned events.[49] As a result all the unions representing these groups were dissolved and many of their members were put in prison. Protests among the political parties increased when al-Asad failed to keep the promise he made on 4 October 1979 to improve the National Progressive Front. Intense activity on the part of both regional and national leaderships to explain the party's position to the unions, the party membership and the general public followed.

There was an extensive campaign of arrests of members of the Muslim Brotherhood. As mentioned in an earlier chapter, Law 49 was passed stating that anyone who belonged to the Muslim Brotherhood and did not withdraw from it in writing within one month would be executed. The law excluded detainees from the implementation of this provision. The 'Long Arm' policy was extended to government enemies abroad through officially sanctioned assassinations. ʿIṣām al-ʿAṭṭār was targeted, but his wife Bayān al-Ṭanṭāwī was killed instead. Muḥammad Bahjah al-Bīṭār, one of the Baʿth founders, was also assassinated in France when he started issuing a magazine in Paris called *Arab Revival*.[51] A number of Lebanese journalists in Beirut who were critical of the regime were killed. Among others these included Salīm al-Lawzī and Riad Taha.

The seventh Baʿth conference held between 22 December and 6 January 1980 attempted to define the crisis as a purely internal one, recognizing that it originated in social, economic and political tensions. The conference closed with a statement about the necessity to 'intensify the campaign both politically and militarily to get rid of the Muslim Brotherhood's gang and demolish its basis in the state and society'.[52] It also admitted to the existence of negative practices in the state, in the party and in society at large, which had resulted in an extensive decline in living conditions. There was great inequality in the distribution of wealth and a very rich covetous new class had grown like a parasite in the shadows of the development plan and its inadequate implementation.[53]

Al-Asad also attempted to form a new government, this time led by a well-known college professor and city planning engineer, ʿAbd al-Raʾūf al-Qāsim, who succeeded the government of Muḥammad al-Ḥalabī. This new government assembled on 30 March 1978 and lasted for a little under two years. It was an indication that structural changes would be made in the wake of rising public protests. The formation of al-Qāsim's government was followed by a referendum on 8 February 1978 that awarded al-Asad another term with a poll of 99.61 per cent.

However, these changes and adjustments, as a whole, did not succeed in stopping the wave of violence that increased rapidly until it subsided and almost vanished after the bombing of Hama in February 1980. The violence of this operation was so extreme that a huge number, estimated at between 5000 and 15,000 civilians were killed, most of them native residents of Hama. Whole quarters were destroyed and it took several months to remove the debris from a city that had lost its characteristic features.[54] Al-Asad followed the example attributed to Napoleon in 1800 when he sent one of his generals to quell an uprising with the advice: 'you have to burn two or three of the worst towns.' Experience had taught him that 'all-inclusive grievous severity is the most humane way in such circumstances. Weakness alone is not humane and a man of power should have his heart in his head.'[55] Al-Asad was following his example when he decided to bomb Hama in February 1982, destroying the city and its residential quarters, and killing a large number of civilians.[56]

A campaign of random arrests occurred, during which thousands of activists and supporters of the opposition, including even those who were suspected of being so, were arrested. The prisons became overcrowded with people given very long prison sentences, usually more than ten years. These measures had negative effects on Syrian society, which was unable to forget its 'national catastrophe'.[57] One Syrian writer aptly described it as 'the regime's victory over its society in its war against it'.[58] No government should engage in a war against its own citizens. The harsh methods the administration used, especially in dealing with the Islamists, inflicted permanent scars on the wider movement whose members remained cut off from the outside world for many years. News spread of the physical and mental torture to which detainees were subjected by way of 'discipline' and the effects of this are still visible. The generation that came after the 'disaster of the 1980s', as it came to be known, particularly those who are religious or who practise Islam, are wary about their personal safety. They not only shy away from political work, but also even avoid discussing it or listening to news about it. It amounts almost to a 'phobia',[59] which stops them from participating in politics or in anything that might lead to it.

This is probably one of the most important political and social legacies of the violent conflict between the Muslim Brotherhood and the Syrian security apparatus. In addition, it deepened the splits between the different factions of the Muslim Brotherhood, each of which blamed the other for embarking on an 'unequal confrontation' with the authorities. President Hafez al-Asad, however, was intelligent enough to benefit from these divisions and to use them to his advantage. On 22 December 1979, he drew a distinction between those:

> who cause affront to religion in the name of religion, but who are misguided and unaware of the harm that their actions cause to their religion and their world, and those who are aware of what they are doing, and whose suspicious movements are intended to undermine the aims of Camp David.[60]

Trying to deflect what public support the Muslim Brotherhood might gain from their religious and conservative base, al-Asad also made a distinction between the Muslim Brotherhood and those conservative Muslims 'who form a large and important part of our country and deserve the greatest respect'.[61]

The authorities' indiscriminate violence created disagreement among the Muslim Brotherhood's leaders, who not only expected the violence to happen, but also thought that it might negatively affect the state by dividing its elite, though this did not in fact happen. The disputes arising from the different political positions within the Muslim Brotherhood's leadership, which the 'Combatant Vanguard' seemed to be leading, gradually hardened into three very clear divisions. These were (a) the general organization of Muslim Brotherhood that had selected ʿAdnān Saʿd al-Dīn as a general guide in 1975; (b) the Damascus Group that was still under the influence of ʿIṣām al-ʿAṭṭār, who was leading it from abroad, as mentioned above; and (c) the Combatant Vanguard organization.

After a number of public and secret debates, conversations and accusations, the three parties agreed, in 1980, to a common leadership in which four officers would represent each faction; Ḥasan al-Huḍaybī from Dayr al-Zawr was chosen as the new general guide. The new leadership included Saʿīd Ḥawwá from Hama, ʿAlī Ṣadr al-Dīn al-Bayānūnī from Aleppo and ʿAdnān Saʿd al-Dīn. ʿAdnān ʿUqlah, who was one of the most active members of the group, represented the Combatant Vanguard.[62] The three parties signed what is known as the 'Statement of the Islamic Revolution in Syria and its Programme', which accused the regime of responsibility for the 'misery' in the country and announced that it had reached the 'point of no return'. This new grouping declared that there would be no armistice or 'laying down of arms' until the regime collapsed.[63]

It started building alliances with the regimes in Iraq and Jordan. This led ʿAdnān ʿUqlah to refuse to attend the meetings, which resulted, on 11 March 1982, in the establishment of the 'National Coalition for Liberating Syria'. When ʿUqlah described this move as cooperation between 'ignorance and atheism',[64] the general organization decided to discharge him, but his dismissal was not announced until after the tragic events of Hama in 1982. This created confusion about whether or not the Muslim Brotherhood, as an organization, were responsible for involving their bases in an unequal battle, so there was an ongoing argument about the legitimacy of an independent decision that the fighting group had made without official guidance.

The dissension in the Muslim Brotherhood's leadership reached a climax in 1986 when a conflict arose over the leadership of the organization between ʿAdnān Saʿd al-Dīn, residing in Iraq and refusing to engage in any form of negotiations with the regime, and Sheik ʿAbd al-Fattāḥ Abū Ghuddah from Aleppo, who held the view that 'dialogue is the basic tool for reaching the desired aim'.[65] The struggles in the group consultative council then resulted in the choice of Munīr al-Ghaḍbān[66] from the al-Tall area in the vicinity of Damascus as the new general guide. This, however, did not put an end to the conflicts and eventually two *shūrá* (consultative councils) were formed, each of which raised doubts about the legality of the other. ʿAdnān Saʿd al-Dīn led the first and ʿAbd al-Fattāḥ Abū Ghuddah the second. Saad adopted what became known as a jihad policy, while Abdal Fattah Abū Ghuddah, with the support of the international organization of Muslim Brotherhood, adopted a conciliatory policy.[67]

Following Saddam Hussein's invasion of Kuwait in August 1990, the two wings, supporting Iraq and Saudi Arabia respectively, entered a direct confrontation and the divisions between them widened, especially after the resignation of the secretary general Abū Ghuddah and the election of ʿAlī Ṣadr al-Dīn al-Bayānūnī as the new secretary general who is still in his position.

None of the negotiations held between al-Bayānūnī and the Syrian security forces managed to solve the problem either of the Muslim Brotherhood's role as a political party or of the return of its leaders. The Syrian authorities were prepared to issue individual pardons and to negotiate the return of several members as individuals, but not as leaders of the Muslim Brotherhood. This applied to the case of the former leader Sheikh ʿAbd al-Fattāḥ Abū Ghuddah, who returned at the end of 1995. Individual, factional and regional mediations also failed to settle the question of the Muslim Brotherhood's role as a political Islamic movement in Syria.

The uninterrupted enforcement of Law 49 was a reflection of the severity of the regime's stand against the Muslim Brotherhood since the end of the 1980s, both in terms of issuing pardons and of allowing its members to return to the fold. However, the imposition of the death sentence was suspended and replaced by sentences of between ten and sixteen years imprisonment, which became the fate of many people whom the authorities accused of being associated with the prohibited Muslim Brotherhood group.[68]

President Hafez al-Asad's death in June 2000 and the advent of his son Bashar as his successor had no effect on the government's position on this issue, which remained unchanged: Muslim Brotherhood's leaders have been denied any opportunity to discuss their situation, despite the accumulation of social, humanitarian and familial problems involved. With the state having placed security at the top of its agenda, the new generation, as well as members of the older generation who have recently been released from prison, is hypersensitive about working in politics or, for that matter, playing any kind of active role in society.

In the wake of the suppression of the Muslim Brotherhood, Islamic life in Syria returned to a situation in which individual religious scholars maintained good relations with the government yet nonetheless made an impact on society, manifested at the regional level by a return to traditional religious practices, as well as an increase in the number of mosques and the number of people attending them. These developments were not necessarily connected with the politicization of religion. Rather, they should be seen as filling the spiritual gaps caused by years of political repression and the suppression of all social activities related to openness and individual initiative. Thus, a state of 'domesticated Islam', so to speak, was established, for the Syrian regime had largely succeeded in containing its prominent symbols through a series of carefully calculated steps.

Members of the Muslim Brotherhood have either ended up in exile or remained at home as an ineffective force, too afraid to declare or even hint at their affiliation to this 'forbidden group'. It is true that the Muslim Brotherhood took some political steps after President Bashar al-Asad's accession to power in June 2000 by publishing the so-called 'National Honor Pact for Political Work', in which they renounced all forms of violence and their support for the 'civil state'.[69] They also published their political programme, which in both its policies and rhetoric represented a significant break with the past. However, these had no effect on the way the authorities dealt with the organization.

The 'National Honor Pact for Political Work' talks about what it calls 'the modern state', which is 'a contractual one, whose contract springs from a free and conscious will between the ruler and the ruled. The contractual form of the state is one of the things offered by Islamic Sharī'ah to human civilization'. The *Statement* lays stress on the equal right for all to 'benefit from the state's capabilities, to explain their positions, to advocate their viewpoints and to put forth their programmes'. The state must reject violence as a means of solving the security problems of society and the executive power of the state must not become corrupted by threats of violence.

This is a radical change of discourse for the most prominent Syrian Islamic movement, especially with regard to its acceptance of democracy and the peaceful transfer of power. Its commitment to work as a civic political party within a basically Islamic country puts it on very much the same footing as the democratic Christian parties in Europe.

This is an extremely important step towards encouraging the most prominent Islamic movement to become involved in the democratic process. The movement's political alliances with the internal political opposition, which issued the Damascus Declaration on 1 November 2005, and its later cooperation with the former vice-president ʿAbd al-Ḥalīm Khaddām to form the National Salvation Front, show how this movement is making pragmatic political alliances with a view to guaranteeing both its existence in the political arena and its political role in the event of dramatic changes in the future.

The Rise of the Religious Tide in Syria

The state maintained its firm control over the position of the mufti of the republic. After the death in 2005 of Sheikh Aḥmad Kuftārū, who had been allowed to maintain his personal establishment in his name and to continue with his preaching and missionary activities, Aḥmad Ḥassūn (born in Aleppo in 1949) was appointed mufti of the republic by presidential decree, thus breaking the tradition requiring the mufti to be chosen from an influential traditional Damascus family. His strongly biased political statements have played a part in his considerable loss of credibility in significant sections of Syrian society. One of the most recent of these statements was in May 2007 when he described President Bashar al-Asad's election for a second presidential term as a '*bai'a* [pledge of allegiance] similar to that of the Prophet'.[70] Despite that, he is given credit for his courageous and forward looking position in defending women's rights, including their right to grant nationality to their children, and for his position towards what are known as 'honour crimes'.[71]

Religious institutions are subsumed into the categories of education and propaganda, both under the supervision of the Ministry of Religious Endowments (*Awqaf*) whose minister is appointed with care and attention. After the death of ʿAbd al-Majīd al-Ṭarābulsī, who had formerly been an active member of the Muslim Brotherhood and one of its radical leaders, the newly appointed ministers were in effect technocrats rather than religious or jurisprudential authorities with influence in Syrian society. Muḥammad Ziyād al-Ayyūbī and the present minister of endowments had previously worked in administrative positions in the ministry, but had no religious or political authority.

The influence of religion, however, can be gauged by the number of legal educational institutions spread throughout the country. The Sharīʿah secondary schools fall within the administrative jurisdiction of *al-Awqaf*, which funds them and decides their religious curriculum. They have been in existence since 1971, are becoming increasingly widespread in all parts of Syria, and the number of students in them is rising continuously.[72] As a result, it became necessary to establish middle and higher legal institutes, the most prominent of which is the Abu Noor Islamic Centre, which the mufti Aḥmad Kuftārū manages. This has a college for teaching Arabic as a foreign language to non-Arabs undertaking Sharīʿah and Islamic studies, and is linked to the Islamic university in Um Durman in Sudan.[73] Another institute, al-Fatḥ al-Islāmī, is a branch of Jāmiʿat al-Azhar in Damascus and is directed by the mufti of Damascus, ʿAbd al-Fattāḥ al-Bizam. It offers three levels of study – primary and secondary school, university, and postgraduate. The centre also runs two-year preparatory courses to give non-Arabic speakers a firm foundation in Sharīʿah studies. In 1998, on this course there were 218 students representing 34 nationalities.[74]

Syrian universities do not recognize most of the higher certificates these Sharīʿah institutes issue. The Syrian government tried to organize religious education in 2006 by making the completion of the basic phase of teaching obligatory for those who wished to enter Sharīʿah schools, but this upset many influential and prominent religious men, 39 of whom signed a letter to the Syrian president accusing the Ministry of Education of forming a 'conspiratorial' plan 'designed to dry up and destroy the streams of the Sharīʿah secondary schools'. They also criticized 'mixed schools'. In the letter they claimed that 'Shiite *ḥawzah* [schools] continuously ignore this circulated note and are determined not to respond to it, whereas *Shweifat* private schools and foreign (French, American and Pakistani) missionary schools are carrying on with their own special curriculum and teaching methods without any opposition.'[75]

The letter was exceedingly effective because its signatories were the most active and influential scholars in Syria. Among them, for example, were Muḥammad Saʿīd Ramaḍān al-Būṭī, who was close to President Hafez al-Asad; Ṣalāḥ Kuftārū, son of the deceased Mufti Aḥmad Kuftārū and now, following his father's death, director of the Abu Noor Islamic Centre; the former minister of *Awqaf*, Muḥammad al-Khaṭīb; the sheikhs Ṣādiq Ḥabanakah and ʿAbd al-Razzāq al-Ḥalabī; Muḥammad ʿAbd al-Karīm Rājiḥ (nicknamed Sheikh al Qoraʾ); Wahba al-Zaḥīlī, a teacher in the Sharīʿah college at the University of Damascus; and Osama Rifaʾee, a preacher in the Rifaʾee mosque in the area of *Kafr Sūsah* and highly influential in Damascus society.

On receiving the letter, President Bashar al-Asad held a meeting with a delegation of its signatories, including Sheikh Rafa'ee, Dr al-Būṭī and the mufti of the republic Aḥmad Ḥassūn, and immediately promised to solve the problem by reverting to the government approved combined curriculum.[76]

This event drew attention to the extent of the religious scholars' influence in Syrian society and of the Syrian government's sensitivity to conflict with this religious element. The government wanted to contain and enclose it as much as possible and, for this reason, took a number of measures, which included founding a Sharīʿah college in Aleppo and establishing several Islamic banks, among which were the Bank al-Shām, the Syrian State Islamic Bank and the Bank al-Barakah. Each of these banks holds capital in the region of US$ 100 million, which is three times the legal limit for non-Islamic banks.[77] In addition, institutes for memorizing the Quran have been set up in most Syrian mosques. They are called 'al-Asad institutes for memorizing the Quran'.

The number of the students in the Sharīʿah faculty at the University of Damascus is gradually increasing. Of the 48,000 students at the university, 7603 are in that faculty (of whom 3337 are female). Every year 650 students graduate from the college. In addition, there are now more than 9000 mosques in Syria and around 30 per cent of Syrians participate in Friday prayers.[78] The al-Qubaysīyāt movement, which has some backing, works towards forming a network of women with widespread religious influence.[79] This growing enthusiasm for religious practices cannot, however, be explained in purely social or political terms. It is rather an expression of spiritual needs in a region considered as the source of religion, the influence of which is always dominant. Given the political, social and cultural isolation in which we live, we should expect more and more people to cling to religious practices.

After the US invasion of Iraq in March 2003, a number of violent operations, usually targeting official residences and foreign embassies, were directed against Syria. The most famous of these was an attack on the radio and television building in June 2006 and another on the US embassy in Damascus.[80] The Syrian security services accused Islamic extremists who belonged to Al Qaeda of carrying out these attacks, and took precautions by putting visible pressure on and constantly surveying the various religious organizations. On 28 February 2006, the Ministry of Religious Endowments issued a ten-point order to all mosques, including:

> Mosques must not be opened between prayer times; the sound of the dawn and afternoon calls to prayer should not be too loud in order not to disturb the neighbourhood at rest; religious lessons are prohibited, and Quran lessons must be cut from being held daily to once or twice a week; financial or material donations may not be accepted unless they are accompanied by the necessary endorsement from the Directorate of Religious Endowments (*Awqaf*).[81]

All preachers of Friday sermons were instructed to speak about 'moderate Islam' and to encourage fathers to protect their sons from exposure to expatriates in an attempt to increase young people's awareness and prevent them from slipping into extremist ideological movements.[82]

A change could even be noticed in the political discourse of the

Ba'th Party, which was founded as a secular party but was moving towards a closer association with the Islamic movements. In addition to its political alliances with Hamas, with the Palestinian Islamic party, and with Hezbollah in Lebanon, it still has special relations with the Turkish Justice and Development Party, the Islamic Labour Front in Jordan, and other Islamic parties. Some of those, like Hamas and the Jordanian Islamic Labour Front, are no more than regional branches of the international Muslim Brotherhood, though the Ba'th Party forbids any affiliation with the Muslim Brotherhood in Syria.

The Ba'th Party also began to celebrate Muslim festivals, such as the anniversary of the birth of the Prophet,[83] and frequently reiterates the need for a nationalist–Islamist alliance 'to face external pressure'.[84]

These policies are no more than part of the containment strategy that the Syrian regime has practised for decades, and through which it aims to gain legitimacy by becoming closer to the most popular movements. It exploits this closeness to ensure, in a new way, the non-return of either the Muslim Brotherhood or their political demands. It is a strategy for survival that consists of building useful alliances against unforeseen circumstances.

The same policy seems to apply when dealing with other religious minorities in Syria. It is well known that Syria contains a plurality of religious sects, denominations and ethnicities. This has greatly affected the nature and balance of the ruling power, which has continuously tried to win the friendship of the different minorities or, at least, to avoid entering into direct conflict with them. For this reason, Syria has not witnessed furious sectarian conflicts like those seen by its close neighbour, Lebanon, during the periods of civil war. Consequently, relations between the different sects in Syria, especially Muslim and Christian ones, have remained good, characterized by respect and mutual friendship, and the political authority continues to support the policy of Muslim–Christian dialogue by organizing many conferences and discussion groups within the concept of 'national unity'.

Conclusion

Accommodating religion has clearly become part of the Syrian regime's strategy. It is, in fact, necessary to ensure its survival in power. Although there is no parallel political discourse trying openly to invest in religion, as there was in more than one Arab country, including Egypt, Algeria and Iraq during the period in which Saddam Hussein was in power, the attitudes and political statements of the Syrian president and government officials are clearly taking an explicit ideological position towards respecting religious sensibilities, as was manifest, for example, during the crisis of the Danish cartoons.

This discourse is unlikely to presage a sweeping return to religious extremism in Syrian society, among either the older or even the younger generation that might have found religious activity a substitute for the political life denied to them. On the other hand, because so many restrictions curtailed so much other social activity, to a greater or lesser degree many people found themselves affected by religious discourse.

As we have said, these manifestations do not necessarily mean an overwhelming presence of political Islam in Syria, especially since the severe repression the Muslim Brotherhood suffered prevents the younger generation from even thinking of joining that movement. The Syrian political system is not expected to allow the movement to return, or for that matter even to improve its internal position. With heightened external pressures on Syria, the regime fears that any step towards reconciliation might be interpreted as a huge political concession. Therefore, internally, political Islam is likely to remain relatively stable, as it has been for the last three decades. This, however, will not prevent the emergence of fundamentalist and extremist groups, which may carry out armed operations from time to time, but they will not have any political or social impact.

Notes

1. Birth of the Third Republic and Establishing Syrian Authoritarianism

1. By the first republic, we mean the time following independence in 1946 until 1958, the year of Syria–Egyptian Unity. Though Syria witnessed many *coups d'état*, no significant change in its political system or structure was recorded, which means that whoever carried out the military coup wanted to legalize the act through parliamentary and constitutional actions, just like Husni al-Zaʾim in his first military coup in March 1949, and Adīb al-Shīshaklī in his *coup d'état* at the end of 1949. The second republic lasted from the Unity in 1958 to 8 March 1963 when the al-Baʿth Party took over power in Syria. Constitutional institutions were established then to imitate rebellious countries in which social democracy took priority over political considerations, and that is justified through 'revolutionary legitimacy'. The Egyptian side insisted on an integrated unity, while Syria 'voluntarily' gave up its multiple political parties, democratic parliament and free journalism. Though Unity only lasted for three years, 1958–61, it deeply affected the perceptions of the political elite in Syria, making it impossible for its members to re-establish constitutional institutions in the 1961–63 period '*Fatrat al-Infiṣāl*' as they were before 1958. Revolutionary malaise would lead to the third republic being formed in 1963 with artificial changes in dealing with power.
2. See Radwan Ziadeh, 'Loss of Constitutional Perception in the Political Education in Syria', *Riwaq Arabi*, no. 45, 2006.
3. Patrick Seale, *The Struggle for Syria: A Study of Post-War Arab Politics, 1945–1958* (London: I.B.Tauris, 1988) p. 65.
4. For more on this see Radwan Ziadeh, *Al-Muthaqqaf Dudd al-Sultah: Hiwarat al-Mujtamaʿ al-Madani fii Suriyya* [*The Intellectual against the Regime: Discussions of Civil Society in Syria*] (Cairo: Cairo Institute for Human Rights Studies, 2005) pp. 46–7.
5. See Muṣṭafá al-Sibāʿī, *ʾIshtirakiyyat al-ʾIslam* [*The Socialism of Islam*] (Damascus: Damascus University Press, 1959).
6. See Muḥammad Musleh, *Al-Jawlan: Al-Tariq ila al-ʾIhtilal* [*The Golan: Path to Occupation*] (Beirut: Palestinian Studies Foundation, 2000). For more on

the same subject, see Moshe Maʿoz, *Syria and Israel: From War to Peacemaking* (Oxford: Clarendon Press, 1995); Itamar Rabinovich, *The Road not Taken: Early Arab-Israeli Negotiations* (New York: Oxford University Press, 1991); Radwan Ziadeh, *Assʿlam Adanie: al-Moufawdat a Suriyya al-israiliaia* [*Approaching Peace: Israeli-Syria Negotiation*] (Beirut: Centre for Arab Unity Studies, 2005).

7. Khaled al-ʿAzem's reservations were not so much about the principle of unity with Egypt, but about the Syrian politicians' rush towards it given that they were such completely different systems – one parliamentary and the other military. Khālid Bakdāsh shared the Soviet Union's reservations. See Khaled al-ʿAzem, *Diary* (Beirut: United Company for Publishing, 1996) part 3.
8. To follow the debate for and against the separation, see Muṣṭafá Ram Hamadani, *Shahid ʿala ʾAhdath Suriyya wa ʿArabiyya wa ʾAsrar al-Infisal* [*A Witness to Syrian and Arab Events and the Secrets of Separation*] (Damascus: Dar Tlas, 2001). Others glorified the separation, calling it an 'Intifada'. See Dr Fuʾad al-ʿAdel, *Qissat Suriyya bayna al-Intikhab wa-l-Inqilab: Taqnin li-l-Fitra ma bayna 1942–1962* [*The Story of Syria between the Elections and the Coup, 1942–1962*] (Damascus: Dar al-Yanabiʿa, 2001).
9. The term 'fragile state' implies the weakness of the state's constitutional, judicial, legislative and executive institutions.
10. ʿAbd Allāh al-ʿArawī, *Mafhūm al-dawlah* [*Concept of the State*] (Beirut: Arab Cultural Centre, 1987).
11. Muḥammad Jamāl Bārūt, *Isteqtabat al-Kuwa Fi al-noukhbaʿ assouria* [*Power Polarization in the Syrian Elite*] (Amman: Dar Sindbad, 2003).
12. Ibid., p. 19.
13. ʿIzz al-Din Diab, *Al-Tahlil al-Ijtimaʿi li-Zhahirat al-Inqisam al-Siyyasi fii al-Watan al-ʿArabi* [*A Social Analysis of the Political Split in the Arab World*] (Cairo: Madbouli Library, 1993) p. 257.
14. For more information, see Bū ʿAlī Yāsīn, 'Arab Socialist Baʿath Party: Establishment and Ideological Development', in Fayṣal Darrāj and Muḥammad Jamāl Baroot (eds) *al-Aḥzāb wa-al-ḥarakāt al-qawmīyah al-ʿArabīyah* [*The Encyclopedia of Arab National Movements and Parties*] (Damascus: The Arabic Centre for Strategic Studies, 2000) vol. 1, pp. 283–6.
15. Ibid., p. 21
16. Ibid, p. 22.
17. For more information, see Muḥammad Ḥaydar, *Al-Baʿth: al-inqisām al-kabīr* [*Al-Baʿth and the Big Division*] (Damascus: Dar al-Ahalie, 1998).
18. Dr Ghassān Salāmah, *Al-Mujtamaʿ wa-l-Dawla fii al-Mashreq al-ʿArabi* [*Society and the State in the Arab Levant: Predicting the Future of the Arab Homeland*] (Beirut: Centre for Arab Unity Studies, 1987) p. 164.

19. Ibid., p. 229.
20. Ibid., pp. 129–30.
21. Diab, *A Social Analysis of the Political Split*, p. 420.
22. Ibid, p. 164.
23. Bārūt, *Power Polarization in the Syrian Elite*, p. 27.
24. See Steven Heydemann, *Authoritarianism in Syria: Institutions and Social Conflict, 1946–1970* (Ithaca: Cornell University Press, 1999); and Raymond Hinnebuch, *Syria: Revolution from Above* (London: Routledge, 2001).
25. Patrick Seale, *Asad of Syria: The Struggle for the Middle East* (Berkeley, CA: University of California Press, 1989).
26. Lucian Peterlan, *Hafez al-Asad: The Career of a Combatant*, translated by Ilias Bdewi (Damascus: Tlas, 1987).
27. See Moshe Ma'oz, *The Sphinx of Damascus: A Political Biography* (New York: Weidenfeld & Nicholson, 1988).
28. Raymond A. Hinnebusch, *Authoritarian Power and state Formation in Ba'thist Syria: Army, Party and Peasant* (Boulder: Westview Press, 1998).
29. Steven Heydemann, *Authoritarianism in Syria.*
30. Hanna Batatu, *Syria's Peasantry, the Descendant of its Lesser Rural Notables, and their Politics* (Princeton: Princeton University Press, 1999).
31. Volker Perthes, *The Political Economy of Syria under Asad* (London: I.B.Tauris, 1995).
32. Eyal Zisser, *Decision Making in Asad's Syria* (Washington, DC: Washington Institute for Near East Policy, 1998); and Eyal Zisser, *Asad's Legacy: Syria in Transition* (London: Hurst & Company, 2001).
33. See Anon, *The 1973 Constitution of the Syrian Arab Republic* (Damascus: Mu'assasat al-Nuri, 2002); also see 'Abd al-Aziz Shehada Mansour, *Al-Mas'ala al-Ma'iyya fii al-Siyasa al-Suriyya Tujah Turkiyya* [*The Issue of Water in Syrian Policy towards Turkey*] (Beirut: Centre for Arab Unity Studies, 2000).
34. Anon, *The 1973 Constitution of the Syrian Arab Republic*. For more on this see Kamal al-Ghali, *Mabade' al-Qanun al-Dustouri wa-l-Nazm al-Siyasiyya* [*Basics of Constitutional Law and Political Regimes*] (Dar al-'Urouba, 1987).
35. For more, see Batatu, *Syria's Peasantry.*
36. Muḥammad Jamāl Bārūt, 'The Ba'th Party in Syria since 1970', in Fayṣal Darrāj and Muḥammad Jamāl Bārūt (eds) *Mawsu'at al-Ahzab wa-l-Harakat al-Qawmiyya al-'Arabiyya* [*The Encyclopedia of Arab Nationalist Movements and Parties*] (Damascus: The Arabic Centre for Strategic Studies, 2000) p. 427; Patrick Seale, *Asad and the Struggle for the Middle East* (London: al-Saqi Press, 1988).
37. Muḥammad Jamal Bārūt, *The Ba'th Party in Syria since 1970*, p. 425.
38. Ibid., p. 432.
39. Perthes, *The Political Economy of Syria under Asad*, pp. 135–40.

40. Ibid., p. 138.
41. Kamel Abu Jaber, *The Arab Ba'th Socialist Party: History, Ideology and Organization* (Syracuse: Syracuse University press, 1966) p. 144.
42. See Ba'th Party, *The Arab Socialist Ba'th Party, Reports and Decisions of the Fifth Exceptional Regional Conference held in Damascus between 30 May and 13 June 1974* (Damascus: Ba'th Party Publications, 1974) p. 33.
43. Ba'th Party, *Arab Socialist Party, Reports of the ninth Regional Conference held between 17 and 20 June 2000* (Damascus: Ba'th Party Publications, 2000) the organizational report.
44. The organizational report of the Arab socialist Ba'th Party, the ninth conference held 17–20 June 2000, p. 57.
45. For more about the history, splits and ideological principles of the Ba'th Party, See Muḥammad Jamāl Bārūt, 'The "Nationalist" Ba'th Party: Origin, Development and Retraction', in Fayṣal Darrāj and Muḥammad Jamāl Bārūt (eds) *Mawsu'at al-Ahzab wa-l-Harakat al-Qawmiyya al-'Arabiyya* [*The Encyclopedia of Arab Nationalist Movements and Parties*] (2 vols, Damascus: Arab Centre for Strategic studies, 2000) vol. 1, pp. 289ff., 366ff.; John F. Devlin, *The Ba'th Party: A History from its Origins to 1966* (Stanford, CA: Hoover Institution Press, 1976) p. 156; Diab, *Social Analysis for the Political Split in the Arab World*; Muḥammad Ḥaydar, *Al-Ba'th: al-inqisām al-kabīr* [*Al-Ba'th and the Big Division*]; Pirch Pirproglo, *Disturbance in the Middle East: Imperialism, War and Instability*, translated by Fakhri Labib, revised by Naser al-Safadi (Cairo: High Council of Culture, 2002); Itamar Rabinovich, *Syria under the Ba'th, 1963–66: The Army Party Symbiosis* (Jerusalem: Israel University Press, 1972); David Roberts, *The Ba'th and the Creation of Modern Syria* (New York: St Martin's Press, 1987); Muta' al-Safadi, *Hizb al-Ba'th: ma'sat al-mawlid, ma'sat al-nihaya* [*Ba'th Party: The Tragedy of Beginning and Ending*] (Beirut: Dar al-Adab, 1964); Naṣr Shamālī, *Ayyām ḥāsimah fī tārīkh al-Ba'th* [*Critical Days in the History of the Party*] (Damascus: Al-Wahdah, 1969).
46. Refer to the organizational report of the Socialist Arab Ba'th Party, the seventh regional conference (*almout 'amar al-quṭrī*), pp. 15ff., 30ff.
47. See Patrick Seale, *Asad and the Struggle for the Middle East*, pp. 439 ff.
48. Radwan Ziadeh, 'The Limits of "the Syrian Reform": The Mechanism of Power Transition and Change Stakes', in Radwan Ziadeh (ed.) *Al-iṣlāḥ fī Sūriyah bayna al-siyāsāt al-dākhilīyah wa-al-taḥawwulāt al-iqlīmīyah wa-al-duwalīyah* [*Reform in Syria between Internal Policies and International and Regional Transformations*] (Jeddah: Al-Raya Centre for Intellectual Development, 2005) p. 95.
49. For more about the role of both regional (*quṭrī*) and national (*qawmi*) leaderships and the conflict between the two, see Muḥammad Jamāl Bārūt, 'The Ba'th Party in Syria since 1970', vol. 2, pp. 450 ff.

50. Volker Perthes, *The Political Economy of Syria under Asad*, p. 157.
51. Ibid., p. 158.
52. For more see Middle East Watch Committee (ed.) *Syria Unmasked: The Suppression of Human Rights by the Regime* (New Haven: Yale University Press, 1991).
53. The state of emergency was imposed on Syria by military command no. 2 issued from the national council of the revolutionary leadership on 8 March 1963. Security organizations and administrative authorities had benefited from wide powers originally outside their sphere of competence. This situation imposed wide-ranging fetters on informational, political, personal and other kinds of freedoms, since it led to the passing of anti-revolutionary laws. Legislative decree no. 6 of 7 January 1965 passed a law to create a field court martial (legislative decree no. 109) on 17 August 1968, which is considered exceptional. Legislative decree no. 14 of 15 January 1969, which originated in the state security administration, created numerous security and intelligence departments, whose functions frequently overlapped. Article 16 of this law protects security personnel from prosecution if they commit torture, though it describes them as crimes because this same article states: 'Any one of the personnel working in state security shall not be prosecuted for crimes they commit during or on the occasion of carrying out the assignments with which they are charged except according to a prosecuting command issued from the director.' All these laws remained in effect despite the operative constitution issued on 3 March 1973. For more, see Razan Zeitouneh, *Can Extraordinary Courts Ensure Justice: Supreme State Security Court in Syria* (Damascus: Centre for Human Rights Studies, December 2007).
54. See Alan George, *Syria: Neither Bread nor Freedom* (London: Zed Books, 2003) pp. 2-3.
55. Perthes, *The Political Economy of Syria under Asad*, pp. 141–5.
56. Ziadeh, 'The Limits of "the Syrian Reform"', pp. 84–5.
57. Lisa Wedeen, *Ambiguities of Domination: Politics, Rhetoric, and Symbols in Contemporary Syria* (Chicago: University of Chicago Press, 1999).
58. When Asad died Syria had had only seven ambassadors in more than 60 Syrian embassies abroad. Foreign Minister Farouk al-Shar'a had appointed consuls instead of ambassadors because the latter are likely to be as equally competent as the republic's president.
59. Perthes, *The Political Economy of Syria under Asad*, pp. 162–6. See also the Charter of the Nationalist Progressive Front (Damascus, 7 March 1972).
60. Muḥammad Jamāl Bārūt, 'The Origins and Path of the Syrian Muslim Brotherhood', in Fayṣal Darrāj and Muḥammad Jamāl Bārūt (eds)

Mawsuʿat al-Ahzab wa-l-Harakat al-Qawmiyya al-ʿArabiyya [*The Encyclopedia of Arab Parties and Nationalist Movements*] (Damascus: The Arab Centre for Strategic Studies, 2001) vol. 1, p. 432.

61. The NPF parties have become inherited familial parties subsisting on politics, since all of them witnessed a kind of struggle on the succession of their originator, as well as various splits. Generally, the Syrians find it very difficult to keep up with these parties, or even to remember their names.
62. George, *Syria*, pp. 86–9; Perthes, *The Political Economy of Syria under Asad*, pp. 162–86.
63. Middle East Watch Committee (ed.) *Syria Unmasked*, pp. 163–85.
64. The law (Act 49) was issued on 7 July 1980. In April 1982 the official paper (no. 17) published the discussions of the People's Assembly regarding this law.
65. Seale, *Asad and the Struggle for the Middle East*, p. 533.
66. Middle East Watch Committee (ed.) *Syria Unmasked*, p. 319.
67. Baʿth Party, *Arab Socialist Party, Reports and Decisions of the Seventh Regional Conference* (*almout ʿamar al-quṭrī*) (Damascus: Baʿth Party Publications, 1980) political report, p. 25.
68. Robert Fisk, *The Times* (London) 19 February 1982. Robert Fisk was the first foreign reporter who visited the city of Hama after the violent battles that had been carried out there. In his report he estimated the number of casualties to be about 12,000. To know the viewpoint of the Muslim Brotherhood, one can consult the book entitled *Magzaraʿt Hamah* [*The Massacre of Hama*] (Cairo: no publisher, n.d.) and *Hama: The Tragedy of the Period*, which was published by the National Alliance for liberating Syria, an assembly of a number of parties and opposing political personalities living abroad which was announced in 1982. See also Thomas Friedman, *From Beirut to Jerusalem* (New York: Farrar, Straus & Giroux, 1989) pp. 76–105; Raymond Hinnebusch, *Authoritarian Power and State Formation in Baʿthist Syria*, pp. 291–300; Fred H. Lawson, *Social Bases for the Hama Revolt*, Merip Reports, November/December 1982, pp. 24–8; al-Ḥabīb al-Janhani, 'The Islamic Wakefulness in Greater Syria: The Syrian Example', in Anon, *Contemporary Islamic Movement in the Arab Homeland* (Beirut: Centre for Arab Unity Studies, 1987); David Roberts, *The Baʿth and the Creation of Modern Syria*, p. 128; Maḥmūd Ṣādiq, *Ḥiwār ḥawla Sūriyah* [*A Dialogue about Syria*] (Cairo: no publisher, n.d.) pp. 166–7; Seale, *Asad and the Struggle for the Middle East*, pp. 537–40; the most prominent book in this regard written in French by Michel Seurat, *L'État de Barbarie* (Paris: Éditions du Seuil, 1989); Nikolaos van Dam, *The Struggle for Power in Syria: Politics and Society Under Asad and the Baʿth Party* (London: I.B.Tauris, 1996) pp. 165–72.

69. Violate Daguerre (ed.) *Democracy and Human Rights in Syria*, translated by Zayna Larbi (Paris: Arab Commission for Human Rights and European Commission, Europe Publishers, 2000).
70. See Anon, 'Arrests in Syria Focusing on the Islamic Liberation Party exceeds more than 800 Persons', *al-Hayat*, editorial (London) 4 January 2000.
71. See the report of Human Rights Association in Syria, 2003.
72. Volker Perthes argues that economic affairs had never much interested President Asad, for he was concerned primarily with political issues such as defence, home security and foreign policy, as well as supervising the oil situation and the media. He regarded economic policies as secondary matters with which he personally dealt only insofar as they served his immediate political objectives. He exemplified this by cutting electricity supplies, which the Syrian electricity board called 'rationing', which in the late 1980s and early 1990s led to widespread public discontent and an economic impasse in the Syrian industrial sector, particularly in faraway cities and governorates where the cuts sometimes lasted for up to 20 hours a day. The city of Damascus was not immune from this crisis. When, on 13 September 1993, al-Asad accidentally heard about this at one of the periodic meetings of the National Progressive Front, which he rarely attended, he declared that electricity was a most important issue and getting access to it was the right of every citizen. Within only two weeks new generators had been installed, external finance had been secured and the establishment of a common sector for producing electricity had been legalized by the government, thereby breaking a state monopoly of this industry since 1963. See Sawsan Khalifah, 'Personal Concern of President Asad, Electricity Sector: From Meeting the Local Need to Exportation', *Al-Thawra* (Damascus) 28 January 1999; Volker Perthes, *The Political Economy of Syria under Asad*, pp. 218–20.
73. President Asad issued legislative decree no. 24 in September 1986 which came to be known as the law of currency smuggling that imposed hard penalties on anyone who illegally dealt in foreign currency. For more information about the economic crisis of 1986, see Nabil Sucker, 'The Crisis of 1986 and Syrian Plan for Reform', in Eberhard Kienle (ed.) *Contemporary Syria: Liberalization between Cold War and Cold Peace* (London: British Academic Press, 1994) pp. 26–43.
74. Volker Perthes, *The Political Economy of Syria under Asad*, p. 54. In 1986 Syria reached a period of partial openness, particularly with regard to the agricultural sector, and joint-stock agricultural companies were allowed to operate at a time when this sector had previously been

wholly monopolized by the government. A second phase of openness occurred in 1990 when investment policy was opened up and private production encouraged, particularly in industry. This gave immigrants special rights to import certain prohibited goods into the country and some private-sector merchants were given permission to import consumer goods previously monopolized by the government such as rice, sugar, tea and fat, though the government retained its monopoly to trade with some agricultural products such as cotton, wheat and sugar beet.

75. Bārūt, 'The Ba'th Party in Syria since 1970', p. 450. For more information about the organizational development of al-Ba'th and the network of political and military elites in it, see Batatu, *Syria's Peasantry*. This book is the best source on the rural and social origins of the Ba'th Party in Syria, whether in the context of its political or military elite.
76. Ibid., p. 167. See also Belal al-Hasan, 'The Ba'th Party and Economic Decisions', al-*Hayat* (London) 7 December 2000.
77. Bassam Haddad, 'The Formation and Development of Economic Networks in Syria: Implications for Economic and Fiscal Reform, 1986–2000', in Steven Heydemann (ed.) *Networks of Privilege in the Middle East: The Politics of Economic Reform Revisited* (New York: Palgrave Macmillan, 2004) pp. 37–75.
78. See Nader Kabbani and Noura Kamel, *Youth Exclusion in Syria: Social, Economic and Industrial Dimensions* (Middle East Youth Initiative, Wolfensohn Centre for Development at Brookings Institution and Dubai School for Government, working paper no. 4, September 2007).
79. See UNDP National Human Development Report, *Education and Human Development: Towards Better Efficiency* (Council of Ministers, UN Development Programme, 2005).
80. Volker Perthes, *The Political Economy of Syria under Asad*, p. 61.
81. See Heydemann, *Authoritarianism in Syria*, pp. 84–105; Hinnebusch, *Syria: Revolution from Above*, pp. 89–114; Raymond A. Hinnebusch, *Authoritarian Power and State Formation in Ba'thist Syria: Army, Party and Peasant* (Boulder: Westview Press).
82. Perthes, *The Political Economy of Syria under Asad*, pp. 170–3.
83. For more about this, consult Hinnebusch's pioneering research on the revolutionary Youth Federation and its role in Ba'thist social recruitment. Raymond Hinnebusch, 'Political Recruitment and Socialization in Syria: The Case of the Revolutionary Youth Federation', *International Journal of Middle East Studies*, vol. 11, 1980, pp. 143–74.
84. Raymond Hinnebusch, 'State and Civil Society in Syria', *Middle East Journal*, vol. 47, no. 2, spring 1993, pp. 243–57.

85. Perthes, *The Political Economy of Syria under Asad*, pp. 168–71.
86. Volker Perthes, 'Private Sector, Economic Liberation and the Possibilities of Moving towards Democracy', in Ghasan Salāmah (ed.) *Democracy Without Democrats: Politics Openness in the Islamic Arab World* (Beirut: Centre for Arab Unity Studies, 1995) p. 335.
87. See Radwan Ziadeh, 'Istishrāf mustaqbal al-ḥayāh al-siyāsīyah wa-quwá al-mujtama' al-madanī fī Sūriyah' ['Overlooking the Horizons of Political Life and Forces of Civil Society in Syria'], in UNDP, *An Overview of Development Tendencies in Syria* (Damascus: UNDP in cooperation with the Syrian State Planning Corps, 2005).
88. See Fā'iq 'Alī Ḥuwayjah, *Maḥaṭṭāt tārīkhīyah fī al-Dustūr* [*Historical Development of the Constitution: A Comparative Analytical Study*] (Damascus: University School of Law, 2005).
89. For more, see Yāsīn al-Ḥāfiẓ, *Ḥawla ba'ḍ qaḍāyā al-thawrah al-'Arabīyah* [*About Some Issues of the Arab Revolution*] (Damascus: al-Hasad, 1997); Yāsīn al-Ḥāfiẓ, *The Defeat and the Defeated Ideology* (Damascus: al-Hasad, 1997).
90. This applies particularly to the political bureau of the Communist Party or what is known as the Riyāḍ al-Turk wing. For more about this see 'Abd Allāh Turkmani, *Al-Ahzab al-Shiyu'iyya fii al-Mashreq al-'Arabi wa-l-Mas'ala al-Qawmiyya fii al-'Ashriniyyat ila Harb al-Khalij al-Thaniya* [*Communist Parties in the Levant and Arab Nationalism, 1920s–Second Gulf War*] (Beirut: al-Aan Press, 2002) pp, 709–20, 733–40.

2. Inheriting Syria from Father to Son: Hafez al-Asad's Last Days

1. All these quotations are from Hafez al-Asad's speech before the Syrian Parliament on the occasion of taking the constitutional oath on 11 March 1999. See *al-Monadel*, the Ba'th Party's internal magazine, no. 295, March–April 1999.
2. Hesham al-Dedjani, 'What does Modernization Mean in Syria and Who are its Agents?', *an-Nahar* (Beirut) 30 March 1999; Hesham al-Dedjani, 'Combating Corruption and Modernizing Laws are the Highest Priority of Reform', *al-Hayat* (London) 27 May 1999; Ismail Jradat, 'Modernization is a Patriot Duty', *al-Thawra* (Damascus) 13 March 1999; Ibrāhīm Muḥammad, 'Reform is the Priority in Education and Judiciary Sectors', *al-Hayat* (London) 9 June 1999; Mahmoud Salameh, 'Reform and Modernization in the Plurality-Based National Scene', *al-Hayat* (London) 4 June 1999; Imad Faozi Sho'aibi, 'Combating and Changing Corruption in Syria', *al-Hayat* (London) 4 June 1999; Joseph Smaha, 'The Needs, Pace and Forces of Change in Syria', *al-Hayat*, London (14–15 May 1999) which concentrated primarily on combating the corruption associated with

Bashar al-Asad's rise and induced wide debate. In any case, these open debates were rare, especially as far as the internal concern in Syria is concerned. See also *al-Hayat* (London) 8 May 1999. The official newspapers started to talk about corruption as a 'cancer' that must be combated, see *Tishreen* (Damascus) 3 May 1999) and *al-Thawra* (Damascus) 6 May 1999.

3. Riyāḍ Sayf and ʿĀrif Dalīlah were arrested during the so-called 'Damascus Spring' of September 2001. Sayf was sentenced to five years imprisonment on charges of attempting to change the state constitution by illegal means, disrupt state institutions, and spread false news that would weaken the nation in wartime, while Dalīlah was sentenced to ten years on the same charges.
4. *Al-Hayat* (London) 3 and 5 July 1998; *al-Majalah Magazine*, no. 963, 26 July–1 August 1998, pp. 22–3; and Zisser, *Asad's Legacy*, pp. 166–7.
5. *Al-Wasat*, London, no. 337, 19 July 1998, pp. 5.
6. *Al-Hayat*, London, 24 September 1999.
7. *Al-Hayat*, London, 14 June 1999.
8. Bashar al-Asad visited Saudi Arabia and met King Fahd and Crown Prince Abdullah, *an-Nahar*, Beirut, 13 July 1999; Kuwait where he met the Kuwaiti Prince Sheikh Jaber al-Ahmad, *al-Itehad*, Abu Dhabi, 24 August 1999; the UAE where he met the president of the UAE Sheikh Zayed; Bahrain where he met Crown Prince Salman Bin Hamad, *al-Hayat*, London, 14 November 1999; Iran and Egypt, *al-Hayat*, London, 3 November 1999. The first Western country he visited was France, where former President Jacques Chirac received him warmly and where he attracted rare media interest, *al-Hayat*, London, 7–8 November 1999. See also Michael Janson, 'Bashar in Paris', *Middle East International*, no. 612, 12 November 1999. His visits to Beirut, however, started in 1995, but they were not publicized until 1996, *Al-Hayat*, London, 24 June 1997; and *Tishreen*, Damascus, 26 December 1998.
9. See, for example, *al-Baʿth*, Damascus, 13 July 1996, when the newspaper, on the first page, highlighted Bashar al-Asad's visit to Saudi Arabia and meeting with the late King Fahd. Mounaf Tlass, the former defence minister, was his permanent companion on those visits and later became an officer with the rank of staff colonel in the Republican Guard.
10. The first interview with Bashar al-Asad was with the newspaper *al-Kefah al-Arabi* (Beirut) 4 February 1999; then with *al-Wasat*, no. 395, 23–29 August 1999. These interviews attracted interest and comment by Syrian newspapers, See Asʾad Abboud, 'We All Hope and Wait', *al-Thawra* (Damascus) 20 February 1999; Burhan Bukhari, 'It is Our Issues First and Foremost', *Tishreen* (Damascus) 29 August 1999.

11. Benjamin Orbach and David Schenker, *The Rise of Bashar al-Asad* (Washington: Institute for Near East Policy, Policy Watch, no. 371, 5 March 1999).
12. *Al-Hayat*, London, 3 January 1999. Bashar al-Asad had exceptionally been promoted from major to staff colonel after completing the staff course and receiving a first-class degree for presenting a 'distinct' essay in the military sciences entitled 'Quality in Military Practice', which became part of a course taught to the Syrian military forces.
13. *Al-Sharq al-Awsat*, London, 16 November 1999. Also, *al-Quds al-Arabi*, London, no. 4, November 1999, p. 24.
14. *Al-Hayat*, London, 25 February 1999. See also Salim Nassar, 'Why Hafez al-Asad Suddenly Decided to Participate in King Hussein's Funeral', *al-Hayat*, London, 13 February 1999.
15. *Al-Hayat*, London, 21 April 1999. See also King Abdullah II's interview with *al-Hayat*, London, 12 May 1999.
16. *Al-Hayat*, London, 27 March 1999. The gradual openness to Iraq began during the rule of Saddam Hussein, towards whom al-Asad had maintained a personal animosity. In May 1997 the first overture was made when a Syrian economic delegation visited Baghdad to discuss joint projects. In turn, the chairperson of the Federation of Trade visited Damascus in July of the same year. Syria was given priority in relation to certain contracts, which was considered to be an obvious political coup at that time (*al-Hayat*, London, 18 July 1997). The contracts were worth up to $70 million, which was reflected in the Syrian officials' dialogues. See ʿAbd al-Ḥalīm Khaddām, the Syrian vice president's interview in *al-Hayat*, London, 18 July 1997. For more details, see *al-Wasat*, no. 270, 31 March 1997.
17. *Al-Hayat*, London, 26 March 1999. These agreements were signed following the visit of Salīm Yāsīn, then deputy prime minister for economic affairs, to Turkey on 23 March 1999. In October 1998, the Syrian–Turkish crisis had reached boiling point with Turkey threatening to launch a military campaign against Syria unless the latter withdrew its support from the Kurdistan Workers Party (PKK) and closed the party's offices on its territory. In an immediate response, al-Asad expelled Abdullah Ojalan and closed the active PKK camps in Lebanon and Syria. With the signing of the Adana Convention on 21 October 1998, the crisis was defused. The convention's provisions focus on security arrangements regarding the interaction of Syria with the PKK. See the Convention text: www.mfa.gov.tr/group
18. See *Al-Hayat* (London) 14 May 1999. See also the final joint Syrian–Iranian statement in *As-Safir*, Beirut, 17 May 1999, which emphasized

provisional support for al-Moqawama (Resistance) and rejection of 'normalization' with Israel. For more details, see Anon, 'Khatami in Damascus', editorial, *an-Nour Magazine*, no. 97, June 1999, pp. 17–18.

19. See Dennis Ross, *The Missing Peace: The Inside Story of the Fight for Middle East Peace* (New York: Farrar, Straus & Giroux, 2004); see also Radwan Ziadeh, *Approaching Peace*.
20. Eyal Zisser, *Syria's Asad: The Approach of a Fifth Term of Office* (Washington: Institute of Near East Policy, Policy Watch, no. 366, 6 February 1999).
21. *Al-Hayat* (London) 20 February 2000.
22. This phrase was first reported by Major General Muṣṭafá Ṭalās, the minister of defence, in one of his television interviews.
23. *Al-Ba'th* (Damascus) 14 March 2000; *As-Safir* (Beirut) 14 March 2000; and *al-Hayat* (London) 14 March 2000.
24. *Al-Hayat* (London) 29 March 2000; see also Abdul Ra'ouf al-Kafri, 'The New Syrian Government between Constancy and Change', *al-Shahr*, no. 83, May 2000, pp 22–3.
25. *Al-Hayat* (London) 26 April 2000; and see also *al-Hayat* (London) 9 May 2000.
26. *Al-Hayat* (London) 13 July 2000; *al-Hayat* (London) 14 July 2000; and *al-Hayat* (London) 19 July 2000.
27. *Al-Hayat* (London) 10 July 2000; *al-Hayat* (London) 19 July 2000 and *al-Hayat* (London) 22 July 2000.
28. In June 1998 French television asked al-Asad if he were preparing his son for his succession. 'No', he said, 'I do not prepare him to succeed me and I have never heard him say anything about this subject. It seems that these sayings repeated about him come from the fact that he is active as well as loved and highly estimated by his friends. As for succession there is nothing in our constitution and laws that gives the relative the right to succession, and I remember that he was asked more than once and denied this thing. However, he is free and my answer in short is that there is no preparation for succession.' What is worth mentioning is that al-Asad was asked in the same interview about what he would like his successor to take from him and he answered: 'I would like him to be straight and fight against corruption.' See al-Asad's discussion with the first channel of the French television in *al-Ba'th* (Damascus) 16 July 1998.
29. *Al-Hayat* (London) 11 May 2000; and *As-Safir* (Beirut) 12 May 2000.
30. *Al-Hayat* (London) 23 May 2000; and see 'How and Why Did al-Ze'bi Commit Suicide?' *Al-Muharrer News* (Beirut) 2–8 June 2000; and also al-Ze'bi put an end to his life according to the 'Perokovwa' scenario, *al-Shira*, June 2000; Hisham al-Dajani, 'What is Going on in Present Day Syria?' *an-Nahar* (Beirut) 26 May 2000.
31. Later on they were sentenced to ten years' imprisonment and given a

large penalty on the charge of having received bribes, *As-Safir* (Beirut) 8 December 2001; *al-Hayat* (London) 9 December 2001; and *al-Ittihad* (Abu Dhabi) 9 December 2001.

32. *Al-Hayat* (London) 2 June 2000.
33. *Tichreen* (Damascus) 4 June 2000; *al-Sharq al-Awsat* (London) 5 June 2000; and *As-Safir* (Beirut) 9 June 2000. In August 2002 al-Najjār died in prison after a fine of a billion Syrian pounds (US$ 20 million dollars) had been imposed on him.
34. See Ibrāhīm Ḥumaydī, 'The Ba'th Conference Lays the Foundations of the Ongoing Change Option', *al-Wasat*, no. 427, 12 June 2000; Haitham Manna, 'The Democratic Option in Syria', *al-Hayat* (London) 11 June 2000; Imad Naddaf, 'On the Margin of the Ninth Conference: The Peculiarity of the Syrian Ba'th', *al-Hayat* (London) 21 May 2000; Ayman Abdul Noor, 'What is Required from the Ninth Regional Conference: To Envisage the Economic Future of Syria', *al-Muharrer News* (Beirut) no. 247, 9–15 June 2000; Karim al-Shibani, 'What Do the Syrians Want from the Ninth Conference of the Ba'th Party?', *As-Safir* (Beirut) 6 June 2000.
35. Hinnebusch, *Syria: Revolution from Above*, pp. 47–64.
36. *Al-Quds al-Arabi* (London) 5 and 6 June 1999.
37. *Al-Wasat* (London) no. 367, 8 February 1999, pp. 10–11.
38. *Al-Mustaqbal* (Beirut) 10 April 2000. Western and Arab journalists started to talk with great confidence about a possible role for the Syrian president's son in succeeding his father.
39. In an interview with *al-Hayat* on the occasion of retiring from his position as minister of defence, which he had occupied for 34 years, he spoke openly about this subject, see dialogue in *al-Hayat* (London) 21 May 2004.
40. In November 1999 General Asef Shawkat had a difference of opinion with Maher al-Asad and the latter shot Shawkat, who was treated in Paris. See Anon, 'Assef Shawkat', editorial, *Middle East Intelligence Bulletin*, vol. 2, no. 6, 1 July 2000; Eyal Zisser, *Where is Asad? The Renewed Struggle for Succession in Syria* (Washington, DC: Institute of Near East Policy, Policy Watch, no. 234, 14 December 1999).
41. See Patrick Seale, 'From Father to Son: The New Regime in Syria', *al-Hayat* (London) 12 June 2000. After that Bahjat Sulaymān headed the internal security branch of general intelligence before being expelled at the end of 2004 in the wake of the assassination of Rafiq al Hariri, the former Lebanese prime minister.
42. *Al-Hayat* (London) 12 June 2000, see the texts of the two legislative decrees in *al-Munadel*, no. 302, June 2000, pp. 16–17.
43. *Al-Hayat* (London) 21 June 2000.

44. *Al-Hayat* (London) 12 July 2000.
45. Volker Perthes, 'The Political Economy of the Syrian Succession', *Survival*, no. 1, Spring 2001, pp. 143–5.
46. *Al-Hayat* (London) 13 June 2000. In one of his speeches at the Arab-American Institute Clinton offered his condolences to the Syrian people on al-Asad's death, and called on Dr Bashar to continue supporting the peace process, *al-Hayat* (London) 15 June 2000.
47. *Al-Hayat* (London) 14 June 2000.
48. See Yossi Baidatz, *Bashar's First Year: From Ophthalmology to a National Vision* (Washington, DC: Washington Institute for Near East Policy, Policy Focus 41, July 2001); Volker Perthes, *The Political Economy of the Syrian Succession*, pp. 143–154; Eyal Zisser, 'Will Bashar al-Asad Rule?', *Middle East Quarterly*, vol. 7, no. 3, September 2000; Eyal Zisser, 'Does Bashar al-Asad Rule Syria?' *Middle East Quarterly*, vol. 10, no. 1, winter 2003.
49. For more information on the country's leadership and on the central committee members who emerged from the ninth national conference, see *al-Munadel* (the internal magazine of the Arab Socialist Baʿth Party) no. 302, May–June 2002, pp. 83–6.
50. See the memo of the party's national leadership no. 1075 of 17 February 2001, which described intellectual opponents and civil society activists as being hell bent on 'destruction, weakening the state and creating a state of disorder and indiscipline', adding that 'they are hateful and collaborators' (*al-Munadel*, no. 306, January–February 2001, pp. 45–52).
51. Flynt Leverett, *Inheriting Syria: Bashar's Trial by Fire* (Washington, DC: Brookings Institution Press, 2005) pp. 57–98. See, also, the decrees and laws issued in the first year of Bashar al-Asad's rule in Anon, *al-Sana al-Oula fi tareq altatweer wa altahdeeth* [*The First Year on the Way to Development and Modernization*] (Damascus: Tishreen Foundation Press and Publication, 2001); also Anon, *Syria 2000: A General Study on the Syrian Arab Republic* (Damascus: National Information Centre, 2001).
52. Ibid, p. 167. See also Belal al-Hasan, 'Baʿth Party and Economic Decrees', *al-Hayat* (London) 12 July 2001.
53. Haddad, 'The Formation and Development of Economic Networks in Syria', pp. 37–75.
54. For more information about the 'Damascus Spring', see George, *Syria*. See also Radwan Ziadeh (ed.) *Min Agel Mojtamaʿ Madanie fi Syria* [*For a Civil society in Syria: National Dialogues Forum*] (Paris: Arab Committee for Human Rights, 2003); and Radwan Ziadeh, *Rabeaa Dimisheq: Itejehat-tayarat-Nihayat* [*Damascus Spring: Issues-Trends-Results*] (Cairo: Cairo Institute for Human Rights, 2007).

55. Alan Makovsky, *Syria under Bashar al-Asad: The Domestic Scene and the 'Chinese Model' of Reform* (Washington: Institute for Near East Policy, Policy Watch, no. 512, 17 January 2001).
56. See Bashar al-Asad interview with the Greek television channel ART in *Tishreen*, Damascus, 15 December 2003.
57. To look into the decrees, laws and legislations issued during the term of President Bashar al-Asad, see Anon, *Arbaa sanwat baʿad bidaet al-theqaa* [*Four Years After the Confident Starting Off*] (Damascus: Tishreen Foundation for Press and Publication, 2004).
58. See President Bashar al-Asad's interviews with *al-Hayat* (London) 7 October 2003, and the *New York Times*, 1 December 2003.
59. David W. Lesch, *The New Lion of Damascus: Bashar al-Asad and Modern Syria* (New Haven: Yale University Press, 2005) pp. 57–80; Flynt Leverett, *Inheriting Syria*, pp. 57–98.
60. Christine Binzel, Tilman Brück and Lars Handrich, 'The Progress of Economic Reform in Syria', paper presented at the Centre for Syrian Studies conference, 10–12 April 2008, St Andrews, UK; Aurora Sottimano, 'Ideology and Discourse in the Era of Baʿthist Reforms', paper presented at the Centre for Syrian Studies conference, 10–12 April 2008, St Andrews, UK.
61. *Newsweek*, Arabic edition, 16–21 August 2007.
62. Søren Schmidt, 'The Developmental Role of the State in the Middle East', paper presented at the Centre for Syrian Studies conference, 10–12 April 2008, St Andrews, UK; Kjetil Selvik, 'Syria's Turn to the Private Sector', paper presented at the Centre for Syrian Studies conference, 10–12 April 2008, St Andrews, UK.
63. See Baʿth Party, *Arab Socialist Party, Reports of the Ninth Regional Conference (almout ʿamar al-quṭrī) held between 17 and 20 of June 2000.*
64. Anon, 'Almalaf al-Kamel al-Azab wa al-Harakat al-Seyasia fi Souria' ['The Contemporary Political Parties and Movements in Syria'], *White and Black Magazine*, vol. 3, no. 129, 30 May 2005, pp. 81–9.
65. *Al-Zaman*, London, 12 May 2001.
66. Anon, 'The Contemporary Political Parties and Movements in Syria', pp. 81–3.
67. See Muḥammad Jamāl Bārūt, 'Booty Mind and Reform Thinking', *Orient News Web Site*, 17 October 2002.
68. See *al-Hayat* (London) 19 July 2000; Ebrahim Hemaidi, 'Permission to Issue Open Newspapers Poses Three New Challenges to the Front Parties', *al-Hayat* (London) 16 December 2000; Imad Naddaf, 'Factious Press and its Need to be Studied', *al-Hayat* (London) 16 December 2000; Nasr al-Deen al-Bahra, 'The Significance of Allowing Syrian Parties to

Issue Open Newspapers', *al-Hayat* (London) 16 December 2000; *Araie al-Aaa'm* (Kuwait) 6 August 2000.

69. See *al-Hayat* (London) 10 February 2007; on political party law see Radwan Ziadeh, 'The Promised Political Party Law', *al-Watan* (Damascus) 9 January 2007.
70. Perthes, *The Political Economy of Syria under Asad*, pp. 168–71.
71. For more on Riyāḍ Sayf and his parliamentary role, see the reports submitted to the People's Assembly, the Sixth Legislative Turn (1994–98); Riyāḍ Sayf, *Experience: Concerns for Industry and Policy* (Damascus: Limited Edition, 1999). And on the transaction over mobile phone contracts, see the report he submitted to the People's Assembly, namely Riyāḍ Sayf, *Ṣafqat ʿuqūdal-khalawī* [*Transaction of Cellular Contracts*] (Damascus: Limited Edition, 2001). On his role in establishing the Forum for National Dialogue, which initiated the so-called 'Damascus Spring', see Ziadeh, *For a Civil Society in Syria.*
72. *Al-Mustaqbal* (Beirut) 6 March 2003; regarding 'the unofficial percentage', see *Orient News* website, 7 March 2003; on opposition and the Kurdish parties that boycotted the elections, see Levant news website (www.thisissyria.net), 24 February 2003, and *an-Nahar* (Beirut) 6 March 2003. For more information, see Ibrahim Makhus, 'The Previous (Elections) in Syria and the State of Continuous Blockage', *Orient News* website, 15 April 2003.
73. This happened more than once with former chairman of the People's Assembly, ʿAbd al-Qādir Qaddūrah, whose name Damascus people would strike off the Baʿth Party's list, but who would get the highest number of votes in the final 'official' results.
74. See Radwan Ziadeh, 'Political Regime in Syria: Elections without Electors', *Democracy Magazine*, no. 28, 2007. This can be measured in various ways. On asking a random sample of Syrians, or taxi drivers who are representative of the man in the street, you get the same answer, 'I shall not vote for anybody', 'they all work for their own interests', 'what shall I get out of it?' Some will tell you that they have never voted or elected a candidate. One can also view Syrians' comments on the Internet, which is a real and free port for them to comment and express themselves; one can sense their views from the political jokes they make.
75. See Radwan Ziadeh, 'The Coming Election Year', *al-Watan* (Damascus) 27 November 2006; Radwan Ziadeh, 'People's Assembly and the Election Law', *al-Watan* (Damascus) 4 December 2006.
76. See *Tishreen* (Damascus) 11 April 2007. It mentioned that the number of candidates in a big governorate like Rural Damascus never exceeds 128, that 562 of the 700 candidates were from the Baʿth Party, and that they

were all standing on 'party orders'. Ba'thist candidates withdraw their applications if the Ba'th Party's national leadership does not select them. Thus, though the governorate's population exceeds 1.5 million according to official figures, there are only 128 candidates, even though the governorate contains several major cities, such as Douma, Darayya, at-Tal, Qatana, Yabroud, an-Nabk, Quteifeh, Zabadani, Erbin, Jaramana, Mleiha, Kiswah and Qudssayya, so includes industrial and agricultural populations. Knowing that no one has stood as an independent candidate in those elections, and that the others depend on tribal support to win a seat in the People's Assembly, we realize why participation is so low in the parliamentary elections.

3. Damascus Spring: The Rise of the Opposition in Syria

1. Perthes, *The Political Economy of Syria under Asad.*
2. In Arabic, 'Moukhatat'.
3. See 'The Attitude of Syrian Intellectuals Towards the Peace Test', *an-Nahar* newspaper supplement (Beirut) 29 April 2000; and Hisham Dajani, 'Voices in Syrian Public Opinion and the Strange Silence towards the Peace Issue', *al-Hayat* (London) 9 February 2000.
4. See Radwan Ziadeh, 'Muntadá al-Ḥiwār al-Waṭanī: al-takwīn al-ijtimā'ī wa-al-ḥarāk al-siyāsī' ['The Forum of National Dialogue: The Social Component and the Political Movement'], in Radwan Ziadeh, *Min ajl mujtama'madanī fī Sūriyah* [*Towards a Civil Society in Syria*] (Paris: Arab Committee for Human Rights, Arab European Publication Association, 2004) pp. 7–26.
5. See Abdel Razzaq Eid, 'Civil Society in Syria: From Association of Friends to Committees of Revival', *al-Adaab Magazine*, nos 1–2, January and February 2001.
6. Ibrāhīm Ḥumaydī, 'The Story of the "Principal Document" for the Committees of Civil Society in Syria', *al-Hayat*, London, 21 January 2001. See, the full text of the communiqué in *Riwaq Arabbi*, no. 20, 2000.
7. See text of the communiqué in *As-Safir* newspaper (Beirut) 27 September 2000, and *al-Hayat* (London) 27 September 2000.
8. See Bilal Khbiz, 'Memorandum of the 99 Intellectuals of Syria', *an-Nahar* supplement (Beirut) 7 October 2000; Samir Qaseer, 'Syria Alive', *an-Nahar*, 29 September 2000; Mohamad al-Rumayhie, 'The Ambition to Change in Syria', *an-Nahar* (Beirut) 2 October 2000.
9. See *al-Thawra* (Damascus) 16 October 2000.
10. Radwan Ziadeh, 'Traffic in Syrian Policy', *an-Nahar* supplement (Beirut) 17 July 2001.

11. *Al-Zaman* (London) 15 November 2000; Ibrahim Ḥumaydī, 'Intellectuals Establishing Forums for Civil Society and Human Rights', *al-Awsat* (London) no. 467, 8 January 2001.
12. Michel Kilo (writer, leftist activist), ʿĀrif Dalīlah (economist, leftist), Khairi al-Zahabi (novelist, communist), Sadek Jalal al-ʿAzem (university professor, leftist), Yūsuf Salman (university professor, translator, leftist), Muḥammad Najati Tayyara (researcher, nationalist), Qasem Azawi (physician, poet, nationalist), Abdelrazak Eid (writer, researcher, leftist), Muḥammad Qarisli (film director), Adel Mahmoud (poet), Walīd al-Bunnī (physician), Jad Elkareem Aljaba'i (writer, researcher, nationalist), Zainab Natfaji (social activist), Yasin Shakor (journalist).
13. Muṣṭafá Ṭalās, the Syrian minister of defence, accused Syrian intellectuals who called for civil society of 'ripping apart national unity and decomposing the country in which it serves Zionism', *The Magazine*, no. 1108, 6–12 May 2001.
14. The Syrian minster of communications Muḥammad ʿUmrān considered 'the claimers of civil society are a part of new colonialism', in *al-Hayat* (London) 30 January 2001.
15. Khalaf Aljarad called 'civil society' off tangent, *Weekly Tishreen Magazine*, 2001; Muṣṭafá Abdelhalim, 'The Democracy of Civil Society', *al-Thawra* cultural supplement (Damascus) no. 251, 18 February 2001.
16. See Nabil Alghadiri, 'National Unity and Civil Society', *al-Muharrer al-Arabi* (Beirut) no. 283, 24 February 2001; Nihad Alghadiri, 'Yes to Opposition in Syria in a National Society not Civil Framework', *al-Muharrer al-Arabi* (Beirut) no. 282, 17–23 February 2001; Munzer Musilli, 'The Civil Society Group: Dreaming Ambitions and Wondering Lectures', *al-Muharrer al-Arabi* (Beirut) no. 281, 16 February 2001;
17. They are Walīd al-Bunnī (physician), Ghaleb Ibrahim (writer and activist), Muḥammad Samer al-Itri (researcher in political science), Izziddin Jouni (university lecturer), Muḥammad Kamāl al-Lubwānī (physician), Ḥasan Saʿdūn (activist), Yusef Salman (university lecturer, translator), Riyāḍ Sayf, MP (a member in the popular council), Muḥammad Maher Zaza (lawyer), Radwan Ziadeh (writer and researcher).
18. See Riyāḍ Sayf, 'Movement of Social Peace: Elemental Principles for Dialogue', *al-Zaman*, London, 3–4 February 2001.
19. See the polemics provoked by Sayf's paper, 'Movement of Social Peace'; Zyad Haidar, 'Baʿth Members Participate in the Dialogue and Criticize Sayf's Paper', *As-Safir* newspaper (Beirut) 2 February 2001; Thaʾer Salloum, 'Syrian Baʿth Members Accuse Founder of Social Peace Movement of Falsification', *al-Zaman* (London) 2 February 2001. Afterwards

Abdelkader Qaddoura, chief of the People's Assembly, lifted the parliamentary immunity on deputy Sayf after the period of official holidays of the assembly and brought him to public prosecution for establishing the social peace movement. See *al-Zaman* (London) 19 February 2001.

20. ʿAbd al-Ḥalīm Khaddām, 'We Shall Not Allow the Partition of Syria and Return to the Times of Revolutions', *al-Hayat*, 10 July 2001. In response to Khaddām's speech, see Hamdan Hamdan, 'The Mediocre Totalitarian Response Against the Affiliates of Social Society: The Speech of ʿAbd al-Ḥalīm Khaddām as an Example', *an-Nahar*, 5 September 2001.
21. For more information, see Radwan Ziadeh, 'The Limits of Syrian Reform'.
22. *Al-Hayat* (London) 17 February 2001.
23. *Al-Hayat* (London) 19 March 2001. See the declarations of the national leadership number 1075 dated 17 February 2001 in *al-Munadel* (an internal magazine that belongs to the Baʿth national socialist party) no. 306, January–February 2001, pp. 45–52.
24. Ibrāhīm Ḥumaydī, 'The Baʿth Party Mounts a Campaign against Intellectuals', *al-Hayat* (London) 16 February 2001. The NPF parties joined the Baʿth protest against the 'enemy actions' of those Syrian intellectuals intent on bringing Syria towards revolution.
25. President Bashar al-Asad in his interview with the Jordanian newspaper *al-Majd* excluded Jamal al-Atāsī's forum from the 'organizational' procedures, as it was named and implemented by the Syrian authorities, *al-Majd* (Amman) 5 March 2001. At that time the Syrian vice-president ʿAbd al-Ḥalīm Khaddām had met Hasan Abdelazim, the spokesperson of the opposing National Democratic coalition in March 2001, *al-Hayat* (London) 21 March 2001. Later, in June 2005, it was closed due to a paper presented on behalf of a general guide of the Muslim Brotherhood party in Syria during a meeting aimed at studying the future objectives of all parties in Syria, including the Baʿth Party.
26. See Hazem Sagieh, 'Society of the Civil Guesthouse', *al-Hayat* (London) February 2001.
27. Deputy Riyāḍ Sayf was the first to coin the name 'Spring of Damascus' in an interview with the agency, France Presse, in February 2001 after legal measures were taken against him over that issue. See Shabban Abboud, 'The Short Spring of Damascus', *an-Nahar* (Beirut) 22 February 2001; also check the file prepared by the *an-Nahar* supplement, which claims that 11 Syrian intellectuals participated in their separation for the Spring of Damascus, *an-Nahar* supplement (Beirut) 'Is the Spring of Damascus over?, no. 546, Sunday 25 August 2002. See also, Judith Cohen, 'The Unsuccessful Spring of Damascus', *Le Monde Diplomatique*, November 2002.

28. See Revival of Civil Society Committees in Syria, 'Towards a National Social Contract in Syria: General National Concurrences,' *an-Nahar*, 18 April 2001. There was a number of Syrian activists and intellectuals abroad who declared the establishment of a working group to support both Syrian intellectuals living in the country and those living abroad to act in a direct and effective way to reactivate civil society. See *an-Nahar*, 30 March 2001.
29. See Abdel Razzaq Eid, 'The Culture of Intimidation', lecture given at Jamal Al-Atāsī Forum for Democratic Dialogue in May 2001, which coincided with the declaration of the Syrian Muslim Brotherhood, in which their presence was prohibited in Syria. See Muslim Brotherhood in Syria, 'Project of National Honorary Pact for Political Work Insists on Dialogue and Democratic Work while Assuring its Abandonment of Violence', *al-Hayat* (London) 4 May 2001.
30. See *al-Zaman* (London) 19 February 2001.
31. *Al-Hayat* (London) 18 August 2001, also *al-Hayat* (London) 10 August 2001.
32. Riyāḍ al-Turk was released in December 2002 although he had been sentenced for two and a half years (*al-Hayat*, 2 September 2001).
33. Burhan Ghalion, 'The Future of Reforms in Syria: Towards a New National Contract', speech given at the Forum of National Dialogue, 5 September 2001, in *al-Hayat* (London) 7 September 2001.
34. *As-Safir* (Beirut) 7 September 2001, and *al-Althawra*, 7 September 2001; see full report on detention conditions of two deputies, al-Humṣī and Sayf, in *Tayarat*, no. 1, 2002, pp. 117–23.
35. *Al-Rai al-Am*, 7 September 2001.
36. *Al-Hayat* (London) 10 September 2001. Ḥasan Sadun and Ḥabīb Ṣāliḥ were released after two and a half years in prison, Kamāl Lubwānī was released after three years in prison, while the two deputies Riyāḍ Sayf and Muḥammad Mamoun al-Humṣī, as well as Dr Walīd al-Bunnī and Fawwāz Tal-lū were sentenced to five years each, and ʿĀrif Dalīlah was sentenced to ten years.
37. *Al-Hayat* (London) 12 September 2001, see a report written on the prison conditions of activists in *Tayarat*, no. 1, 2002, pp 124–6.
38. *Al-Hayat*, 4 May 2001.
39. For the political programme of the Syrian Popular Democratic Party as announced in its sixth conference in May 2005, see www.arraee.com
40. See websites such as Akhbar al-Sharq (Levant News) (http://www.thisissyria.net/), the Kuluna Shuraka bulletin (http:// all4syria.info), al-Rai (http://www. alrai. com/) al-Muaten.

4. Bashar al-Asad and Foreign Policy

1. See Anon, *The 1973 Constitution of the Syrian Arab Republic*; Mansour, *The Issue of Water in Syrian Policy towards Turkey*.
2. Mansour, *The Issue of Water in Syrian Policy towards Turkey*, pp. 73–4.
3. Ibid., p. 74.
4. See Ziadeh, *Approaching Peace: Israeli–Syria Negotiations*.
5. See Radwan Ziadeh, 'Al-iṣlāḥ fī Sūriyah bayna taḥaddiyāt al-iṣlāḥ al-dākhilī wa-rihānāt al-taghyīr al-khārijī' ['Reform in Syria between the Internal Reform Challenges and the Bets of External Change'], paper presented to conference on The Great Middle East Project: Interior and Exterior Controversy and the Future of the Arab Region, Cairo University Faculty of Economic and Political Sciences, 26–29 December 2005.
6. *Al-Hayat* (London) 18 February 2006.
7. Radwan Ziadeh, 'Crisis of the Syrian Foreign Policy Discourse', *al-Hayat* (London) 7 January 2007. Al-Mua'alem is known for his political moderation and he may have been chosen for his position to present a new more flexible approach to foreign policy than the previous more rigid one with which Syria had been characterized. This was reflected in the welcome his appointment received in European circles, but he turned out to be too weak to express or state 'moderate' political positions. Instead, he turned so far to the right that he can be said to have exceeded even the Baʿth Party eagles at the end of the 1960s when a high level of political and economic naiveté characterized the Syrian regime and had a disastrous outcome in losing Syria not only Golan but also international credibility. When, for example, al-Mua'alem offered to review Syrian foreign policy before the People's Assembly (parliament) in May 2006, it was the first time a foreign minister had done so for decades. While required 'to explain' his policy to the MPs rather than discuss it with them, when a Baʿthist deputy posed the question: 'where did Syrian policy hit the mark and where did it fail?' al-Mua'alem answered that Syrian policy was right in everything it did and had not made any mistakes. Then he said that Syria's relations were good with all states of the world except Europe and America! Many people may attribute this to the weakness of al-Mua'alem's position in the hierarchy of the Syrian political system, which obliges him to comply with the present inflexible and populist nature of Syrian foreign policy. This, however, operates simultaneously with a two-sided discourse – one, which takes place behind closed doors, to convince foreign diplomats and journalists of the need to support his moderate stand of encouraging reformists inside the 'regime' and another quite different one for

consumption by 'the Syrian people' and the Arab communities behind them. This dualism may succeed in diplomacy, but it renders the diplomacy itself incapable of taking any initiatives that go beyond mere rhetoric. For example, during negotiations with Israel President Hafez al-Asad had always kept his words in check, negotiating rather about the expressions and statements themselves, while now – when al-Mua'alem is the main player –there is an abundance, even overabundance, of 'revolutionary' statements, but with no backing to turn them into matching policies.

8. See *Al-Hayat* (London) 7 March 2005.
9. See al-Asad's speech to the Syrian People's Assembly in *al-Hayat* (London) 6 March 2005.
10. See *al-Hayat* (London) 10 January 2006.
11. For more on Syrian–Lebanese relations, see Michael Kilo, 'Transformations of Syrian Regional Policy with Regard to Relations with Lebanon', in Radwan Ziadeh (ed.) *Maʿrakat al-iṣlāḥ fī Sūriyah* [*Battle of Reform in Syria*] (Cairo: Cairo Institute for Human Rights Studies, 2006) pp. 47–60; see also Radwan Ziadeh, 'Al-ʿalāqāt al-Sūrīyah al-Lubnānīyah: mashaqqat al-ukhūwah' ['Syrian–Lebanese Relations: Hardship of Brotherhood'], in Radwan Ziadeh (ed.) *Maʿrakat al-iṣlāḥ fī Sūriyah* [*Battle of Reform in Syria*] (Cairo: Cairo Institute for Human Rights Studies, 2006) pp. 69–85.
12. *Al-Hayat* (London) 10 February 2005.
13. *Al-Hayat* (London) 18 July 2000, and look up the complete text of the speech of the oath in *As-Safir* (Beirut) 18 July 2000, and *al-Mustaqbal* (Beirut) 18 July 2000.
14. Georges Malbrunot, *Des Pierres aux Fusils: Les Secrets de l'Intifada* (Paris: Flammarion, 2002).
15. Ibid., p. 120.
16. Bashar al-Asad's interview with *al-Majd* newspaper (Amman) 9 March 2001.
17. *Al-Hayat* (London) 22 October 2000, and look up the complete text of President Bashar al-Asad's words in the casual conference of the Arab summit in *Tishreen* newspaper (Damascus) 22 October 2000.
18. *Al-Hayat* (London) 14 November 2000, and look up the complete text of President Bashar al-Asad's word at the 55th conference of the Islamic summit in *Tishreen* (Damascus) 12 November 2000.
19. *Al-Hayat* (London) 25 November 2000.
20. *Al-Hayat* (London) 3 December 2000.
21. President Bashar al-Asad's interview with *al-Sharq al-Awsat* newspaper (London) 7 February 2001.
22. *Al-Hayat* (London) 24 January 2001.

23. *Al-Hayat* (London) 30 and 31 January 2001.
24. *Tishreen* (Damascus) 28 March 2001.
25. See *Haaretz* (Tel Aviv) 24 April 2001.
26. *Tishreen* (Damascus) 17 April 2001; see also Salim Nassar, 'Sharon Changes the Rules of the Syrian Confrontation in Lebanon', *al-Hayat* (London) 21 April 2001.
27. *Al-Hayat* (London) 29 April 2001, which is what President Bashar al-Asad also mentioned in his interview with the Spanish newspaper *El País*. See *Tishreen* (Damascus) 2 May 2001.
28. *As-Safir* (Beirut) 5 April 2001.
29. President Bashar al-Asad's interview on the second French television channel, 21 June 2001. See *al-Thawra* (Damascus) 22 June 2001 and for more about the change in Bashar al-Asad's discourse see George Bakasini, 'Al-Asad's Speech is a Successful Preamble for a Successful Visit', *al-Mustaqbal* (Beirut) 24 June 2001. See also al-Asad's interview with the French newspaper *Le Figaro*, 23 June 2001, and with *Der Spiegel* in July 2001.
30. *Al-Hayat* (London) 2 July 2001; Siril Taoutsand, 'Israel and the Postponed Syrian Response', *al-Hayat* (London) 30 July 2001.
31. President Bashar al-Asad's discussion with *Der Spiegel* in July 2001; see *Tishreen* (Damascus) 9 July 2001.
32. President Bashar al-Asad's discussion with *As-Safir* newspaper (Beirut) 16 July 2001.
33. *Al-Hayat* (London) 9 October 2001. In the election Syria got a comfortable majority despite the Israeli opposition; see Ghi Bakhour, 'Unwise Israeli Isolation because of the Syrian Seat', *Haaretz* (Tel Aviv) 15 October 2001.
34. *As-Safir* (Beirut) 12 October 2001.
35. *Al-Mustaqbal* (Beirut) 13 October 2001.
36. *Al-Hayat* (London) 28 October 2001.
37. *Al-Hayat* (London) 1 November 2001.
38. *Al-Hayat* (London) 18 and 20 November 2001; *Tishreen* (Damascus) 9 January 2002.
39. *As-Safir* (Beirut) 14 December 2001.
40. *As-Safir* (Beirut) 27 December 2001.
41. This was mentioned by William Burns, the US assistant secretary of state, *an-Nahar* (Beirut) 14 January 2002; and about this see also Subhi al-Hadidi, 'Damascus and the Cost of the Dissolution of "Terrorist" Organizations: The Consequences of the Double-Faced Game', *al-Quds al-Arabi* (London) 28 December 2001; and Sarkis Na'oum, 'Syria and the United States', *an-Nahar*, 11 December 2001. In a telephone call between al-Asad and Bush, the former said that America was a novice at fighting

terrorism and should make use of the Syrian experience in this field, *As-Safir* (Beirut) 15 January 2002.

42. Look up the complete text of Bush's speech about peace in the Middle East in *As-Safir* (Beirut) 25 June 2002, and *al-Hayat* (London) 25 June 2002.
43. Bin Kasbit, 'One of the Most Successful Weeks', *Maarif* (Tel Aviv) 28 June 2002; Joel Marcus, 'Another Text Like This', *Haaretz* (Tel Aviv) 28 June 2002; Yusi Sarid, 'What is Bad in a Good Speech?' *Yedioth Ahronoth*, 27 June 2006; Shamoun Shiver, 'Sharon: We Did Our Duty', *Yedioth Ahronoth* (Tel Aviv) 28 June 2002.
44. See Anon, 'A Vision that Does not Lead to Peace', editorial, *Tishreen* (Damascus) 29 June 2002; Marwan Bshara, 'Bush's Imaginary Plan Repeats the Previous Mistakes', *International Herald Tribune*, 27 June 2002; Martin Indyk, 'The White House and the Middle East Crisis', *New York Times*, 12 August 2002; Khalaf al-Jarad, 'An Obscure "Viewpoint" and a Queer Logic', *Tishreen* (Damascus) 1 July 2002.
45. Bashar al-Asad's interview with *al-Liwa* newspaper (Beirut) 1 July 2002; for more about Prince Abdullah's peace plan, see Murhaf Jouejati, 'The Abdullah Plan and the Arab States', *Middle East Institute*, 4 March 2002.
46. *Tishreen* (Damascus) 6 March 2002. Later on al-Asad revealed that in his meeting with a delegation from the union of Arab lawyers, see *al-Quds al-Arabi* (London) 31 May 2002.
47. *New York Times*, 13 March 2002.
48. Review Prince Abdullah's discussion with the US television station ABC, 15 March 2002; see *al-Mustaqbal* (Beirut) 16 March 2002; Raghida Dergham, 'Towards an Arab Peace "Viewpoint" that Complies with the American "Viewpoint"', *al-Hayat* (London) 1 March 2002; Najib al-Khunizi, 'The Crown Prince Initiative and the Horizons of Settlement', *al-Watan* (Abha) 8 March 2002; Patrick Seale, 'In the Context of the Saudi Initiative', *al-Hayat* (London) 1 March 2002.
49. See the public opinion survey carried out by Market Watch and issued by *Maarif* (Tel Aviv) 31 September 2002. Other surveys also indicate that the majority of Israelis have lost confidence in the peace process and support all-inclusive American interference, *Haaretz* (Tel Aviv) 3 September 2002.
50. See *As-Safir* (Beirut) 29 March 2002; *al-Hayat* (London) 29 March 2002; and Murhaf Jouejati, 'The Arab Summit: Israeli Opportunity?' *Middle East Institute*, 5 April 2002.
51. See Audid Ghranout, 'The Crown Prince Bomb', *Maarif* (Tel Aviv) 1 March 2002; Dan Margalit, 'The Saudi Initiative', *Maarif*, 1 March 2002; Tasvi Para'el, 'Saudi on the Horizon', *Haaretz*, 10 March 2002; Aouzi Patriman, 'Abdullah's Good Omen', *Yedioth Ahronoth* (Tel Aviv) 1 March 2002.

52. *Washington Post*, 25 July 2002.
53. *As-Safir* (Beirut) 9 October 2002, and see Hasan Mnimna, 'A New Call for Account for Syria or Usual American Internal Pull Back and Forth', *al-Hayat* (London) 16 September 2002.
54. *As-Safir* (Beirut) 11 October 2002. Damascus had strongly responded to these allegations, called for the recall of the US ambassador in Damascus and officially protested against Bolton's allegations.
55. *Al-Hayat* (London) 11 November 2002; *an-Nahar* (Beirut) 10 November 2002; *As-Safir* (Beirut) 19 November 2002; and see a discussion with Faisal Meqdad, the Syrian permanent delegate at the United Nations Security Council, in which he explains the details of Syrian voting on Security Council Resolution no. 1441, *al-Hayat* (London) 11 November 2002.
56. *Al-Mustaqbal* (Beirut) 18 January 2003.
57. See Bashar al-Asad's speech in *al-Thawra* (Damascus) 2 March 2003.
58. Bashar al-Asad's interview with *As-Safir* newspaper (Beirut) 27 March 2003. On the violent American and Israeli response to the interview, see Walter Pincus, 'Syrian–US Ties Strained by Iraq War', *Washington Post*, 4 April 2003; Eyal Zisser, 'Bashar's Game: What is Syria Up To?' *Tel Aviv Notes*, 4 April 2003.
59. Uri Dan, 'Game Over for Syria's Double-Dealer', *New York Post*, 30 March 2003. Later on, the Israeli officials and Israeli mass media continued to repeat the same accusations, see Shaul Movaz, 'The Israeli Minister of Defence who alleged that Syria had Provided the Iraqi Army with Antitank Weapons', *Haaretz* (Tel Aviv) 2 April 2003. A few months before that, the newspaper claimed that the Syrians had bought weapons for Iraq from states in eastern Europe.
60. *Al-Mustaqbal* (Beirut) 14 April 2003.
61. *Al-Mustaqbal* (Beirut) 17 April 2003.
62. Anon, 'Israel Wants US to Attack Syria', editorial, *Pravda*, 17 April 2003; William A. Cook, 'Sharon Recruits US Mercenaries against Syria of Pariahs and Pre-emptive Strikes', *Counter Punch*, 26 April 2003; for a report on Syrian military capabilities see Anthony H. Cordesman, *If it's Syria: Syrian Military Forces and Capabilities* (Washington, DC: Centre for Strategic and International Studies, 15 April 2003); Khaled Ezzelarab, 'Syria's Turn', *Cairo Times*, vol. 7, no. 8, 24–30 April 2003; Colonel Dan Smith, 'From Baghdad, Turn Left: On the Road to Damascus?', *Foreign Policy in Focus*, 22 April 2003.
63. *Al-Hayat* (London) 3 May 2003, *al-Sharq al-Awsat* (London) 3 May 2003 and Condoleezza Rice's interview with *Yedioth Ahronoth* (Tel Aviv) 2 May 2003. For more about this, see Anon, 'Powell Presses Syria to Change its Middle East Policies', *Reuters Report*, 3 May 2003; Anon, 'Syria to Urge

Powell to Back Weapons Ban', editorial, *New York Times*, 3 May 2003; also Anon, 'Powell Demands Syria Cooperate with US in Mideast', *New York Times*, 3 May 2003; David Lamb, 'Hezbollah Feeling the Squeeze', *Los Angeles Times*, 3 May 2003; Flynt Leverett, 'How to Get Syria out of the Terrorism Business', *New York Times*, 3 May 2003; Sonya Ross, 'Syria Mast Down on Terror Groups, Powell Says', *Associated Press Report*, 3 May 2003; Howard Witt, 'In Syria, Powell to Press for Change', *Chicago Tribune*, 3 May 2003; Robin Wright, 'Powell Plans to Deliver Tough Message to Syria', *Los Angeles Times*, 3 May 2003; Robin Wright, 'Syria Faces Hard Choices', *Los Angeles Times*, 4 May 2003.

64. *As-Safir* (Beirut) 8 May 2003, *Maarif* (Tel Aviv) 5 May 2003, but Damascus denied the occurrence of any secret contacts between Maher al-Asad, brother of the Syrian president, and Itan Pentsor, ex-general manager of the Israeli foreign ministry, *al-Hayat* (London) 8 May 2003. Sharon openly denied the existence of such contacts, See Shamoun Shiver, 'Sharon has to Give the Evidence', *Yedioth Ahronoth* (Tel Aviv) 11 May 2003.
65. *An-Nahar* (Beirut) 19 May 2003, and see *Yedioth Ahronoth* (Tel Aviv) 24 May 2003; Glenn Kessler, 'Syria Shut Offices of Palestinian Groups: US Labels Terrorists, Powell Says', *Washington Post*, 4 May 2003; Matthew Levitt, 'Terror from Damascus: The Palestinian Terrorist Presence in Syria', *Peace Watch* (Washington Institute for Near East Policy) no. 420, 7 May 2003; Daniel J. Wakin, 'Powell says Syria is Taking Action on Terror Groups', *New York Times*, 4 May 2003; Robin Wright and David Lamb, 'Syria Puts New Curbs on Militants', *Los Angeles Times*, 4 May 2003.
66. *Al-Hayat* (London) 24 May 2003; and see Karen Deyoung, 'US Warns Syria it is Watching its Actions', *Washington Post*, 5 May 2003.
67. Volker Perthes, 'Managing Modernization: Domestic Politics and the Limits of Change', in Radwan Ziadeh (ed.) *Reform in Syria between Domestic Politics and Regional and International Changes* (Jeddah: al-Raya Centre for Intellectual Development, 2004) pp. 7–26.
68. Ibid., p. 16.
69. *As-Safir* (Beirut) 17 May 2003.
70. *As-Safir* (Beirut) 29 May 2003.
71. *An-Nahar* (Beirut) 26 June 2003, and see Seymour M. Hersh, 'The Syrian Bet', *New Yorker*, 28 July 2003.
72. *As-Safir* (Beirut) 4 June 2003.
73. *As-Safir* (Beirut) 5 June 2003; and see William Dalrymple, 'Tolerance Thrives amid Syria's Repression', *International Herald Tribune*, 10 June 2003.
74. For more about the Syrian position on the US war against Iraq, see Raymond A. Hinnebusch, 'Syria after the Iraq War: Between Domestic

Reform and the New Conservatives' Attack', in Radwan Ziadeh (ed.) *Al-iṣlāḥ fī Sūriyah bayna al-siyāsāt al-dākhilīyah wa-al-taḥawwulāt al-iqlīmīyah wa-al-duwalīyah* [*Reform in Syria between Internal Policies and International and Regional Transformations*] (Jeddah: Al-Raya Centre for Intellectual Development, 2005) pp. 111–148. On the Israeli reading of this position, see Eyal Zisser, 'Syria and the War in Iraq', *Middle East Review of International Affairs* (MERIA) vol. 7, no. 2, June 2003.

75. Syrian Foreign Minister Farouk al-Shar'a described the US adminstration as the most stupid in history. See *As-Safir* (Beirut) 28 July 2003; and Bashar al-Asad's interview with the Italian newspaper *Corriere della Sera* in *Tishreen* (Damascus) 30 September 2003.
76. *As-Safir* (Beirut) 6 October 2003, *Tishreen* (Damascus) 6 October 2003 and *Al-Hayat* (London) 6 October 2003. See also Felicity Barringer, 'The Mideast Turmoil: United Nations: Syria Offers a Resolution to Condemn Israeli Raid', *New York Times*, 6 October 2003; Robert Fisk, 'Israel's Attack is a Lethal Step towards War in Middle East', *Independent*, October 2003; Richard W. Murphy, 'Raid against Syria sets Regrettable Precedent', Council of Foreign Relations, 8 October 2003; Za'if Shif, 'Against the Outward Slide of Confrontation', *Haaretz* (Tel Aviv) 10 October 2003.
77. *Al-Hayat* (London) 7 October 2003. Bush openly stated: 'We would have done the same', *al-Hayat* (London) 8 October 2003. Fred Goldstein, 'Bush Hails Israel: Attack on Syria', *Workers World Newspaper*, and 16 October 2003.
78. See Mahdi Dakhlallah, 'Let's Give them the Opposite of What they Expect', *al-Ba'th* (Damascus) 8 October 2003; David Harrison, 'Syria Threatens to Attack Golan Settlers if Israel Strikes Again', *Daily Telegraph*, 26 October 2003; Neil MacFarquhar, 'Syria Leader Says Israel Aims to Stir Region', *New York Times*, 8 October 2003.
79. *As-Safir* (Beirut) 16 October 2003. Peter Brown Field, 'The Syria Accountability Act', *Fox News*, 6 November 2003.
80. *An-Nahar* (Beirut) 22 October 2003, and *an-Nahar* (Beirut) 16 November 2003.
81. *An-Nahar* (Beirut) 12 November 2003, also see proceedings of the American senate session about voting on the 'Syrian Accountability Act' in *al-Mustaqbal* (Beirut) 13 and 14 October 2003, and Carl Hulse, 'Panel Approves Sanctions on Syria with White House Support', *New York Times*, 9 October 2003.
82. *New York Times*, 1 December 2003. See also the text of Bashar al-Asad interview with the same newspaper in *al-Sharq al-Awsat* (London) 2 December 2003.
83. *Al-Ba'th* (Damascus) 1 January 2003; *al-Mustaqbal* (Beirut) 3 January 2004.

84. *As-Safir* (Beirut) 3 January 2004.
85. *An-Nahar* (Beirut) 13 January 2004.
86. *An-Nahar* (Beirut) 17 January 2004.
87. *As-Safir* (Beirut) 27 August 2004.
88. *As-Safir* (Beirut) 27 September 2004.
89. *Al-Mustaqbal* (Beirut) 3 September 2004; *al-Mustaqbal* (Beirut) 4 September 2004; *As-Safir* (Beirut) 3 September 2004.
90. Ghassān Salāmah, *Society and the State in the Arab Levant: Predicting the Future of the Arab Homeland* (Beirut: Centre for Arab Unity Studies, 1987) p. 65; Radwan Ziadeh, 'The Political Crisis and the Problem of Democratic Obstruction in Syria', *al-Zaman* (London) 15 February 2001.
91. Moshe Maʿoz, 'The Emergence of Modern Syria', in Moshe Maʿoz and Amer Yanir (eds) *Syria under Asad* (London: Croom Helm, 1986) p. 9. See also Maʿoz, *The Sphinx of Damascus.*
92. For information about the beginning of the Lebanese civil war and the conditions that kept it going, see John Bulloch, *Death of a Country: The Civil War in Lebanon* (London: Weidenfeld & Nicholson, 1977); Kamal S. Salibi, *Crossroads to Civil War: Lebanon, 1958–1976* (Delmar, NY: Caravan Books, 1976).
93. Adeed I. Dawisha, *Syria and the Lebanese Crisis* (London: Macmillan Press, 1980) p. 120.
94. For more on Jumblatt's personality and leadership, see Igorʿ Timofeev, *Kamāl Jumblāṭ: al-rajul wa-al-usṭūrah* (Beirut: Dar an-Nahar, 2000).
95. Moshe Maʿoz, *Sūriyah wa-Isrāʾīl min al-ḥarb ilá ṣanʿ al-salām* [*Syria and Israel from War to Peace-making*] (Amman: Dar al-Jalil, 1993) p. 161; Zaif Schiff, 'Dealing with Syria', *Foreign Policy*, no. 55, Summer 1984; Zaif Schiff, *Peace with Security: Israel Minimum Security Requirements in its Negotiations with Syria*, translated by Military Studies Centre (Damascus: Military Research Centre, 1992) pp. 40–3; Seale, *Asad and the Struggle for the Middle East*, p. 453.
96. Muḥammad Jamāl Bārūt, 'The Socialist Arab Baʿth Party in Syria: From the Corrective Movement to the Liquidation of the Generals' Centres', *Al-Hayat* (London) 15 June 2000.
97. Dawisha, *Syria and the Lebanese Crisis*, p. 136.
98. Seale, *Asad and the Struggle for the Middle East*, p. 460.
99. Dawisha, *Syria and the Lebanese Crisis*, p. 163.
100. Ziadeh, *Approaching Peace: Israeli–Syria Negotiations.*
101. Maḥmūd Suwayd, *Janūb Lubnān fī muwājahat Isrāʾīl* [*Southern Lebanon in the Face of Israel: 50 Years of Steadfastness and Resistance*] (Beirut: Palestinian Studies Foundation, 1988) p. 23.
102. Maḥmūd Suwayd (ed.) *Ḥarb al-ayyām al-sabʿah fī Lubnān: ʿAmalīyat al-Muḥāsabah* [*The Seven Day War on Lebanon: Operation Accountability*]*, 25–31 July 1993* (Beirut: Palestinian Research Establishment, 1993) p. 7.

103. Ibid, p. 7.
104. *As-Safir* (Beirut) 12 August 1993.
105. *An-Nahar* (Beirut) 29 July 1993.
106. *As-Safir* (Beirut) 22 August 1993. This is what the Lebanese minister of information Michal Smaha declared at that time.
107. *An-Nahar* (Beirut) 25 August 1993.
108. Ziadeh, *Approaching Peace: Israeli–Syria Negotiations.*
109. Raymond Hinnebusch, 'Syrian Foreign Policy between Realism and Idealism', in Radwan Ziadeh (ed.) *Al-iṣlāḥ fī Sūriyah bayna al-siyāsāt al-dākhilīyah wa-al-taḥawwulāt al-iqlīmīyah wa-al-duwalīyah* [*Reform in Syria between Internal Policies and International and Regional Transformations*] (Jeddah: Al-Raya Centre for Intellectual Development, 2005) pp. 651–2; Jamāl ʿAbd al-Jawwād and Muḥammad Munīr Luṭfī, *Sūriyah tufāwiḍ Isrāʾīl* [*Syria Negotiates with Israel*] (Cairo: Centre of Strategic and Political Studies, 1996); Mohammad Abdul Qader, *The Strategy of the Syrian Negotiations with Israel* (Abu Dhabi: Emirates Centre for Strategic Studies and Research Studies, 1999) p. 23.
110. Helena Cobban, *The Israeli–Syrian Peace Talks 1991–96 and Beyond* (Washington DC: US Institute for Peace Press, 1999) p. 157; cf. Helena Cobban, 'The Big Lost Opportunity: Syrian–Israeli Negotiations', *al-Siyasah* (Kuwait) no. 17, 7 July 1999. During his meeting with Asad at the end of March 1996, former US president George Bush asked him to calm down the situation in southern Lebanon to ensure the continuation of peace negotiations, see *al-Hayat* (London) 2 April 1996.
111. Robert Satloff and Alan Makovsky, 'Changing Asad's Incentive Structure: Christopher in the Lion's Den', *Policy Watch*, Washington Institute for Near East Policy, no. 194, 22 April 1996.
112. The numbers are mentioned in a report prepared by a United Nations committee charged with investigating the massacre of Qānā. See Maḥmūd Suwayd, *Southern Lebanon in the Face of Israel*, pp. 24–5; and report prepared by Human Right Watch, September 1997.
113. From Perez's interview with Israeli television, 18 April 1996, transcribed from *As-Safir* (Beirut) 19 April 1996.
114. From an Israeli report on the army radio entitled 'Army Commanders Discuss the Operation of Anger Punches in Lebanon', transcribed from Cobban, *The Israeli–Syrian Peace Talks*, p. 161; cf. Cobban, 'The Big Lost Opportunity'.
115. International condemnation started with UN Secretary General Boutros-Ghali, followed by a long list that included the foreign ministries of Britain, Germany, Denmark, Australia, China, France, Russia, Spain, Romania, the EU and NATO. The Security Council started discussing a Lebanese complaint against Israeli aggression. Following the massacre of Qānā, President Clinton expressed his regret and sorrow for the families

of those killed or injured in southern Lebanon and offered his condolences to the Lebanese government. The condemnation spread so widely that it reached the level of heads of government such as French president Jacques Chirac, British prime minister John Major, and Canadian and French prime ministers, which demonstrated the depth of the crisis into which Peres had put himself.

116. See Joel Marcus, 'Peres's Hard Face', *Haaretz* (Tel Aviv) 19 April 1996.
117. See the full text of the April accord in Muḥammad Suwayd, *ʿAmalīyat ʿanāqīd al-ghaḍab* [*Operation Grapes of Wrath*] (Beirut: Palestinian Studies Foundation, 1996) p. 118; see also *As-Safir* (Beirut) 27 April 1996.
118. *Al-Hayat* (London) 21 May 2000. For more on the Israeli withdrawal from southern Lebanon, which was considered a victory for the Lebanese resistance, see the Lebanese newspapers dedicated to celebrating the so-called day of resistance and liberation, namely *al-Hayat* (London) 24 May 2000; *As-Safir* (Beirut) 24 and 25 May 2000; and *al-Mustaqbal*, 24 and 25 May 2000. Israeli newspapers were filled with news of the fall of southern Lebanon and grim predictions for the future. Israel's sudden humiliating withdrawal played a decisive role in the fall of Ehud Barak's popularity, see Josi Filmann, 'Until the Last Gates are Closed', *Haaretz* (Tel Aviv) 25 May 2000; Zaif Schiff, 'The New Security Theory', *Haaretz* (Tel Aviv) 25 April 2000; Awvar Shallah, 'Hezbollah Takes the Decision', *Yedioth Ahronoth* (Tel Aviv) 24 May 2000; Ron bin Yashai, 'The Period of Uncertainty', *Yedioth Ahronoth* (Tel Aviv) 24 May 2000.
119. See Akifa Aldar, 'Shebaʾa Farms are Lebanese', *Haaretz* (Tel Aviv) 25 June 2002; Isam Khalifah, 'A Documented Study Confirming the Lebanese Character of Shebaʾa Farms', *As-Safir* (Beirut) 19 May 2000; Basem Yamut, 'The Economic Strategic Importance of Shebaʾa Farms', *As-Safir* (Beirut) 7 March 2000.
120. On 9 January 2000 the *Sunday Times* mentioned that, through cooperation with Jordanian intelligence, Israeli intelligence (Mossad) had acquired a sample of al-Asad's urine while he was in Amman attending King Hussein's funeral. Through this sample the Israelis were able to gain a lot of information about al-Asad's state of health, including a full list of the drugs he used and the diet he followed. On 20 January 2000 *Maarif* (Tel Aviv) confirmed that Israeli intelligence had files about the health of many Arab leaders, including al-Asad.
121. *Al-Mustaqbal* (Beirut) 4 September 200, *al-Mustaqbal* (Beirut) 3 September 2004, *As-Safir* (Beirut) 3 September 2004.
122. International Crisis Group, 'Syria after Lebanon: Lebanon after Syria', *Middle East Report*, no. 39, 12 April 2005; Michael Young, 'All Eyes Turn to Syria', *International Herald Tribune*, Thursday 17 February 2005.
123. See Abdullah Bu Habib, 'Syria's Strategic Mistakes in its Relations with Washington', *al-Hayat* (London) 11 April 2005.

124. *Al-Hayat* (London) 18 May 2006.
125. *Al-Hayat* (London) 18 May 2006. For more on Syrian–Lebanese relations, see Kilo, 'Transformations of Syrian Regional Policy'; Radwan Ziadeh, 'Al-ʿalāqāt al-Sūrīyah al-Lubnānīyah: mashaqqat al-ukhūwah' ['Syrian–Lebanese Relations: Hardships of Brotherhood'], in Radwan Ziadeh (ed.) *Maʿrakat al-iṣlāḥ fī Sūriyah* [*Battle of Reform in Syria*] (Cairo: Cairo Centre for Human Rights Studies, 2006) pp. 69–85.
126. *Al-Hayat* (London) 18 May 2006.
127. *Al-Mustaqbal* (Beirut) 23 June 2006.
128. *Al-Hayat* (London) 23 June 2006; Radwan Ziadeh, 'Crisis of the Syrian Foreign Policy Discourse'.
129. *Al-Hayat* (London) 23 June 2006.
130. *Al-Thawra* (Damascus) 13 July 2006 mentioned that a culture of resistance is likely to spread because its validity has been proved.
131. *Al-Hayat* (London) 14 July 2006; see also Ahmad Diab, 'International Positions towards the War on Lebanon', *Al-Siyassa al-Dawliya [International Politics]*, vol. 42, no. 166, October 2006, pp. 138–41.
132. *Al-Hayat* (London) 29 July 2006. For more, see Yossi Mekelberg, 'Israel and London: Soul Searching', *World Today*, vol. 62, no. 10, October 2006, pp. 12–13.
133. *An-Nahar* (Beirut) 21 August 2006, while followers of the Israeli peace party called for attacks on Syria. See Yossi Pilin, 'Attacking Syria', translated from Hebrew, *al-Mustaqbal* (Beirut) 14 July 2006.
134. *An-Nahar* (Beirut) 17 July 2006.
135. *Al-Hayat* (London) 7 August 2006.
136. Ibid. In an interview with Al Jazeera in September 2006, after a month of putting an end to this 'regional war', al-Mu'allem belittled the importance of Condoleezza Rice's statements to the *Wall Street Journal* in which she had threatened to impose new sanctions on Syria, confirming that these declarations reflected US dissatisfaction with Syrian diplomacy. He said that Washington did not want to move in the right direction but to continue making mistakes, adding that if it wanted to impose sanctions, he would welcome them (*As-Safir*, 28 September 2006). What is strange is that, unlike the official Syrian position characterized by caution for fear of getting into an unequal confrontation, this was the first time Walīd al-Mu'allem had welcomed the regional war, a rare position in the history of the diplomacy of any country, for no one welcomes the involvement of his or her country in war. A country always tries to present its international position as being a 'defensive' one and the war unwillingly imposed on it, for otherwise it would fail to attract international, regional or even domestic sympathy. Again, when the US foreign minister declared that her country was considering increasing sanctions against Syria, the Syrian foreign minister welcomed them, as if

the diplomatic expressions always betrayed him: for example he could have said that the United States has to think of its interests, or reconsider its policies, as Syrian diplomats have said for decades, but he welcomed the sanctions too.

137. *An-Nahar* (Beirut) 7 August 2006. See also Bashir ʿAbd al-Fattāḥ, 'The Arab Position towards the Israeli Aggression on Lebanon', *Al-Siyassa al-Dawliya* [*International Politics*], vol. 42, no. 166, October 2006, pp. 130–3; *Al-Hayat* (London) 7 August 2006.
138. *Al-Hayat* (London) 23 July 2006. About the military capabilities of Hezbollah, see D. Jamal Mazloum, 'Hezbollah Management of Military Operations in the Lebanese War', *Al-Siyassa al-Dawliya [International Politics]*, vol. 42, no. 166, October 2006, pp. 96–100; and Mohammad Abdul Salam, 'The Military Lessons of the Lebanon War', *Al-Siyassa al-Dawliya [International Politics]*, vol. 42, no. 166, October 2006, pp. 120–5.
139. *An-Nahar* (Beirut) 12 August 2006. See also Hasan Nafeʾa, 'The Israeli War on Lebanon: The International Consequences', *al-Mustaqbal al-Arabi*, vol. 29, no. 332, October 2006, pp. 88–103; and in book form, Hasan Nafeʾa, *The Israeli War against Lebanon: Lebanese and Israeli Consequences and their Arab, Regional and International Effects* (Beirut: Centre for Arab Unity Studies, 2006).
140. *Al-Mustaqbal* (Beirut) 12 August 2006. See also Khalil al-Anani, 'Resolution 1701: Indications and Outcomes', *Al-Siyassa al-Dawliya [International Politics]*, vol. 42, no. 166, October 2006, pp. 142–5.
141. *An-Nahar* (Beirut) 14 August 2006.
142. *An-Nahar* (Beirut) 13 July 2006.
143. *An-Nahar* (Beirut) 23 August 2006. About this, see Nadim Shehadi, 'Iran–US Confrontation in Lebanon: Capitulate or Escalate', *World Today*, vol. 62, no. 10, October 2006, pp. 9–11.
144. *Al-Hayat* (London) 23 August 2006. See also Sameh Rashed, 'Iran and Syria: Agreeing on Lebanon', *Al-Siyassa al-Dawliya [International Politics]*, vol. 42, no. 166, October 2006, pp. 134–7. On the Iranian role, see Nivin Mesed, 'The Israeli War on Lebanon: Regional Consequences, Iran', *al-Mustaqbal al-Arabi*, vol. 29, no. 332, October 2006, pp. 52–72. It was later published as Nivin Mesed, *The Israeli War on Lebanon: Lebanese and Israeli Consequences and their Arab, Regional and International Effects* (Beirut: Centre for Arab Unity Studies, 2006).
145. *As-Safir* (Beirut) 16 August 2006.
146. *Al-Mustaqbal* (Beirut) 21 August 2006. See also Ahmad Yousef Ahmad, 'The Israeli War on Lebanon: The Arabian Consequences', *al-Mustaqbal al-Arabi*, vol. 29, no. 332, October 2006, pp. 3–51. Later published in Nivin Mesed, *The Israeli War on Lebanon: Lebanese and Israeli Consequences and their Arab, Regional and International Effects* (Beirut: Centre for Arab Unity Studies, 2006).

147. *An-Nahar* (Beirut) 23 August 2006.
148. *An-Nahar* (Beirut) 7 October 2006.
149. For more about this, see Burhan Ghalion, 'Asadism in Syrian Policy or the Role of Regional Policy in Realizing Internal Control', in Radwan Ziadeh (ed.) *Maʿrakat al-iṣlāḥ fī Sūriyah* [*Battle of Reform in Syria*] (Cairo: Cairo Institute for Human Rights Studies, 2006) pp. 15–45.

5. The Challenge of Political Islam: Muslim Brotherhood and Democracy

1. David Dean Commins, *Islamic Reform: Politics and Social Change in Late Ottoman Syria* (Oxford: Oxford University Press, 1990).
2. See ʿAbd al-Jabbār Ḥasan al-Jubūrī, *al-Aḥzāb wa-al-jamʿīyāt al-siyāsīyah fī Sūriyah min awākhir al-qarn al-tāsiʿ ʿashar ḥattá 1958* [*Political Parties and Societies in Syria from the Late Nineteenth Century to 1958*] (Baghdad: Dar al-Hurria Publishing House, 1980) pp. 14–16.
3. Johannes Reissner, *Ideologie und Politik der Muslimbrüder Syriens* (Freiburg: Klaus Schwarz Verlag, 1980). The book was also published in Arabic, see Johannes Reissner, *Islamic Movements in Syria*, translated by Mohammad Ibraheem al-Atāsī (Beirut: Dar Riad al-Rayes, 2005) p. 118. I use the Arabic edition.
4. Ibid, p. 119.
5. For more information about Damascene families or what was known as 'urban people' during the early phase of national political awareness, it is essential to consult Philip S. Khoury, *Urban Notables and Arab Nationalism: The Politics of Damascus, 1860–1920* (Cambridge: Cambridge University Press, 1983).
6. *Islamic Urbanization* is a 'social, educational and intellectual Islamic weekly magazine published by the Islamic Urbanization Society'. Its chief editor is Ahmad Muzhar al-ʿAsma, and its executive manager is Mohammad Kamāl al-Khaṭīb. The magazine has carried articles by Mohammad Kurd ʿAlī, ʿAbd al-Raḥmān al-Shahbandar, Lutfi al-Haffar, Ma'arouf al-Dawalibi and others. The author has a few issues in his private archive.
7. al-Janhani, 'The Islamic Wakefulness in Greater Syria', p 114.
8. For more information about the numbers, activities and roles of these societies in that period, see al-Jubūrī, *Political Parties and Societies in Syria*, pp. 121, 204.
9. Reissner, Islamic Movements in Syria, p. 104.
10. On Kāmil al-Qaṣṣāb's character and role, see Seale, *The Struggle for Syria.*
11. Reissner, *Islamic Movements in Syria*, p. 123.
12. Philip S. Khoury, *Syria and the French Mandate: The Politics of Arab Nationalism, 1920–1945* (Princeton: Princeton University Press, 1987) Chapter 8.
13. Reissner, *Islamic Movements in Syria*, pp. 191–201.

14. Ibid, pp. 129–32.
15. Muḥammad Jamāl Bārūt, 'Usul wa Ta'arujat Jama'at al-Ikhwan al-Muslimin fii Suriyya' ['The Origins and Path of the Syrian Muslim Brotherhood'], in Fayṣal Darrāj and Muḥammad Jamāl Bārūt (eds) *Mawsu'at al-'Ahzab wa-l-Jama'aat al-'Islamiyya* [*Encyclopaedia of Arab Parties and Nationalist Movements*] (Damascus: The Arab Centre for Strategic Studies) vol. 1, pp. 255–8.
16. On the organizational structure of the Muslim Brotherhood, see Richard P. Mitchell, *The Society of the Muslim Brothers* (London: I.B.Tauris, 1999) pp. 297 *et seq*.
17. Muṣṭafá al-Sibāʿī was born in Homs in 1915. He finished his studies there in 1930. Through his father, who was a mosque imam, he contacted religious scholars and occasionally substituted for his father at Friday prayers. In 1933, he travelled to Cairo to study in Al-Azhar and received his Ph.D. from there in 1949. His thesis was on 'Al Sunna and its Status in Islam'. He took part in student demonstrations against the British invasion of Cairo and was imprisoned more than once. In 1940, he helped establish a secret organization in Cairo to support A'li Al Kilani's Intifada in Iraq. The French imprisoned him in Syria in 1941 and again in 1943. He worked as a teacher in Homs, but then moved to the Arabic Islamic Institute in Damascus in 1945. Before his election as general guide of the Muslim Brotherhood in Syria he was secretary of the Prophet Mohammad's Youth Society in Homs. In summer 1957 he was elected leader of the Muslim Brotherhood and so handed over his former position in the organization to Isaam al-ʿAṭṭār. He played a significant role in college and educational life; in 1950 he was appointed as a professor at the law school in Damascus, then in 1955 he became the first dean of the Sharia school in the university. He published a number of books, the most significant of which was *Islam Socialism*. In 1956 there was an attempt to assassinate him and he died after a chronic disease in October 1964. For more on this see Sāmī Ibrāhīm al-Dallāl, *Al-Islām wa-'l-dīmūqrāṭiyah fī Sūriyah* [*Islam and Democracy in Syria: Haseer and Sareem*] (Cairo: Madbouli Library, 2007) pp. 19–43; al-Janhani, 'The Islamic Wakefulness in Greater Syria', pp. 115–16; Muṣṭafá al-Sibāʿī, *Akhlaquna al-Ijtemaeia* [*Our Social Ethics*] (Beirut: Islamic Office, 1987); Muṣṭafá al-Sibāʿī, *Hādhā mā 'allamatnī al-ḥayāh* [*That Is What Life Taught Me*] (Beirut: Islamic Office, 1987); Muṣṭafá al-Sibāʿī, *al-Mar'ah bayna al-wāqiʿ wa-al-qānūn*[*Women between Jurisprudence and Law*] (Beirut: Islamic Office, 1987).
18. Nasouh Babel, *Sahafa wa Seyassa* [*Journalism and Politics: Syria in the 20th Century*] (Beirut: Dar Riad al-Rayes, 2001); Akram al-Ḥawrānī, *Diary* (Cairo: Madbouli Library, 2000) 4 parts; Seale, *The Struggle for Syria*; Ziadeh, *The Intellectual against Power*.

19. See Abdula Hanna, *Al-Mujtamʿa al-ʾAhli wa-l-Madani fii al-Dawla al-ʿArabiyya al-Haditha* [*Native and Civil Society in the Modern Arab State*] (Damascus: Dar al-Mada, 2002) p. 349–63; Reissner, *Ideologie und Politik der Muslimbrruder Syriens*, pp. 379–91.
20. Hanna, *The Civil Society in the Arabic Modern State*, p. 389; Jonathan Owen, *Akram al-Hourani: A Study of Politics in Syria from 1943 to 1954*, translated by Wafaa al-Hourani (Homs: Dar al-Maʾaref, 1997) p. 131.
21. Owen, *Akram al-Hourani*, pp. 389–90.
22. Jamal Bārūt, 'The Muslim Brotherhood in Syria', p. 258; Abdul Rahman Al Haj, 'Political Islam's Phenomena and Trends in Syria', in Radwan Ziadeh (ed.) *Maʿrakat al-iṣlāḥ fī Sūriyah* [*Battle of Reform in Syria*] (Cairo: Cairo Centre for Human Right Studies, 2006) pp. 132–3.
23. Reissner, *Islamic Movements in Syria*, p 156; see also Hans Günter Lobmeyer, 'Islamic Ideology and Secular Discourse: The Islamists of Syria', *Orient*, vol. 32, 1991, pp. 395–418.
24. Bārūt, 'The Muslim Brotherhood in Syria', pp. 261–3. For more about the consecutive military coups that took place in Syria, see Andrew Rathmell, *Secret War in the Middle East: The Covert Struggle for Syria, 1949–1961* (London: I.B.Tauris, 1995).
25. Rathmell, *Secret War in the Middle East*, p. 262.
26. See Muṣṭafá al-Sibāʿī, *Ishtirakiyyat al-ʾIslam* [*The Socialism of Islam*] (Damascus: Damascus University Press, 1959).
27. Bārūt, 'The Muslim Brotherhood in Syria', p. 264.
28. There was much debate among Syrian elites in the 1956–63 period about the unity with and then subsequent separation from Egypt. See al-Adel, *The Story of Syria Between Elections and Revolution*; Hamadani, *An Eyewitness to Arab and Syrian Events, and the Secrets of Separation*.
29. For more on this subject see Heydemann, *Authoritarianism in Syria*; Hinnebusch, *Authoritarian Power and State Formation in Baʿthist Syria*; Hinnebusch, *Syria: Revolution from Above*; Radwan Ziadeh, *Sanʾal-Qarar wa-l-Siyasa al-Kharijiyya fii Suriyya* [*Decision Making and Syrian Foreign Policy*] (Cairo: Al-Ahram Centre for Political and Strategic Studies, 2007).
30. Hanna Batatu, *Syria's Peasantry*, p. 261.
31. Seale, *Asad of Syria: the Struggle for the Middle East*.
32. Ibid.
33. Article 3 from the Syrian constitution of 1973.
34. Batatu, *Syria's Peasantry*, p. 261.
35. Ibid, p. 261; and Patrick Seale, *Asad of Syria*, p. 279.
36. Batatu, *Syria's Peasantry*, p. 262; Seale, *Asad of Syria*, pp. 279–80.
37. For more on Sheikh Ḥasan Habanakah al-Medani and his role in Damascus city, see Reissner, *Islamic Movements in Syria*, p. 124.

38. Batatu, *Syria's Peasantry*, p. 263.
39. Ibid, p. 264.
40. For more about the writings of Sayyid Quṭb and their influence, see Radwan Ziadeh, *Su'al al-Tajdid fii al-Khitab al-Islami al-Mu'aser* [*The Question of Renewal in Contemporary Islamic Discourse*] (Beirut: Dar al-Madar al-Islami, 2004) pp. 93–114. Also see Mohamed Tawfiq Barakat, *Sayyid Quṭb: A Summary of His Life and his Method in Movement* (Beirut: Dar at-Tawhid, n.d.); and ʿAdel Hammouda, *Sayyid Quṭb: From Village to Gallows: A Documentary Investigation* (Cairo: Sina Publishing House, 1987).
41. For more about the concept of *Hakimiyya* (governorship), see Hisham Ahmad Jaʿfar, *Political Dimensions of the Concept of 'Hakemiya': Epistemological Vision* (Herndon, VA: International Institute for Islamic Thought, 1995). The concept of *Hakimiyya* was spread by Abu al-ʿAla Mawdudi, the founder of al-Jemaa e-Islami in India (then in Pakistan after secession from India) who invented this concept based on his own experience in Pakistan. Sayyid Quṭb translated this book into Arabic. The term *Hakimiyya* is derived from several verses in the Qur'an. 'No one has to rule, but God' and 'It is not judged by what Allah hath revealed, they are the disbelievers', or 'they are debauched' as said in another verse.
42. On this subject see Bārūt, 'The Muslim Brotherhood in Syria', pp. 266–9; Saʿīd Ḥawwá, *This is My Experience and My Proof* (Algeria: Dar Alwafa, 1991) pp. 72–5.
43. Perthes, *The Political Economy of Syria under Asad*, p. 28.
44. Perthes, *The Political Economy of Syria under Asad*, pp. 109–14, describes in details the rise of a new class composed of no more than a few hundred people who benefited enormously from their friendships with powerful political and military figures. See also Seale, *Asad of Syria*, p. 517.
45. Bārūt, 'The Socialist Arab Baʿth Party in Syria'.
46. Alasdair Drysdale, 'The Succession Question in Syria', *Middle East Journal*, vol. 39, no. 2, Spring 1985, pp. 93–111; al-Ḥawrānī, *Diary*, Part 4, p. 254; Tomas Kozynovsky, 'Rifaat al-Asad', *Orient*, vol. 4, 1984, pp. 465–70; Middle East Watch Committee, *Syria Unmasked*; Volker Perthes, *The Political Economy of Syria under Asad*, pp. 147–53.
47. See report of 'massacre' of 16 June 2002 by London Syrian Human Rights Committee, www.shrc.org. See also Baʿth Party, *Muslim Brotherhood: Suspected Establishment and Black History* (Damascus: Party Preparation Office, 1985) part 3, pp. 68 *et seq*; Bārūt, 'The "Nationalist" Baʿth Party: Origin, Development and Retraction', vol. 1, pp. 279 *et seq*; Hanna Batatu, 'Syria's Muslim Brotherhood', *MERIP Reports*, vol. 12, no. 110, November/December 1982, pp. 12–20.
48. Seale, *Asad and the Struggle for the Middle East*, pp. 532–3. See also report

by Syrian Committee for Human Rights, London, 26 June 2001, www.shrc.org

49. See Bārūt, 'The Muslim Brotherhood in Syria', pp. 285 *et seq*; Middle East Watch Committee, *Syria Unmasked*, pp. 163–85; Hāshim 'Uthmān, *al-Aḥzāb al-siyāsīyah fī Sūriyah: al-sirrīyah wa-al-'alanīyah* [*Public and Secret Political Parties in Syria*] (Beirut: Dar Riad al-Rayes, 2001).
50. The congregation involved five national and leftist parties – the Syrian Communist Party (Riyāḍ al-Turk); the Arab Socialist Union Party (Jamal al-Atāsī); the Revolutionary Labourers' Party (Hamdi Abdul Majeed); the Arab Socialist Movement (Abdul Ghani Ayash); and the Ba'th Arab Socialist Democratic Party (Ibraheem Makhus).
51. Al-Ḥawrānī, *Diary*, part 4, pp. 3506–14; Seale, *The Struggle for Syria*, pp. 533–4.
52. Ba'th Party, *Arab Socialist Party, reports and decisions of the regional seventh conference*, p. 25.
53. Bārūt, 'The Ba'th Party in Syria since 1970', p. 450. To learn more about the Ba'th Party's growth and development among the military and political elite, see Batatu, *Syria's Peasantry*.
54. Muslim Brotherhood in Syria, *Ḥamāh: ma'sāt al-'aṣr* [*Hama: Tragedy of our Time*] (Cairo: National Alliance to Liberate Syria, 1984). See Robert Fisk, 'Hama', *The Times*, 19 February 1982. Robert Fisk was of the first foreign correspondents to visit Hama after the fierce battles took place in it. In his report he estimated the victims at around 12,000. See also Friedman, *From Beirut to Jerusalem*, pp. 76–105; Hinnebusch, *Authoritarian Power and State Formation in Ba'thist Syria*, pp. 291–300; al-Janhani, 'Islamic Awakening in Bilad as-Sham'; Lawson, *Social Bases for the Hamah Revolt*, pp. 24–8; Roberts, *The Ba'th and the Creation of Modern Syria*, p. 128; Sadek, *A Dialogue about Syria*, pp. 166–7; Seale, *The Struggle for the Middle East*, pp. 537–40; Michel Seurat, *L'État de Barbarie* (Paris: Éditions du Seuil, 1989); van Dam, *The Struggle for Power in Syria*, pp. 165–72.
55. Batatu, *Syria's Peasantry*, p. 274.
56. Lawson, *Social Bases for the Hamah Revolt*, pp. 24–8; and van Dam, *The Struggle for Power in Syria*.
57. Ziadeh, 'The Limits of Syrian Reform', p. 104.
58. This phrase is quoted from an article by Abd al-Razzaq Eid in the Lebanese newspaper *an-Nahar*.
59. Husam Jazmattie, 'Youth and Islam in Syria', *Al-A'dab Magazine*, nos 11–12, November–December 2005, p. 111.
60. Batatu, *Syria's Peasantry*, p. 270.
61. Ibid, p. 271; Eyal Zisser, 'Hafiz al-Asad Discovers Islam', *Middle East Quarterly*, vol. 6, no. 1, March 1999.

62. Bārūt, 'The Muslim Brotherhood in Syria', pp. 302–10; ʿAdnān Saʿd al-Dīn, 'The Traditions of Political Action of the Contemporary Islamic Movement', in Abdullah an-Nufaisi (ed.) *Islamic Movement: Futuristic Vision* (Cairo: Madbouli Library, 1989) pp. 269–98.
63. Bārūt, 'The Muslim Brotherhood in Syria', pp. 203–98. For the formal authority's account, see Baʿth Party (1985) *Muslim Brotherhood: Suspected Establishment and Black History*, part 4.
64. Ibid., p. 299.
65. Ibid., pp. 308–13; Ibrahim Ḥumaydī, 'History of Secret Relations between Damascus and Syrian Muslim Brotherhood', *al-Hayat* (London) 23 February 1997.
66. See Munīr al-Ghaḍbān, *Al-Taḥāluf al-siyāsī fī al-Islām* [*Political Alliance in Islam*] (Amman: no publisher, 1982).
67. Bārūt, 'The Muslim Brotherhood in Syria', pp. 310–15.
68. Razan Zeitouneh and Abdul Haï al-Sayyed, *Can Extraordinary Courts Ensure Justice: Supreme State Security Court* (Damascus: Damascus Centre for Human Rights Studies, May 2007).
69. *Al-Hayat*, London, 4 May 2001.
70. Sheikh Abdul Salam Rājiḥ, teacher of religious principles at Al Fatah Islamic Institute and member of the Syrian People's Assembly, spoke of 'participation in the referendum as an individual's religious duty'.
71. *Al Hayat*, London, 1 March 2007.
72. According to statistics of the Syrian Ministry of Religious Endowments, the number of students in Sharia schools doubled in six years from 5574 in 1991 to 9647 in 1998, and from 38 institutes and schools to 50.
73. UNDP National Human Development Report, *Education and Human Development*, pp 82–3.
74. Shabban Abboud, 'Religious Education in Syria', *al-Hayat* (London) 23 July 2000.
75. *Al-Hayat* (London) 6 July 2006; and *an-Nahar* (Beirut) 6 July 2007.
76. *Al-Hayat* (London) 6 July 2006.
77. *Al-Hayat* (London) 10 April 2006.
78. *An-Nahar* (Beirut) 30 January 2006.
79. There is a long report on Qubeysiat, its traditions, influence and role in Syrian society in *al-Hayat* (London) 3 May 2006. Qubeysiat is a group of women followers of the female Muneerah al-Qubeysi, which exists in all the Syrian governorates, especially Damascus, as well as in some Arab countries and even in some European capitals and American states. Although there are different religious viewpoints on the ethics of this group, some distinguished Islamic scholars see it as a moderate religious movement that adopts the Sunna doctrine. Muneerah al-Qubeysi was

born in Damascus in 1933 to a family of ten children. She went to school in Damascus and studied for a degree in geology, after which she taught in the Muhajereen quarter of Damascus. According to the sheikhs and various other interested people, she has at least 75,000 female followers. She has greatly benefited from her close neighbourhood and relationship with the Abu Noor mosque of the late Aḥmad Kuftārū, the former mufti of Syria.

80. *Al-Hayat* (London) 10 April 2006.
81. *As-Safir* (Beirut) 19 June 2006.
82. Ibid.
83. *Al-Hayat* (London) 10 April 2006.
84. See *al-Hayat* (London) 12 April 2006; and Shabban Abboud, 'The Danger of Islamist Extremism', *an-Nahar* (Beirut) 17 September 2006.

References

Abboud, As'ad (1999) 'We All Hope and Wait', *al-Thawra* (Damascus) 20 February

Abboud, Shabban (2000) 'Religious Education in Syria', *al-Hayat* (London) 23 July

Abboud, Shabban (2001) 'The Short Spring of Damascus', *an-Nahar* (Beirut) 22 February

Abboud, Shabban (2006) 'The Danger of Islamist Extremism', *an-Nahar* (Beirut) 17 September

Abdelhalim, Muṣṭafá (2001) 'The Democracy of Civil Society', *al-Thawra* cultural supplement (Damascus) no. 251, 18 February

Abdul Rahman, Al Haj (2006) 'Political Islam's Phenomena and Trends in Syria', in Radwan Ziadeh (ed.) *Ma'rakat al-iṣlāḥ fī Sūriyah* [*Battle of Reform in Syria*] (Cairo: Cairo Centre for Human Right Studies) pp. 132–3

al-'Adel, Dr Fu'ad (2001) *Qissat Suriyya bayna al-Intikhab wa-l-Inqilab: Taqnin li-l-Fitra ma bayna 1942–1962* [*The Story of Syria between the Elections and the Coup, 1942–1962*] (Damascus: Dar al-Yanabi'a)

Ahmad, Ahmad Yousef (2006) 'The Israeli War on Lebanon: The Arabian Consequences', *al-Mustaqbal al-Arabi*, vol. 29, no. 332, October, pp. 3–51

Aldar, Akifa (2002) 'Sheba'a Farms are Lebanese', *Haaretz* (Tel Aviv) 25 June

Alghadiri, Nabil (2001) 'National Unity and Civil Society', *al-Muharrer al-Arabi* (Beirut) no. 283, 24 February

Alghadiri, Nihad (2001) 'Yes to Opposition in Syria in a National Society not Civil Framework', *al-Muharrer al-Arabi* (Beirut) no. 282, 17–23 February al-Anani, Khalil (2006) 'Resolution 1701: Indications and Outcomes', *Al-Siyassa al-Dawliya [International Politics]*, vol. 42, no. 166, October, pp. 142–5

Anon (1999) 'Khatami in Damascus', editorial, *an-Nour Magazine*, no. 97, June, pp. 17–18

Anon (2000) 'Assef Shawkat', editorial, *Middle East Intelligence Bulletin*, vol. 2, no. 6, 1 July

Anon (2000) 'Arrests in Syria Focusing on the Islamic Liberation Party exceeds more than 800 Persons', *al-Hayat*, editorial (London), 4 January

Anon (2001) *al-Sana al-Oula fi tareq altatweer wa altahdeeth* [*The First Year on the Way to Development and Modernization*] (Damascus: Tishreen Foundation Press and Publication)

Anon (2001) *Syria 2000: a general study on the Syrian Arab Republic* (Damascus: National Information Centre)

Anon (2002) *The 1973 Constitution of the Syrian Arab Republic* (Damascus: Muʾassasat al-Nuri)

Anon (2002) 'A Vision that Does not Lead to Peace', editorial, *Tishreen* (Damascus) 29 June

Anon (2003) 'Israel Wants US to Attack Syria', editorial, *Pravda*, 17 April

Anon (2003) 'Powell Demands Syria Cooperate with US in Mideast', *New York Times*, 3 May

Anon (2003) 'Powell Presses Syria to Change its Middle East Policies', *Reuters Report*, 3 May

Anon (2003) 'Syria to Urge Powell to Back Weapons Ban', editorial, *New York Times*, 3 May

Anon (2004) *Arbaa sanwat baʿad bidaet al-theqaa* [*Four Years after the Confident Starting Off*] (Damascus: Tishreen Foundation for Press and Publication)

Anon (2005) 'Almalaf al-Kamel al-Azab wa al-Harakat al-Seyasia fi Souria' ['The Contemporary Political Parties and Movements in Syria'], *White and Black Magazine*, vol. 3, no. 129, 30 May, pp. 81–9

al-ʿArawī, ʿAbd Allāh (1987) *Mafhūm al-dawlah* [*Concept of the State*] (Beirut: Arab Cultural Centre) al-ʿAzem, Khaled (1996) *Diary* (Beirut: United Company for Publishing)

Babel, Nasouh (2001) *Sahafa wa Seyassa* [*Journalism and Politics: Syria in the 20th Century*] (Beirut: Dar Riad al-Rayes)

al-Bahra, Nasr al-Deen (2000) 'The Significance of Allowing Syrian Parties to Issue Open Newspapers', *al-Hayat* (London) 16 December

Baidatz, Yossi (2001) *Bashar's First Year: From Ophthalmology to a National Vision* (Washington, DC: Washington Institute for Near East Policy, Policy Focus 41, July)

Bakasini, George (2001) 'Al-Asad's Speech is a Successful Preamble for a Successful Visit', *al-Mustaqbal* (Beirut) 24 June

Bakhour, Ghi (2001) 'Unwise Israeli Isolation because of the Syrian Seat', *Haaretz* (Tel Aviv) 15 October

Barakat, Mohamed Tawfiq (n.d.) *Sayyid Quṭb: A Summary of His Life and his Method in Movement* (Beirut: Dar at-Tawhid)

Barringer, Felicity (2003) 'The Mideast Turmoil: United Nations: Syria Offers a Resolution to Condemn Israeli Raid', *New York Times*, 6 October

Bārūt, Muḥammad Jamāl (2000) 'The Baʿth Party in Syria since 1970', in Fayṣal Darrāj and Muḥammad Jamāl Bārūt (eds) *Mawsuʿat al-Ahzab wa-l-Harakat al-Qawmiyya al-ʿArabiyya* [*The Encyclopedia of Arab Nationalist Movements and Parties*] (Damascus: The Arabic Centre for Strategic Studies)

Bārūt, Muḥammad Jamāl (2000) 'The "Nationalist" Baʿth Party: Origin, Development and Retraction', in Fayṣal Darrāj and Muḥammad Jamāl Bārūt (eds) *Mawsuʿat al-Ahzab wa-l-Harakat al-Qawmiyya al-ʿArabiyya* [*The Encyclopedia of Arab Nationalist Movements and Parties*] (2 vols, Damascus: Arab Centre for Strategic studies)

Bārūt, Muḥammad Jamāl (2000) 'The Socialist Arab Baʿth Party in Syria: From the Corrective Movement to the Liquidation of the Generals' Centres', *Al-Hayat* (London) 15 June

Bārūt, Muḥammad Jamāl (2000) 'The Muslim Brotherhood in Syria: Origins and Continuities of Conflict between Traditional and Radical Schools', in Fayṣal Darrāj and Muḥammad Jamāl Bārūt (eds) *Encyclopedia of Arab Parties and Nationalist Movements* (Damascus: The Arab Centre for Strategic Studies) vol. 1, pp. 255–63

Bārūt, Muḥammad Jamāl (2001) 'Usul wa Ta'arujat Jama'at al-Ikhwan al-Muslimin fii Suriyya' ['The Origins and Path of the Syrian Muslim Brotherhood'], in Fayṣal Darrāj and Muḥammad Jamāl Bārūt (eds) *Mawsu'at al-Ahzab wa-l-Harakat al-Qawmiyya al-'Arabiyya* [*Encyclopedia of Arab Parties and Nationalist Movements*] 2 vols (Damascus: The Arab Centre for Strategic Studies)

Bārūt, Muḥammad Jamāl (2002) 'Booty Mind and Reform Thinking', *Orient News Web Site*, 17 October

Bārūt, Muḥammad Jamāl (2003) *Isteqtabat al-Kuwa Fi al-noukhba' assouria* [*Power Polarization in the Syrian Elite*] (Amman: Dar Sindbad)

Batatu, Hanna (1982) 'Syria's Muslim Brotherhood', *MERIP Reports*, vol. 12, no. 110, November/December, pp. 12–20

Batatu, Hanna (1999) *Syria's Peasantry, the Descendants of its Lesser Rural Notables, and their Politics* (Princeton: Princeton University Press)

Ba'th Party (1974) *The Arab Socialist Ba'th Party, Reports and Decisions of the Fifth Exceptional Regional Conference held in Damascus between 30 May and 13 June 1974* (Damascus: Ba'th Party Publications)

Ba'th Party (1980) *Arab Socialist Party, Reports and Decisions of the Seventh Regional Conference* (Damascus: Ba'th Party Publications)

Ba'th Party (1985) *Muslim Brotherhood: Suspected Establishment and Black History* (Damascus: Ba'th Party Party Preparation Office)

Ba'th Party (2000) *Arab Socialist Party, Reports of the Ninth Regional Conference held between 17 and 20 of June 2000* (Damascus: Ba'th Party Publications)

Binzel, Christine, Tilman Brück and Lars Handrich (2008) 'The Progress of Economic Reform in Syria', paper presented at the Centre for Syrian Studies conference, 10–12 April, St Andrews, UK

Bshara, Marwan (2002) 'Bush's Imaginary Plan Repeats the Previous Mistakes', *International Herald Tribune*, 27 June

Bukhari, Burhan (1999) 'It is Our Issues First and Foremost', *Tishreen* (Damascus) 29 August

Bulloch, John (1977) *Death of a Country: The Civil War in Lebanon* (London: Weidenfeld & Nicholson)

Cobban, Helena (1999) *The Israeli–Syrian Peace Talks 1991–96 and Beyond* (Washington DC: US Institute for Peace Press)

Cobban, Helena (1999) 'The Big Lost Opportunity: Syrian–Israeli Negotiations', *al-Siyasah* (Kuwait) no. 17, 7 July

Cohen, Judith (2002) 'The Unsuccessful Spring of Damascus', *Le Monde Diplomatique*, November

Commins, David Dean (1990) *Islamic Reform: Politics and Social Change in Late Ottoman Syria* (Oxford: Oxford University Press)

Cook, William A. (2003) 'Sharon Recruits US Mercenaries against Syria of Pariahs and Pre-emptive Strikes', *Counter Punch*, 26 April

Cordesman, Anthony H. (2003) *If it's Syria: Syrian Military Forces and Capabilities* (Washington, DC: Centre for Strategic and International Studies, 15 April)

Daguerre, Violate (ed.) (2000) *Democracy and Human Rights in Syria*, translated by Zayna Larbi (Paris: Arab Commission for Human Rights and European Commission, Europe Publishers)

al-Dajani, Hisham (2000) 'Voices in Syrian Public Opinion and the Strange Silence towards the Peace Issue', *al-Hayat* (London) 9 February

al-Dajani, Hisham (2000) 'What is Going on in Present Day Syria?' *an-Nahar* (Beirut) 26 May

Dakhlallah, Mahdi (2003) 'Let's Give them the Opposite of What they Expect', *al-Ba'th* (Damascus) 8 October

al-Dallāl, Sāmī Ibrāhīm (2007) *Al-Islām wa-'l-dīmūqrāṭiyah fī Sūriyah* [*Islam and Democracy in Syria: Haseer and Sareem*] (Cairo: Madbouli Library)

Dalrymple, William (2003) 'Tolerance Thrives amid Syria's Repression, *International Herald Tribune*, 10 June

Dan, Uri (2003) 'Game Over for Syria's Double-Dealer', *New York Post*, 30 March

Dawisha, Adeed I. (1980) *Syria and the Lebanese Crisis* (London: Macmillan Press)

al-Dedjani, Hesham (1999) 'Combating Corruption and Modernizing Laws are the Highest Priority of Reform', *al-Hayat*, (London) 27 May al-Dedjani, Hesham (1999) 'What does Modernization Mean in Syria and Who are its Agents?', *an-Nahar*, (Beirut) 30 March

ad-Deen, Sa'd al-Dīn Saad (1989) 'The Traditions of Political Action of the Contemporary Islamic Movement', in Abdullah an-Nufaisi (ed.) *Islamic Movement: Futuristic Vision* (Cairo: Madbouli Library) pp. 269–98

Dergham, Raghida (2002) 'Towards an Arab Peace "Viewpoint" that Complies with the American "Viewpoint"', *al-Hayat* (London) 1 March

Devlin, John F. (1976) *The Ba'th Party: A History from its Origins to 1966* (Stanford, CA: Hoover Institution Press)

Deyoung, Karen (2003) 'US Warns Syria it is Watching its Actions', *Washington Post*, 5 May

Diab, Ahmad (2006) 'International Positions towards the War on Lebanon', *International Politics*, vol. 42, no. 166, October, pp. 138–41

Diab, 'Izz al-Din (1933) *Al-Tahlil al-Ijtima'i li-Zhahirat al-Inqisam al-Siyyasi fii al-Watan al-'Arabi* [*A Social Analysis of the Political Split in the Arab World*] (Cairo: Madbouli Library)

Drysdale, Alasdair (1985) 'The Succession Question in Syria', *Middle East Journal*, vol. 39, no. 2, Spring, pp. 93–111

Eid, Abdel Razzaq (2001) 'Civil Society in Syria: From Association of Friends to Committees of Revival', *al- Adaab Magazine*, nos 1–2, January and February

Eid, Abdel Razzaq (2001) 'The Culture of Intimidation', lecture given at Jamal al-Atāsī Forum for Democratic Dialogue in May

Ezzelarab, Khaled (2003) 'Syria's Turn', *Cairo Times*, vol. 7, no. 8, 24–30 April

Fattah, Bashir Abdul (2006) 'The Arab Position towards the Israeli Agression on Lebanon', *Al-Siyassa al-Dawliya [International Politics]*, vol. 42, no. 166, October, pp. 130–3

Field, Peter Brown (2003) 'The Syria Accountability Act', *Fox News*, 6 November

Filmann, Josi (2000) 'Until the Last Gates are Closed', *Haaretz* (Tel Aviv) 25 May

Fisk, Robert (1982) 'Hama', *The Times*, 19 February

Fisk, Robert (2003) 'Israel's Attack is a Lethal Step towards War in Middle East', *Independent*, October

Friedman, Thomas (1989) *From Beirut to Jerusalem* (New York: Farrar, Straus & Giroux)

George, Alan (2003) *Syria: Neither Bread nor Freedom* (London: Zed Books)

al-Ghaḍbān, Munīr (1982) *Al-Taḥāluf al-siyāsī fī al-Islām* [*Political Alliance in Islam*] (Amman: no publisher)

al-Ghali, Kamāl (1987) *Mabadeʾ al-Qanun al-Dustouri wa-l-Nazm al-Siyasiyya* [*Basics of Constitutional Law and Political Regimes*] (Damascus: Dar al-ʿUrouba)

Ghalion, Burhan (2001) 'The Future of Reforms in Syria: Towards a New National Contract', speech given at the Forum of National Dialogue, 5 September 2001, *al-Hayat* (London) 7 September

Ghalion, Burhan (2006) 'Asadism in Syrian Policy or the Role of Regional Policy in Realizing Internal Control', in Radwan Ziadeh (ed.) *Maʿrakat al-iṣlāḥ fī Sūriyah* [*Battle of Reform in Syria*] (Cairo: Cairo Institute for Human Rights Studies) pp. 15–45

Ghranout, Audid (2002) 'The Crown Prince Bomb', *Maarif* (Tel Aviv) 1 March

Goldstein, Fred (2003) 'Bush Hails Israel: Attack on Syria', *Workers World Newspaper*, and 16 October

Habib, Abdullah Bu (2005) 'Syria's Strategic Mistakes in its Relations with Washington', *al-Hayat* (London) 11 April

Haddad, Bassam (2004) 'The Formation and Development of Economic Networks in Syria: Implications for Economic and Fiscal Reform, 1986–2000', in Steven Heydemann (ed.) *Networks of Privilege in the Middle East: The Politics of Economic Reform Revisited* (New York: Palgrave Macmillan) pp. 37–75

al-Hadidi, Subhi (2001) 'Damascus and the Cost of the Dissolution of "Terrorist" Organizations: The Consequences of the Double-Faced Game', *al-Quds al-Arabi* (London) 28 December al-Ḥāfiẓ, Yāsīn (1997) *Al-Hazemaa' and Fekh Al-Hazemaa'* [*The Defeat and the Defeated Ideology*] (Damascus: al-Hasad)

al-Ḥāfiẓ, Yāsīn (1997) *Ḥawla ba'ḍ qaḍāyā al-thawrah al-'Arabīyah* [*About Some Issues of the Arab Revolution*] (Damascus: al-Hasad)

Haidar, Zyad (2001) 'Ba'th Members Participate in the Dialogue and Criticize Seif's Paper', *As-Safir* newspaper (Beirut) 2 February

Hamdan, Hamdan (2001) 'The Mediocre Totalitarian Response Against the Affiliates of Social Society: The Speech of 'Abd al-Ḥalīm Khaddām as an Example', *an-Nahar*, 5 September

Hamdani, Muṣṭafá Ram (2001) *Shahid 'ala 'Ahdath Suriyya wa 'Arabiyya wa 'Asrar al-Infisal* [*A Witness to Syrian and Arab Events and the Secrets of Separation*] (Damascus: dar Tlas)

Hammouda, 'Adel (1987) *Sayyid Quṭb: From Village to Gallows: A Documentary Investigation* (Cairo: Sina Publishing House)

Hanna, Abdula (2002) *Al-Mujtam'a al-'Ahli wa-l-Madani fii al-Dawla al-'Arabiyya al-Haditha* [*Native and Civil Society in the Modern Arab State*] (Damascus: Dar al-Mada)

Harrison, David (2003) 'Syria Threatens to Attack Golan Settlers if Israel Strikes Again', *Daily Telegraph*, 26 October

al-Hasan, Belal (2000) 'The Ba'th Party and Economic Decisions', al-*Hayat* (London), 7 December

al-Hasan, Belal (2001) 'Ba'th Party and Economic Decrees', *al-Hayat* (London) 12 July

al-Ḥawrānī, Akram (2000) *Diary* (Cairo: Madbouli Library)

Ḥawwá, Sa'īd (1991) *This is My Experience and My Proof* (Algeria: Dar Alwafa)

Ḥaydar, Muḥammad (1998) *Al-Ba'th: al-inqisām al-kabīr* [*Al-Ba'th and the Big Division*] (Damascus: Dar al-Ahalie)

Hemaidi, Ebrahim (2000) 'Permission to Issue Open Newspapers Poses Three New Challenges to the Front Parties', *al-Hayat* (London) 16 December

Hersh, Seymour M. (2003) 'The Syrian Bet', *New Yorker*, 28 July

Heydemann, Steven (1999) *Authorianism in Syria: Institutions and Social Conflict 1946–1970* (Ithaca: Cornell University Press)

Hinnebusch, Raymond (1980) 'Political Recruitment and Socialization in Syria: The Case of the Revolutionary Youth Federation', *International Journal of Middle East Studies*, vol. 11, pp. 143–74

Hinnebusch, Raymond (1993) 'State and Civil Society in Syria', *Middle East Journal*, vol. 47, no. 2, spring, pp. 243–57

Hinnebusch, Raymond A. (1998) *Authoritarian Power and State Formation in Baʿthist Syria: Army, Party and Peasant* (Boulder: Westview Press)

Hinnebuch, Raymond (2001) *Syria: Revolution from Above* (London: Routledge)

Hinnebusch, Raymond A. (2005) 'Syria after the Iraq War: Between Domestic Reform and the New Conservatives' Attack', in Radwan Ziadeh (ed.) *Al-iṣlāḥ fī Sūriyah bayna al-siyāsāt al-dākhilīyah wa-al-taḥawwulāt al-iqlīmīyah wa-al-duwalīyah [Reform in Syria between Internal Policies and International and Regional Transformations]* (Jeddah: Al-Raya Centre for Intellectual Development)

Hinnebusch, Raymond (2005) 'Syrian Foreign Policy between Realism and Idealism', in Radwan Ziadeh (ed.) *Al-iṣlāḥ fī Sūriyah bayna al-siyāsāt al-dākhilīyah wa-al-taḥawwulāt al-iqlīmīyah wa-al-duwalīyah [Reform in Syria between Internal Policies and International and Regional Transformations]* (Jeddah: Al-Raya Centre for Intellectual Development)

Hulse, Carl (2003) 'Panel Approves Sanctions on Syria with White House Support', *New York Times*, 9 October

Ḥumaydī, Ibrāhīm (2000) 'The Baʿth Conference Lays the Foundations of the Ongoing Change Option', *al-Wasat*, no. 427, 12 June

Ḥumaydī, Ibrāhīm (2001) 'Intellectuals Establishing Forums for Civil Society and Human Rights', *al-Awsat* (London) no. 467, 8 January

Ḥumaydī, Ibrāhīm (2001) 'The Story of the "Principal Document" for the Committees of Civil Society in Syria', *al- Hayat*, London, 21 January

Ḥumaydī, Ibrāhīm (2001) 'The Baʿth Party Mounts a Campaign against Intellectuals', *al-Hayat* (London) 16 February

Ḥumaydī, Ibrāhīm (1997) 'History of Secret Relations between Damascus and Syrian Muslim Brotherhood', *al-Hayat* (London) 23 February

Ḥuwayjah, Fāʾiq ʿAlī (2005) *Maḥaṭṭāt tārīkhīyah fī al-Dustūr* [*Historical Development of the Constitution: A Comparative Analytical Study*] (Damascus: University School of Law)

Indyk, Martin (2002) 'The White House and the Middle East Crisis', *New York Times*, 12 August

International Crisis Group (2005) 'Syria after Lebanon: Lebanon after Syria', *Middle East Report*, no. 39, 12 April

Jaber, Kamel Abu (1966) *The Arab Baʿth Socialist Party: History, Ideology and Organization* (Syracuse: Syracuse University Press)

Jaʿfar, Hisham Ahmad (1995) *Political Dimensions of the Concept of 'Hakemiya': Epistemological Vision* (Herndon, VA: International Institute for Islamic Thought)

al-Janhani, al-Habib (1987) 'The Islamic Wakefulness in Greater Syria: The Syrian Example', in Anon, *Contemporary Islamic Movement in the Arab Homeland* (Beirut: Centre for Arab Unity Studies)

Janson, Michael (1999) 'Bashar in Paris', *Middle East International*, no. 612, 12 November

al-Jarad, Khalaf (2002) 'An Obscure "Viewpoint" and a Queer Logic', *Tishreen* (Damascus) 1 July

ʿAbd al-Jawwād, Jamāl and Muḥammad Munīr Luṭfī (1996) *Sūriyah tufāwiḍ Isrāʾīl* [*Syria Negotiates with Israel*] (Cairo: Centre of Strategic and Political Studies)

Jazmattie, Husam (2005) 'Youth and Islam in Syria', *Al-Aʿdab Magazine*, nos 11–12, November–December, p. 111

Jouejati, Murhaf (2002) 'The Abdullah Plan and the Arab States', *Middle East Institute*, 4 March

Jouejati, Murhaf (2002) 'The Arab Summit: Israeli Opportunity?' *Middle East Institute*, 5 April

Jradat, Ismail (1999) 'Modernization is a Patriot Duty', *al-Thawra* (Damascus) 13 March

al-Jubūrī, ʿAbd al-Jabbār Ḥasan (1980) *al-Aḥzāb wa-al-jamʿīyāt al-siyāsīyah fī Sūriyah min awākhir al-qarn al-tāsiʿ ʿashar ḥattá 1958* [Political Parties *and Societies in Syria from the Late Nineteenth Century to 1958*] (Baghdad: Dar al-Hurria Publishing House)

Kabbani, Nader and Noura Kamel (2007) *Youth Exclusion in Syria: Social, Economic and Industrial Dimensions* (Middle East Youth Initiative, Wolfensohn Centre for Development at Brookings Institution and Dubai School for Government, working paper no. 4, September)

al-Kafri, Abdul Ra'ouf (2000) 'The New Syrian Government between Constancy and Change', *al-Shahr*, no. 83, May, pp 22–3

Kasbit, Bin (2002) 'One of the Most Successful Weeks', *Maarif* (Tel Aviv) 28 June

Kessler, Glenn (2003) 'Syria Shut Offices of Palestinian Groups: US Labels Terrorists, Powell Says', *Washington Post*, 4 May

Khaddām, ʿAbd al-Ḥalīm (2001) 'We Shall Not Allow the Partition of Syria and Return to the Times of Revolutions', *al-Hayat*, 10 July

Khalifah, Isam (2000) 'A Documented Study Confirming the Lebanese Character of Sheba'a Farms', *As-Safir* (Beirut) 19 May

Khalifah, Sawsan (1999) 'Personal Concern of President Asad, Electricity Sector: From Meeting the Local Need to Exportation', *Al-Thawra* (Damascus), 28 January

Khbiz, Bilal (2000) 'Memorandum of the 99 Intellectuals of Syria', *an-Nahar* supplement (Beirut) 7 October

Khoury, Philip S. (1983) *Urban Notables and Arab Nationalism: The Politics of Damascus, 1860–1920* (Cambridge: Cambridge University Press)

Khoury, Philip S. (1987) *Syria and the French Mandate: The Politics of Arab Nationalism, 1920–1945* (Princeton: Princeton University Press)

al-Khunizi, Najib (2002) 'The Crown Prince Initiative and the Horizons of Settlement', *al-Watan* (Abha) 8 March

Kilo, Michael (2006) 'Transformations of Syrian Regional Policy with Regard to Relations with Lebanon', in Radwan Ziadeh (ed.) *Maʿrakat al-iṣlāḥ fī Sūriyah* [*Battle of Reform in Syria*] (Cairo: Cairo Institute for Human Rights Studies) pp. 47–60

Kozynovsky, Tomas (1984) 'Rifaat al-Asad', *Orient*, vol. 4, pp. 465–70

Lamb, David (2003) 'Hezbollah Feeling the Squeeze', *Los Angeles Times*, 3 May

Lawson, Fred H. (1982) *Social Bases for the Hamah Revolt*, Merip Reports, November/December

Lesch, David W. (2005) *The New Lion of Damascus: Bashar al-Asad and Modern Syria* (New Haven: Yale University Press)

Leverett, Flynt (2003) 'How to Get Syria out of the Terrorism Business', *New York Times*, 3 May

Leverett, Flynt (2005) *Inheriting Syria: Bashar's Trial by Fire* (Washington, DC: Brookings Institution Press)

Levitt, Matthew (2003) 'Terror from Damascus: The Palestinian Terrorist Presence in Syria', *Peace Watch* (Washington Institute for Near East Policy) no. 420, 7 May

Lobmeyer, Hans Günter (1991) 'Islamic Ideology and Secular Discourse: The Islamists of Syria', *Orient*, vol. 32, pp. 395–418

MacFarquhar, Neil (2003) 'Syria Leader Says Israel Aims to Stir Region', *New York Times*, 8 October

Makhus, Ibrahim (2003) 'The Previous (Elections) in Syria and the State of Continuous Blockage', *Orient News* website, 15 April

Makovsky, Alan (2001) *Syria under Bashar al-Asad: The Domestic Scene and the 'Chinese Model' of Reform* (Washington: Institute for Near East Policy, Policy Watch, no. 512, 17 January)

Malbrunot, Georges (2002) *Des Pierres aux Fusils: Les Secrets de l'Intifada* (Paris: Flammarion)

Manna, Haitham (2000) 'The Democratic Option in Syria', *al-Hayat* (London) 11 June

Mansour, ʿAbd al-Aziz Shehada (2000) *Al-Masʾala al-Maʾiyya fii al-Siyasa al-Suriyya Tujah Turkiyya* [*The Issue of Water in Syrian Policy towards Turkey*] (Beirut: Centre for Arab Unity Studies)

Maʿoz, Moshe (1986) 'The Emergence of Modern Syria', in Moshe Maʿoz and Amer Yanir (eds) *Syria under Asad* (London: Croom Helm)

Maʿoz, Moshe (1988) *The Sphinx of Damascus: A Political Biography* (New York: Weidenfeld & Nicholson)

Ma'oz, Moshe (1993) *Sūriyah wa-Isrā'īl min al-ḥarb ilá ṣan' al-salām* [*Syria and Israel from War to Peace-making*] (Amman: Dar al-Jalil)

Ma'oz, Moshe (1995) *Sūriyah wa-Isrā'īl min al-ḥarb ilá ṣan' al-salām* [*Syria and Israel: From War to Peacemaking*] (Oxford: Clarendon Press)

Marcus, Joel (1996) 'Peres's Hard Face', *Haaretz* (Tel Aviv) 19 April

Marcus, Joel (2002) 'Another Text Like This', *Haaretz* (Tel Aviv) 28 June

Margalit, Dan (2002) 'The Saudi Initiative', *Maarif* (Tel Aviv)1 March

Mazloum, D. Jamal (2006) 'Hezbollah Management of Military Operations in the Lebanese War', *Al-Siyassa al-Dawliya [International Politics]*, vol. 42, no. 166, October, pp. 96–100

Mekelberg, Yossi (2006) 'Israel and London: Soul Searching', *World Today*, vol. 62, no. 10, October, pp. 12–13

Mesed, Nivin (2006) 'The Israeli War on Lebanon: Regional Consequences, Iran', *al-Mustaqbal al-Arabi*, vol. 29, no. 332, October, pp. 52–72

Middle East Watch Committee (ed.) (1991) *Syria Unmasked: The Suppression of Human Rights by the Regime* (New Haven: Yale University Press)

Mitchell, Richard P. (1999) *The Society of the Muslim Brothers* (London: I.B.Tauris, 1999)

Mnimna, Hasan (2002) 'A New Call for Account for Syria or Usual American Internal Pull Back and Forth', *al-Hayat* (London) 16 September

Mohammed, Ibrahim (1999) 'Reform is the Priority in Education and Judiciary Sectors', *al-Hayat* (London) 9 June

Movaz, Shaul (2003) 'The Israeli Minister of Defence who Alleged that Syria had Provided the Iraqi Army with Antitank Weapons', *Haaretz* (Tel Aviv) 2 April

Murphy, Richard W. (2003) 'Raid against Syria sets Regrettable Precedent', Council of Foreign Relations, 8 October

Musilli, Munzer (2001) 'The Civil Society Group: Dreaming Ambitions and Wondering Lectures', *al-Muharrer al-Arabi* (Beirut) no. 281, 16 February

Musleh, Mohammad (2000) *Al-Jawlan: Al-Tariq ila al-ʾIhtilal* [*The Golan: Path to Occupation*] (Beirut: Palestinian Studies Foundation)

Muslim Brotherhood in Syria (1984) *Ḥamāh: maʾsāt al-ʿaṣr* [*Hama: Tragedy of our Time*] (Cairo: National Alliance to Liberate Syria)

Muslim Brotherhood in Syria (2001) 'Project of National Honorary Pact for Political Work Insists on Dialogue and Democratic Work while Assuring its Abandonment of Violence', *al-Hayat* (London) 4 May

Naddaf, Imad (2000) 'On the Margin of the Ninth Conference: The Peculiarity of the Syrian Baʿth', *al-Hayat* (London) 21 May

Naddaf, Imad (2000) 'Factious Press and its Need to be Studied', *al-Hayat* (London) 16 December

Nafeʾa, Hasan (2006) 'The Israeli War on Lebanon: The International Consequences', *al-Mustaqbal al-Arabi*, vol. 29, no. 332, October, pp. 88–103

Nafeʾa, Hasan (2006) *The Israeli War against Lebanon: Lebanese and Israeli Consequences and their Arab, Regional and International Effects* (Beirut: Centre for Arab Unity Studies)

Naʾoum, Sarkis (2001) 'Syria and the United States', *an-Nahar*, 11 December

Nassar, Salim (1999) 'Why Hafez al-Asad Suddenly Decided to Participate in King Hussein's Funeral', *al-Hayat* (London) 13 February

Nassar, Salim (2001) 'Sharon Changes the Rules of the Syrian Confrontation in Lebanon', *al-Hayat* (London) 21 April

Noor, Ayman Abdul (2000) 'What is Required from the Ninth Regional Conference: To Envisage the Economic Future of Syria', *al-Muharrer News* (Beirut) no. 247, 9–15 June

Orbach, Benjamin and David Schenker (1999) *The Rise of Bashar al-Asad* (Washington: Institute for Near East Policy, Policy Watch, no. 371, 5 March)

Owen, Jonathan (1997) *Akram al-Hourani: A Study of Politics in Syria from 1943 to 1954*, translated by Wafaa al-Ḥawrānī (Homs: Dar al-Maʾaref)

Para'el, Tasvi (2002) 'Saudi on the Horizon', *Haaretz* (Tel Aviv) 10 March

Patriman, Aouzi (2002) 'Abdullah's Good Omen', *Yedioth Ahronoth* (Tel Aviv) 1 March

Perthes, Volker (1995) 'Private Sector, Economic Liberation and the Possibilities of Moving towards Democracy', in Ghasan Salāmah (ed.) *Democracy Without Democrats: Politics Openness in the Islamic Arab World* (Beirut: Arab Unity Research Centre) pp. 125–46

Perthes, Volker (1995) *The Political Economy of Syria under Asad* (London: I.B.Tauris)

Perthes, Volker (2001) 'The Political Economy of the Syrian Succession', *Survival*, no. 1, Spring, pp. 143–5

Perthes, Volker (2004) 'Managing Modernization: Domestic Politics and the Limits of Change', in Radwan Ziadeh (ed.) *Reform in Syria between Domestic Politics and Regional and International Changes* (Jeddah: al-Raya Centre for Intellectual Development) pp. 7–26

Peterlan, Lucian (1987) *Hafez al-Asad: The Career of a Combatant*, translated by Ilias Bdewi (Damascus: Tlas)

Pilin, Yossi (2006) 'Attacking Syria', translated from Hebrew, *al-Mustaqbal* (Beirut) 14 July

Pincus, Walter (2003) 'Syrian–US Ties Strained by Iraq War', *Washington Post*, 4 April

Pirproglo, Pirch (2002) *Disturbance in the Middle East: Imperialism, War and Instability*, translated by Fakhri Labib, revised by Naser al-Safadi (Cairo: High Council of Culture)

Qader, Mohammad Abdul (1999) *The Strategy of the Syrian Negotiations with Israel* (Abu Dhabi: Emirates Centre for Strategic Studies and Research Studies)

Qaseer, Samir (2000) 'Syria Alive', *an-Nahar*, 29 September

Rabinovich, Itamar (1972) *Syria under the Baʿth, 1963–66: The Army Party Symbiosis* (Jerusalem: Israel University Press)

Rabinovich, Itamar (1991) *The Road not Taken: Early Arab-Israeli Negotiations* (New York: Oxford University Press)

Rashed, Sameh (2006) 'Iran and Syria: Agreeing on Lebanon', *Al-Siyassa al-Dawliya [International Politics]*, vol. 42, no. 166, October, pp. 134–7

Rathmell, Andrew (1995) *Secret War in the Middle East: The Covert Struggle for Syria, 1949–1961* (London: I.B.Tauris)

Reissner, Johannes (1980) *Ideologie und Politik der Muslimbrüder Syriens* (Freiburg: Klaus Schwarz Verlag)

Reissner, Johannes (2005) *Islamic Movements in Syria*, translated by Mohammad Ibraheem al-Atāsī (Beirut: Dar Riad al-Rayes)

Revival of Civil Society Committees in Syria (2001) 'Towards a National Social Contract in Syria: General National Concurrences', *an-Nahar*, 18 April

Roberts, David (1987) *The Baʿth and the Creation of Modern Syria* (New York: St Martin's Press)

Ross, Dennis (2004) *The Missing Peace: The Inside Story of the Fight for Middle East Peace* (New York: Farrar, Straus & Giroux)

Ross, Sonya (2003) 'Syria Mast Down on Terror Groups, Powell Says', *Associated Press Report*, 3 May

al-Rumayhie, Mohamad (2000) 'The Ambition to Change in Syria', *an-Nahar* (Beirut) 2 October

Ṣādiq, Maḥmūd (n.d.) *Ḥiwār ḥawla Sūriyah* [*A Dialogue about Syria*] (Cairo: no publisher)

al-Safadi, Mutaʿ (1964) *Hizb al-Baʿth: maʿsat al-mawlid, maʿsat al-nihaya* (*The Baʿth Party: The Tragedies of its Birth and End*) (Beirut: Dar al-Adab)

Sagieh, Hazem (2001) 'Society of the Civil Guesthouse', *al-Hayat* (London) February

Salam, Mohammad Abdul (2006) 'The Military Lessons of the Lebanon War', *Al-Siyassa al-Dawliya [International Politics]*, vol. 42, no. 166, October, pp. 120–5

Salāmah, Ghassān (1987) *Al-Mujtamaʿ wa-l-Dawla fii al-Mashreq al-ʿArabi* [*Society and the State in the Arab Levant: Predicting the Future of the Arab Homeland*] (Beirut: Centre for Arab Unity Studies)

Salameh, Mahmoud (1999) 'Reform and Modernization in the Plurality-Based National Scene', *al-Hayat*, (London) 4 June

Salibi, Kamal S. (1976) *Crossroads to Civil War: Lebanon, 1958–1976* (Delmar, NY: Caravan Books)

Salloum, Tha'er (2001) 'Syrian Ba'th Members Accuse Founder of Social Peace Movement of Falsification', *al-Zaman* (London) 2 February

Sarid, Yusi (2006) 'What is Bad in a Good Speech?' *Yedioth Ahronoth*, 27 June

Satloff, Robert and Alan Makovsky (1996) 'Changing Asad's Incentive Structure: Christopher in the Lion's Den', *Policy Watch*, Washington Institute for Near East Policy, no. 194, 22 April

Sayf, Riyāḍ (1999) *Experience: Concerns for Industry and Policy* (Damascus: Limited Edition)

Sayf, Riyāḍ (2001) 'Movement of Social Peace: Elemental Principles for Dialogue', *al-Zaman* (London) 3–4 February

Sayf, Riyāḍ (2001) *Ṣafqat ʿuqūdal-khalawī* [*Transaction of Cellular Contracts*] (Damascus: Limited Edition)

Schiff, Zaif (1984) 'Dealing with Syria', *Foreign Policy*, no. 55, Summer

Schiff, Zaif (1992) *Peace with Security: Israel Minimum Security Requirements in its Negotiations with Syria*, translated by Military Studies Centre (Damascus: Military Research Centre)

Schiff, Zaif (2000) 'The New Security Theory', *Haaretz* (Tel Aviv) 25 April

Schmidt, Søren (2008) 'The Developmental Role of the State in the Middle East', paper presented at the Centre for Syrian Studies conference, 10–12 April, St Andrews, UK

Seale, Patrick (1988) *Asad and the Struggle for the Middle East* (London: al-Saqi Press)

Seale, Patrick (1988) *The Struggle for Syria: A Study of Post-War Arab Politics, 1945–1958* (London: I.B.Tauris)

Seale, Patrick (1989) *Asad of Syria: The Struggle for the Middle East* (Berkeley, CA: University of California Press)

Seale, Patrick (2000) 'From Father to Son: The New Regime in Syria', *al-Hayat* (London) 12 June

Seale, Patrick (2002) 'In the Context of the Saudi Initiative', *al-Hayat* (London) 1 March

Selvik, Kjetil (2008) 'Syria's Turn to the Private Sector', paper presented at the Centre for Syrian Studies conference, 10–12 April, St Andrews, UK

Seurat, Michel (1989) *L'État de Barbarie* (Paris: Editions du Seuil)

Shallah, Awvar (2000) 'Hezbollah Takes the Decision', *Yedioth Ahronoth* (Tel Aviv) 24 May

Shamālī, Naṣr (1969) *Ayyām ḥāsimah fī tārīkh al-Ba'th* [*Critical Days in the History of the Party*] (Damascus: Al-Wahdah)

Shehadi, Nadim (2006) 'Iran–US Confrontation in Lebanon: Capitulate or Escalate', *World Today*, vol. 62, no. 10, October, pp. 9–11

al-Shibani, Karim (2000) 'What Do the Syrians Want from the Ninth Conference of the Ba'th Party?', *As-Safir* (Beirut) 6 June

Shif, Zaʾif (2003) 'Against the Outward Slide of Confrontation', *Haaretz* (Tel Aviv) 10 October

Shiver, Shamoun (2002) 'Sharon: We Did Our Duty', *Yedioth Ahronoth* (Tel Aviv) 28 June

Shiver, Shamoun (2003) 'Sharon has to Give the Evidence', *Yedioth Ahronoth* (Tel Aviv) 11 May

Shoʿaibi, Imad Faozi (1999) 'Combating and Changing Corruption in Syria', *al-Hayat*, (London) 4 June

al-Sibāʿī, Muṣṭafá (1959) *ʾIshtirakiyyat al-ʾIslam* [*The Socialism of Islam*] (Damascus: Damascus University Press)

al-Sibāʿī, Muṣṭafá (1987) *Akhlaquna al-Ijtemaeia* [*Our Social Ethics*] (Beirut: Islamic Office)

al-Sibāʿī, Muṣṭafá (1987) *Hādhā mā 'allamatnī al-ḥayāh* [*That Is What Life Taught Me*] (Beirut: Islamic Office)

al-Sibāʿī, Muṣṭafá (1987) *al-Marʾah bayna al-wāqiʿ wa-al-qānūn* [*Women between Jurisprudence and Law*] (Beirut: Islamic Office)

Smaha, Joseph (1999) 'The Needs, Pace and Forces of Change in Syria', *al-Hayat* (London) 14–15 May

Smith, Colonel Dan (2003) 'From Baghdad, Turn Left: On the Road to Damascus?', *Foreign Policy in Focus*, 22 April

Sottimano, Aurora (2008) 'Ideology and Discourse in the Era of Baʿthist Reforms', paper presented at the Centre for Syrian Studies conference, 10–12 April, St Andrews, UK

Sucker, Nabil (1994) 'The Crisis of 1986 and Syrian Plan for Reform', in Eberhard Kienle (ed.) *Contemporary Syria: Liberalization between Cold War and Cold Peace* (London: British Academic Press) pp. 26–43

Suwayd, Maḥmūd (1988) *Janūb Lubnān fī muwājahat Isrāʾīl* [*Southern Lebanon in the Face of Israel: 50 Years of Steadfastness and Resistance*] (Beirut: Palestinian Studies Foundation)

Suwayd, Maḥmūd (ed.) (1993) *Ḥarb al-ayyām al-sabʿah fī Lubnān: ʿAmalīyat al-Muḥāsabah* [*The Seven Day War on Lebanon: Operation Accountability*], *25–31 July 1993* (Beirut: Palestinian Research Establishment)

Suwayd, Muḥammad (1996) *ʿAmalīyat ʿanāqīd al-ghaḍab* [*Operation Grapes of Wrath*] (Beirut: Palestinian Studies Foundation)

Taoutsand, Siril (2001) 'Israel and the Postponed Syrian Response', *al-Hayat* (London) 30 July

Timofeev, Igorʿ (2000) *Kamāl Junbulāṭ: al-rajul wa-al-usṭūrah* (Beirut: dar an-Nahar)

Turkmani, Abdullah (2002) *Al-Ahzab al-Shiyuʿiyya fii al-Mashreq al-ʿArabi wa-l-Masʾala al-Qawmiyya fii al-ʿAshriniyyat ila Harb al-Khalij al-Thaniya* [*Communist Parties in the Levant and Arab Nationalism, 1920s–Second Gulf War*] (Beirut: al-Aan Press)

UNDP National Human Development Report, *Education and Human Development: Towards Better Efficiency* (Council of Ministers, UN Development Programme, 2005)

ʿUthmān, Hāshim (2001) *al-Aḥzāb al-siyāsīyah fī Sūriyah: al-sirrīyah wa-al-ʿalanīyah* [*Public and Secret Political Parties in Syria*] (Beirut: Dar Riad al-Rayes)

van Dam, Nikolaos (1996) *The Struggle for Power in Syria: Politics and Society Under Asad and the Baʿth Party* (London: I.B.Tauris)

Wakin, Daniel J. (2003) 'Powell says Syria is Taking Action on Terror Groups', *New York Times*, 4 May

Wedeen, Lisa (1999) *Ambiguities of Domination: Politics, Rhetoric, and Symbols in Contemporary Syria* (Chicago: University of Chicago Press)

Witt, Howard (2003) 'In Syria, Powell to Press for Change', *Chicago Tribune*, 3 May

Wright, Robin (2003) 'Powell Plans to Deliver Tough Message to Syria', *Los Angeles Times*, 3 May

Wright, Robin (2003) 'Syria Faces Hard Choices', *Los Angeles Times*, 4 May

Wright, Robin and David Lamb (2003) 'Syria Puts New Curbs on Militants', *Los Angeles Times*, 4 May

Yamut, Basem (2000) 'The Economic Strategic Importance of Sheba'a Farms', *As-Safir* (Beirut) 7 March

Yashai, Ron bin (2000) 'The Period of Uncertainty', *Yedioth Ahronoth* (Tel Aviv) 24 May

Yāsīn, Bū ʿAlī (2000) 'Ḥizb al-Baʿth al-ʿArabī al-Ishtirākī: al-taʾsīs wa-al-taṭawwur al-naẓarī ['Arab Socialist Baʿath Party: Establishment and Ideological Development'], in Fayṣal Darrāj and Muḥammad Jamāl Baroot (eds) *al-Aḥzāb wa-al-ḥarakāt al-qawmīyah al-ʿArabīyah* [*The Encyclopedia of Arab National Movements and Parties*], vol. 1 (Damascus: The Arabic Centre for Strategic Studies)

Young, Michael (2005) 'All Eyes Turn to Syria', *International Herald Tribune*, Thursday 17 February

Zeitouneh, Razan (2007) *Can Extraordinary Courts Ensure Justice: Supreme State Security Court in Syria* (Damascus: Centre for Human Rights Studies, December)

Zeitouneh, Razan and Abdul Haï al-Sayyed (2007) *Can Extraordinary Courts Ensure Justice: Supreme State Security Court* (Damascus: Damascus Centre for Human Rights Studies, May)

Zisser, Eyal (1998) *Decision Making in Asad's Syria* (Washington, DC: Washington Institute for Near East Policy)

Zisser, Eyal (1999) *Syria's Asad: The Approach of a Fifth Term of Office* (Washington, DC: Institute of Near East Policy, Policy Watch, no. 366, 6 February)

Zisser, Eyal (1999) *Where is Asad? The Renewed Struggle for Succession in Syria* (Washington, DC: Institute of Near East Policy, Policy Watch, no. 234, 14 December)

Zisser, Eyal (1999) 'Hafiz al-Asad Discovers Islam', *Middle East Quarterly*, vol. 6, no. 1, March

Zisser, Eyal (2000) 'Will Bashar al-Asad Rule?', *Middle East Quarterly*, vol. 7, no. 3, September, pp. 67–75

Zisser, Eyal (2001) *Asad's Legacy: Syria in Transition* (London: Hurst & Company)

Zisser, Eyal (2003) 'Bashar's Game: What is Syria Up To?' *Tel Aviv Notes*, 4 April

Zisser, Eyal (2003) 'Syria and the War in Iraq', *Middle East International Affairs Journal* (MERIA) vol. 7, no. 2, June

Zisser, Eyal (2003) 'Does Basher al-Asad Rule Syria?' *Middle East Quarterly*, vol. 10, no. 1, winter

Ziadeh, Radwan (2001) 'The Political Crisis and the Problem of Democratic Obstruction in Syria', *al-Zaman* (London) 15 February

Ziadeh, Radwan (2001) 'Traffic in Syrian Policy', *an-Nahar* supplement (Beirut) 17 July

Ziadeh, Radwan (ed.) (2003) *Min Agel Mojtama' Madanie fi Syria* [*For a Civil Society in Syria: National Dialogues Forum*] (Paris: Arab Committee for Human Rights)

Ziadeh, Radwan (2004) 'Muntadá al-Ḥiwār al-Waṭanī: al-takwīn al-ijtimā'ī wa-al-ḥarāk al-siyāsī' ['The Forum of National Dialogue: The Social Component and the Political Movement'], in Radwan Ziadeh, *Min ajl mujtama'madanī fī Sūriyah* [*Towards a Civil Society in Syria*] (Paris: Arab Committee for Human Rights, Arab European Publication Association) pp. 7–26

Ziadeh, Radwan (2004) *Su'al al-Tajdid fii al-Khitab al-Islami al-Mu'aser* [*The Question of Renewal in Contemporary Islamic Discourse*] (Beirut: Dar al-Madar al-Islami)

Ziadeh, Radwan (2005) *Ass'lam Adanie: al-Moufawdat a Suriyya al-israiliaia* [*Approaching Peace: Israeli-Syria Negotiation*] (Beirut: Centre for Arab Unity Studies)

Ziadeh, Radwan (2005) *Al-Muthaqqaf Dudd al-Sultah: Hiwarat al-Mujtama' al-Madani fii Suriyya* [*The Intellectual against Power: Discussions of Civil Society in Syria*] (Cairo: Cairo Centre of Human Rights Studies)

Ziadeh, Radwan (2005) 'Ḥudūd al-iṣlāḥ al-Sūrī: ālīyat intiqāl al-sulṭah wa-rihānāt al-taghyīr' ['The Limits of Syrian Reform: The Methods of Authority Transition and the Bets of Reforms'], in Radwan Ziadeh (ed.) *Al-iṣlāḥ fī Sūriyah bayna al-siyāsāt al-dākhilīyah wa-al-taḥawwulāt al-iqlīmīyah wa-al-duwalīyah* [*Reform in Syria between Internal Policies and International and Regional Transformations*] (Jeddah: Al-Raya Centre for Intellectual Development)

Ziadeh, Radwan (2005) 'Istishrāf mustaqbal al-ḥayāh al-siyāsīyah wa-quwá al-mujtamaʿ al-madanī fī Sūriyah' ['Overlooking the Horizons of Political Life and Forces of Civil Society in Syria'], in UNDP, *An Overview of Development Tendencies in Syria* (Damascus: UNDP in cooperation with the Syrian State Planning Corps)

Ziadeh, Radwan (2005) 'Al-iṣlāḥ fī Sūriyah bayna taḥaddiyāt al-iṣlāḥ al-dākhilī wa-rihānāt al-taghyīr al-khārijī' ['Reform in Syria between the Internal Reform Challenges and the Bets of External Change'], paper presented to conference entitled The Great Middle East Project: Interior and Exterior Controversy and the Future of the Arab Region, Cairo University Faculty of Economic and Political Sciences, 26–29 December

Ziadeh, Radwan (2006) 'Loss of Constitutional Perception in the Political Education in Syria', *Riwaq Arabi*, no. 45

Ziadeh, Radwan (2006) 'The Coming Election Year', *al-Watan* (Damascus) 27 November

Ziadeh, Radwan (2006) 'Al-ʿalāqāt al-Sūrīyah al-Lubnānīyah: mashaqqat al-ukhūwah' ['Syrian–Lebanese Relations: Hardship of Brotherhood'], in Radwan Ziadeh (ed.) *Maʿrakat al-iṣlāḥ fī Sūriyah* [*Battle of Reform in Syria*] (Cairo: Cairo Centre for Human Right Studies) pp. 69–85

Ziadeh, Radwan (2006) 'People's Assembly and the Election Law', *al-Watan* (Damascus) 4 December

Ziadeh, Radwan (2007) 'The Promised Political Party Law', *al-Watan* (Damascus) 9 January

Ziadeh, Radwan (2007) 'Political Regime in Syria: Elections without Electors', *Democracy Magazine*, no. 28, pp. 89–96

Ziadeh, Radwan (2007) *Rabeaa Dimisheq: Itejehat-tayarat-Nihayat* [*Damascus Spring: Issues-Trends-Results*] (Cairo: Cairo Institute for Human Rights)

Ziadeh, Radwan (2007) *San' al-Qarar wa-l-Siyasa al-Kharijiyya fii Suriyya* [*Decision Making and Syrian Foreign Policy*] (Cairo: Al-Ahram Centre for Political and Strategic Studies)

Ziadeh, Radwan (2007) 'Crisis of the Syrian Foreign Policy Discourse', *Al-Hayat* (London) 7 January

Index